Conquering Your Workplace

Books by Dilip Saraf

The 7 Keys to a Dream Job: A Career Nirvana Playbook!
Reinvention through Messaging: The Write Message for the Right Job!
Pathways to Career Nirvana: An Ultimate Success Sourcebook!
Rehired, not Retired: Proven Strategies for the Baby Boomers!

Conquering Your Workplace

From Mail Room to Board Room—A Sourcebook for Today's Workforce!

Dilip G. Saraf

Career Transitions Unlimited
Only for those who dare to practice what we preach...®

www.career-transitions-unl.com

iUniverse, Inc.
New York Lincoln Shanghai

Conquering Your Workplace
From Mail Room to Board Room—A Sourcebook for Today's Workforce!

iUniverse books may be ordered through booksellers or by contacting:

iUniverse
2021 Pine Lake Road, Suite 100
Lincoln, NE 68512
www.iuniverse.com
1-800-Authors (1-800-288-4677)

ISBN-13: 978-0-595-37486-1 (pbk)
ISBN-13: 978-0-595-67511-1 (cloth)
ISBN-13: 978-0-595-81879-2 (ebk)
ISBN-10: 0-595-37486-7 (pbk)
ISBN-10: 0-595-67511-5 (cloth)
ISBN-10: 0-595-81879-X (ebk)

Printed in the United States of America

This book is dedicated to empowering the countless millions who quietly suffer through the daily indignities of the corporate world and who do not know that they have an option!

TABLE OF CONTENT (MACRO)

TABLE OF CONTENTS (MICRO)

PREFACE

"There will be a time when loudmouthed incompetent people seem to be getting the best of you. When that happens, you only have to be patient and wait for them to self destruct. It never fails."
—Richard Rybolt, author, management consultant

This book emerged from the needs expressed by many who wanted continued coaching beyond their job or career transitions. Their coaching sessions typically started during their job transitions. After the 2001 job-market meltdown, my own practice (I am a career counselor and a life coach) focused on helping many professionals displaced by what had happened to the job market. Many high-tech refugees went on to reinvent themselves and reengage in a variety of other roles and industries as a result of their reinvention. The survivors, however, had something else to deal with: how to continue their careers and protect themselves from future uncertainties.

What I discovered, during my clients' experiences, was that many did not know how to make a smooth transition into a new job, industry, or a career and continue their professional pursuits with some semblance of confidence and certainty. Some felt that their career momentum was lost in the process. During their job transition I helped them with their messages, résumés, interviewing skills, negotiating skills, and so on. Once they landed, I thought that they would be able to carry on with their integration into their new role on their own and assimilate in their new workplace without much concern. I thought that this would be particularly true where clients landed in their dream jobs, as many did; often in jobs that did not even exist, but the ones that they conceived, created, and then claimed as theirs (This is what I practice and preach!).

I was surprised by the large number of clients who needed help of a different kind after they had landed, even in their dream jobs that gave them the confidence to complete their transition. In such cases changing the nature of the service I provided from job coaching to career coaching seemed to provide the bridge that they were looking for. After years of practice, I have come to realize that if a small population of clients consistently seeks a certain strain of help, there is a much bigger market that also needs it. This book was born out of that perceived need.

Although my job coaching focused on the transitional nature of the clients' needs, my career coaching focused on how to succeed in the "quiescent" workplace. I think that perhaps turbulent would be a better adjective. A transition is typically prompted by some turmoil or disruption in an otherwise predictable life. So, when a client landed at a new place they were surprised not to find the respite of stability with some security and peace that they were expecting.

In my *job* coaching sessions my focus is on clients' transitional skills, as, how to get an interview, how to position themselves correctly, how to leverage their career momentum, and so on. In *career* coaching, I had to change gears and tutor them in organizational, interpersonal, and management basics. Surprisingly, this tutoring was not limited to junior professionals. There were many senior managers, including executives and CEOs who felt ill-equipped to jump into a new environment and have the confidence to succeed. Most were looking for expert coaching and organizational skills to give them the confidence needed to make their transition successful.

What they were looking for was some foundational knowledge about why things happen the way that they do in organizations. Surprisingly, the different needs that popped up in our sessions had a theme.

What emerged from these sessions with many clients was an acute awareness of a lack of basic organizational and management knowledge. Every so often someone comes up with a "new" management idea. They write a book about it and, if a CEO gets enamored of it enough, it soon becomes a major initiative in the organization, often wreaking havoc. Such fads then take over the entire organization and soon displace the most basic and foundational courses. Over time, the organization drifts aimlessly in the absence of a solid foundational body of knowledge.

There is yet one more reason why the foundational management courses have disappeared over time: In the past, organizations were physically identifiable. Just as we identified a business by its brick-and-mortar façade, an organization was expected to have a physical attribute. That, too, has now changed with the concept of a virtual organization, cyber businesses, and boundaryless thinking. And, as a result of many regulatory and federal guidelines, as Equal Opportunity and American Disabilities Act (ADA) that make the pages of an Employee Handbook these days, the topics that once provided the basic knowledge—theoretical and practical—to the employees who needed it to function effectively, took back seat. The focus of the two types of contents is different.

What is the difference between the two contents? One helps you avoid lawsuits and the other makes you achieve excellence in what you do. In the evolution of priorities of the modern organization, many of these foundational courses eventually got lost in the shuffle. But, the need for the material that provided these basics did not. In fact, this need exacerbated and became more acute. As a result, most employees sought what they needed by trial and error and by experiencing and observing how things happen in the workplace as they witnessed events around them unfold in situations that were relevant to them. In the process they gleaned the working knowledge, but failed to codify what they learned using common lexicon. They also failed to share what they observed and to develop common understanding; typically what a good book does.

The lack of a common source of foundational knowledge of how to succeed in a new organization was not limited to those just transitioning into it. Many veteran employees often felt lost in how things happened around them that they found puzzling. They, too, needed a beacon to illuminate their career paths so that they could safely navigate their own course. They, too, had to resort to trial and error!

This is a frustrating way to learn a new skill; a skill that will help one succeed in the business and the corporate world. Even though the knowledge itself is abundantly available, having the skill is a prerequisite for one's corporate survival. And, yet, trial-and-error is the most available and accepted approach to how new—and old—employees learn organizational skills! Compounding this problem is the current focus on transactional employment, where many employers have become body shops—they bring in the bodies and put them to work until suddenly they no longer need them. The *cost* of on-boarding employees and then training them in the basic organizational and management skills has now become a luxury for most employers. The irony, though, is that the *price* of this practice is high in terms of how things happen inside organizations. The price we pay as a society in chronic and undue stress, our emotional well being, and the loss of productivity from it is incalculable.

The purpose of this book is not to provide a replacement for what has disappeared from many organizations. That would be a daunting task. Its content is aimed at providing career employees some basic knowledge that they can internalize, allowing them to be productive at work in today's flux. In this context the word "employee" is used broadly: it applies to anyone who works inside an organization, including its CEO and the members of its Board. This is how the book's subtitle was chosen.

The material evolved from the everyday demands employees face in what they do: how to deal with an incompetent boss, how to deal with the management that "promises" actions and then does nothing, how to deal with a jealous colleague, how to handle a "Notice of Concern," how to handle the annual performance review, how to handle a termination, and so on. There are many newspaper articles written by syndicated columnists that specifically address these topics on a regular basis, many in a question-and-answer format. Although this is helpful, there is no one source that an employee can go to for relief in addressing their specific problem. Besides, many career columnists dispense their advice by telling its readers the "what," and not the "why" or the "how." What the employees are looking for is something that can be contextualized in general theory or foundational knowledge that they can accept. They need a handbook!

The organization of this book is divided into ten chapters. Each chapter is aimed at providing some basic material around the topic presented. The basic material itself came from over 25 years of my own experience working as an employee at different companies internationally, followed by over 10 years as a business, organization, and leadership development consultant. This is further fortified by working directly with over 2,000 clients who looked to me as their job, career, and life coach during the past five years. I was fortunate to be working in an geography—the Silicon Valley and the greater San Francisco Bay Area—where the region experienced one of the highest unemployment rates in the nation for a long time, starting in 2001. This opportunity allowed me to work with many out-of-work and working professionals. Those working were especially stressed out because of a variety of factors that were getting worse for them. Those out of work, soon landed in jobs that they were after. But, as I kept in touch with those who landed new jobs, I found that they had difficult time transitioning, despite their eagerness to make the new relationship work for them. This is where I saw the need for this book. Yet another need came from those who continued to stay in their jobs, but found that their environment had shifted enough to warrant some new awareness of how to deal with it. What evolved makes the pages of this book. The material is grounded in solid reality of today's corporate world and the challenges professionals face in it, regardless of how long they have been working there.

My own experience suggests that the basic need to understand how organizations behave stems from an employee's inability to see beyond their own situation and to understand why people around them behave in ways that baffle them. Many personalize that treatment and rationalize it by trying to find something that they themselves might have done wrong, regardless of how untoward that treatment was. This gets even more interesting when such treatment comes from their superiors: their boss, someone with seniority, or someone who they consider should know better! This scenario is not much different from someone who gets abused at home and rationalizes that abuse by convincing themselves that they deserved that treatment because they must have done something wrong in the first place. This way to personalize their plight can be pervasive throughout an organization.

Part of the mission of this book is to dispel that apprehension and empower the reader with the knowledge that will allow them to fend for themselves. The foundational knowledge of how organizations are designed, how managers manage—should manage—and how the leadership process drives an organization, will clarify what expectations employees should hold in their daily interactions with others and in their discharge of assigned tasks and their expected outcomes. These insights are provided to make working in most environments a manageable endeavor.

The other aspect of their need is to know how to interact with others in a business setting. This need stems from the required interpersonal skills: Such need becomes acute when they feel that they are interacting with someone who engages in a relationship abuse that they find offensive. Many quietly resign to this treatment and put up with it day in and day out, doing their work in a highly stressed-out state. Some quit their jobs, hoping to find a better place where things would be different, only to discover that their problems have followed them. I know some clients, before they came to see me, who had done nothing wrong and who, after years of such treatment, continued to endure indignities by resorting to therapy and even taking anti-depressants just to cope with something that they could not avoid. The content of this book, which formed part of the coaching sessions, was their best remedy to deal with their predicament. I know of at least one client who stopped his therapy and anti-depressants after he saw the light of the day through these sessions; they freed and empowered him beyond words.

Yet another strain of this book is inspired by the immigrant population of professionals. Somehow, they seem to need the most hand-holding in their periods of job and career transitions and beyond. In everyday interactions at work, they seem ill equipped to be confident in what swirls around them. This book is particularly written with that audience in mind. The treatment provided will remind those ABCs (American Born Citizens), how the immigrant population sees what is happening and how they can accommodate their perceptions to make the workplace more harmonious.

This book is, by no means, a panacea for all the work-related quandaries, obstacles, and setbacks. It is a manual aimed at providing an objective view of how organizations function—or should function—and how to use that knowledge to improve your everyday encounters with others. No book can provide all the resources that will redress or even address every situation. But, it is the purpose of this book to provide enough basic material to allow you to leverage that knowledge into a situation that may not be expressly addressed in what is here. And, if you cannot, you must also work on your own discovery and development areas before you start blaming others for everything that goes wrong in your daily existence. There are also tools provided to help you with your own development. It is hoped that with what is provided, some vigilance, and some commitment to your own ongoing development, working for someone else can be a joyous experience.

Individual Contributors and Managers

What is presented here is for anyone, who is interested in knowing how to succeed in the workplace. For the individual contributor the challenges are plenty. Their focus is to do the best and make a name for themselves. Of course, many are ambitious enough to want to climb the career ladder and move up as their career blossoms. But, some choose to remain in their hands-on role and devote their career to a lifetime of pursuing something they love. Those who want to go into management face different challenges. As they become managers they suddenly realize that they are now in a different world and what is expected from them is also different. This is a surprise—even a shock—to many.

It is here that many of the current corporate training programs could do more in what they deliver to the up-and-coming managers. Most do not even realize that their previous role as an individual contributor, for which they got rewarded for having done it so well and got promoted to a manager, has nothing or very little to do with the challenges they face in their new role. An interesting conflict arises when they intuitively assume that they should continue doing more of what they did to get promoted to be a manager. This is a flawed assumption!

Although the purpose of this book is not to educate a rising manager and impart the basics of managing, there is a chapter devoted to this topic. Chapter-3 is specifically written to present the management basics in a unique way that will allow managers to capture what they missed out on in the corporate training circuit or even in their MBA class rooms. Even MBA curricula do not address these topics in an integrated way. Chapter-2, together with this chapter, is expected to provide the foundational knowledge of managing and of how the organization behaves in a corporate setting. Some estimate that nearly 80 percent of managers are deficient in some aspect of their development. In fact, *Dilbert* is founded on that premise and is one of the most widely syndicated features in today's newspapers. It resonates with today's corporate zeitgeist. Humor apart, I think, that a large percentage of managers could be more effective in what they did if they knew what their functions were (See functions of managing in Chapter-3).

So, from an organization standpoint, this book shows any employee (all the way to the CEO and beyond!) how to succeed in the corporate world by knowing how to manage up, down, and sideways, effectively.

As in all my previous books, a ♠ before a heading represents an important topic worth coming back to get more insights after you have already gone past it and a * represents topics that need your attention.

Acknowledgements

Many have contributed to the motivation of this book, including my clients. My own experience in the corporate world also was instrumental in the development of this book. Of many clients who inspired this book, Susan Chiu provided the most impetus for many topics that appear in the book. She brought to our sessions—first job and then career coaching—her everyday challenges in ways that validated the framework of this book. What other clients brought also followed similar patterns. Once again, my loving wife, Mary Lou, helped me with the editing of this book. Our son, Raj, read many critical narratives and provided his perspective to enrich what I wrote.

Silicon Valley, CA

CHAPTER 1

Today's Workplace

"A positive attitude may not solve all your problems, but it will annoy enough people to make it worth the effort."

—Herm Albright, author

Today's workplace is vastly different from the one that our parents were used to. This is even more so in the U.S. than it is in other western countries and even Japan. The changes to the workplace accelerated after the mid '70s, when the expectations of both the employees the employers started shifting towards each other rather dramatically. Until then, the employers enjoyed an implicit authority and power over their employees and, in return, provided a certain degree of security, protection, and a sense of personal belonging to the organization.

This dynamic rapidly began to change, starting in the mid-'70s, when the implicit covenant between the employer and the employee began to be replaced by "employment at will." Even the psychological contract that was implied began to fray and loyalty, once the hallmark of an employer-employee relationship, began to disappear. It is not that this concept was brand new then, it simply came into vogue after that time in ways that made it undeniable, as to its meaning for both parties. A historical view of how this all came about may be of interest.

Historical Perspective

During the past 50 years the entire employment scene has undergone a sea change. Over time, this pace of change has accelerated, particularly during the past couple of decades. Many of the rules that people had accepted and had steadfastly held as given since the advent of the industrial revolution have dissolved over time and new rules have emerged to replace them. The pace of change of these rules gradually accelerated over time. During the past decade that ushered in the new Millennium, the employment scene resembled the battlefield. Under battleground conditions, you make your own rules.

While these rules have had the most dramatic impact on the employment of the white-collar professionals, the blue-collar and union hands have seen their own share of changes as well. What is unsettling about the trends and their fierce velocity within the U.S. labor pool is that their direction is not favoring the average professional. This trend has accelerated during the past few years with no end in sight, marked by relentless, and sometimes wanton and promiscuous, off shoring, outsourcing, and other practices that have significantly altered and even eroded employee confidence.

What makes these trends and episodes discomposing for someone trying to understand a workplace, so that they can be productive, is that they must now make adjustments to their deeply held mental models. It is these models on which they based their future plans of growth, employment, income, and retirement. Benefits such as healthcare and dependent coverage have similarly been and continue to be eroded as a part of the employment package. It has become important for those in the workforce now to look at their employment in a way never before needed. All of this is due to a yet another paradigm shift—the global workforce—that has hit the job market.

But, what is a paradigm shift?

Shifting Paradigms

A paradigm is a set of rules that defines a certain system or operating environment. It is a pattern of defined rules and behaviors that make those who follow them successful. When a paradigm shifts, everything changes: all the previous rules, success criteria, and outcomes change. In fact, when a paradigm shifts everything goes back to zero. What this means is that new rules and patterns have to be defined for the new paradigm to take root. Those who write their own rules have the power to rule in a shifted paradigm.

Period	Operating Paradigm	Emerging Mindset	Comments
'50-'60	Lifetime employment	Disposable Employees	With fewer producers and many consumers this worked
'60-'70	Employment at Will	Hire and Fire	Getting laid-off was a matter of shame.
'70-'80	Flexible Workforce	Outsourcing	Companies increasingly started to outsource
'90-'95	Virtual Organization	Networked organization	Geographic separation became irrelevant
'95-'00	Core Competencies	Off shoring	Contracting comes into prominence
'01-'05	Value Creation	Global Workforce	Shifting from your having to find work, to work finding you, wherever you are.
'06-	Continual Innovation	Experimental-Markets concept	Innovation in every area of how value is created in an enterprise will change employment models. Experimental-markets model may eventually decimate already lean management ranks.

Table-1: Shifts in Employment Models and their Implications

Table-1 shows a comparison of the old and the new paradigms in employment and the U.S. employment scene. For those outside the U.S., the picture is probably not that different. It may be distorted because of many of the rules of a free economy are tempered by the labor laws, as they are in Europe. This table captures the shifts of the past 55 years. Observe how the trend of shifts is itself accelerating!

Table-1 also shows how major shifts in business models and mindsets have affected employment paradigms. Let us look at each of the entries in the table to understand what the implications are of these trends so that we can prepare for the emerging patterns of change.

Lifetime employment was the expectation of both the employees and the employers in the middle of the last century. In reputable companies it was both expected and offered. Some companies built their reputation on this principle of lifetime employment, which lasted well into the current Millennium. Hewlett-Packard had built its reputation on this primordial human expectation. This all came to a sudden end in early 2001, when an outsider was brought in as a CEO, who reinterpreted the vaunted HP's values and started aligning its business with emerging realities, after merging it with Compaq.

The deeply rooted HP's employment practice was replaced by what the rest of industry had already set in motion by then: considering employees more as a cost than as an asset. In this model, when markets shifted and employee skills could not help companies to remain competitive in the marketplace, many treated employees as disposable, rather than retraining and finding them alternate sources of employment within the company.

The most dramatic impact of the end of lifetime employment was felt in Japan in the mid '80s, when many companies realized that to stay competitive they had to manage their work force to match the output. When layoffs began in Japan at that time, the shock wave hit many very hard. Since one-employer culture was so deeply ingrained in the Japanese psyche, many did not know how to handle being let go. There were rampant stories of those, who, after being laid off, decided to jump off the building where they worked, rather than go home as unemployed and face humiliation. It took nearly a decade for many Japanese to reconcile to the new rules of employment.

Employment at will emerged as a result. This mindset resulted in employees being treated as engaged in an "at will" employment contract. This meant that at any time a company felt that an employee became a cost and their value creation process ceased to benefit it, they were terminated. As the employment-at-will mindset took root during the '80s, a new trend began to emerge. Early in that decade there was a massive military build-up in the U.S. Many defense contractors decided to expand their operations under the apprehension that this expansion might not last, in fact, they feared that when it did run its course, there would be costly layoffs. To avoid this possibility many companies resorted to contract labor.

Flexible workforce was a result of the contract labor force. This option allowed organizations to adopt an "accordion" employee force that quickly expanded and contracted based on the current headcount need. As time passed, more and more people became available in the contract pool. Many contracting agencies saw the opportunity for the market and they started specializing in certain skill sets. This made it easier for the companies to rely on institutional sources—contract agencies—of skilled labor pools, rather that relying on individuals who showed up with a résumé in hand. Often, the contract agency took care of the benefits, as vacation, healthcare premiums, and other amenities.

During the mid '90s, companies began to realize that as technology became a commodity, it was important to focus on their core competencies. There were companies that specialized in many of the administrative and routine functions that did not represent a company's core competency. This mindset resulted in outsourcing many of the rules-based functions.

Outsourcing is a management alternative that growingly became a common practice as the outsourced functions themselves became commoditized, drastically reducing their cost to the contracting organizations. In addition, as the definition of a core competency became more and more exclusive, more and more nontraditional functions got added to the outsourcing list.

In this development the concept of "context" and "core" capabilities drove the outsourcing decisions. Context capabilities are those that are the expected but do not create differentiation. And yet, without them a company simply cannot exist. Once again, this can be compared to the body and soul analogy. The body is context and the soul is core. You can outsource some of your bodily functions by acquiring appropriate aids, such as a wheelchair if you cannot walk, a prosthetic arm if you lost yours in an accident, and so on. You cannot outsource your soul without losing who you are! In the business world all competitors in a market share this—context—set of capabilities. Although the list of what the context capabilities are becomes ever so long in a high-velocity market, the core capabilities remain surprisingly narrow. Many of the workers who staffed the functions—context functions—that were once performed by the companies in-house, were forced to find alternate employment in contract houses that specialized in specific functions. Common were manufacturing, front-office staff, mailroom and administrative functions, security, and many human resource adjuncts as payroll and benefits. Even with this employment model, as overseas labor force began competing with the domestic counterparts, spurred by the ubiquitous Internet and global services, yet another force began to shape the employment scene. This trend was called off shoring. But before off shoring took root, yet another concept in organizational design emerged: Virtual organization.

Virtual Organization emerged out of corporations spreading out in different geographies and growing by mergers and acquisitions, with concomitant ease of communications. The last element in this list—ease of communication—played an increasingly central role as information technology became more and more pervasive and the Intranet—and the Internet—became a critical resource for organizations, starting in the mid nineties.

Off shoring was going beyond outsourcing both conceptually and practically. Off shoring involved having a presence in the country where the cheap labor force was available and then having a close tie to the work that was integral to the company's success. Often off-shored resources excelled at the work of their domestic counterparts, not just by doing it cheaper, but by doing it better and faster as well. This was particularly true with knowledge work, where better-trained workforce and more disciplined work habits made what they did more valuable. Software development process was one example. Using the Capability Maturity Model (CMM) many premier software development companies in India were able to routinely produce quality software at roughly one fourth the costs of their U.S. counterparts, with many-fold increase in quality and speed to boot. The next wave of this capability is the Integrated CMM (CMMI).

Off shoring took with it a company's core competencies, unlike the outsourcing trend, where it was a holy grail. Many companies set up off-shored entities as if they were extensions of their own operations. Interestingly, in some instances, the "core" functions got off shored and the "context" remained back at the home office.

As we see these trends, ostensibly, the U.S. is losing its main competency: skilled labor force. True, many of the manufacturing and "back-end" activities are gone out of the country for good, but that view would be myopic. This needs further discussion. Why? For two reasons: one, it suggests how people should prepare themselves as they grow in their jobs, to make themselves more immune to economic cycles to protect their careers. The second reason is that, to the reader, it will provide a perspective that may help shape their career by taking appropriate action.

Value creation on an *ongoing* basis is the new expectation for employment. It is not that value creation was not the basis of employment in the past; this emergent mindset has made *continuous* value-stream creation (Dynamic Value Creation) a requirement for ongoing employment. This implies that the employees must go beyond their "assignments" to prosecute tasks and identify opportunities to create ongoing value stream that makes the enterprise grow. This shift also resulted in how the selection process changed during this period: unless hiring managers saw demonstrated record of continuous value creation in their résumés, many, who were trying to get jobs, were disappointed because of their inability to understand this shift. Many had great track records; but that was no longer enough, because it failed to show this constancy of value generation!

Global workforce mindset emerged out of the relentless off shoring that changed the employment picture starting 2001. In this model, work goes where the resources are.

Innovation is how value is created in new ways from existing inventions. Inventions bring new ideas to life. Innovations make those ideas spawn new ways to generate value from them. Every employee on their own, and collectively, must innovate value creation to thrive in this complex world economy. Functional boundaries have now been replaced by seamless value creation across the entire supply chain and it now knows no geographic boundaries.

Experimental Markets is an emerging concept, where individual employees use their intimate knowledge of the product, company, and the markets to project how a particular product is going to be performing. They use this knowledge to adjust their plan of action to move forward. The interesting aspect of this model is that individual employees chart this, not their higher ups, eliminating the need for managers as we classically define it. This concept, coupled with the self-directed work teams from the past decade, may change the organizational models of employment in the future.

This discussion may give an impression to a casual reader that, with time, organizations became one-dimensionally identifiable with the labels shown in the table. To infer this would be a mistake. At any given time organizations became a mix of all of these different models. How they continue to evolve is a function of what industry they belong to, and how they adapt to the emerging paradigms, and how fast. It is not unusual to see organizations still dominated by the employment cultures dating back to the early models depicted in the table. By the same token it would not be difficult to find those that are dominated by the employment models reflective of the more recent paradigms listed in that table as well. This discussion is merely provided to guide the thinking of those who want to seriously look at career planning by giving them a historical perspective.

A Seismic Shift

Many wonder if the fallout during the past few years of the paradigm shift is good for the country, the economy, and the future of both the U.S. labor pool and of the rest of the world. To keep things in perspective, let us look at similar shifts that took place a few decades back and their effects on these same factors today.

Let us look at one such shift that occurred nearly thirty years back. In the late 1970s and early 1980s, Japan was eating Detroit's lunch. The U.S. was despondent over losing jobs in the automotive industry and the loss of leadership in that sector to the Japanese. Many had predicted the demise of Detroit, as we had known, similar to the end of the steel industry.

But, that did not happen. In fact, the auto industry emerged stronger as a result, selling over 15 million autos annually in 2004. During that era the annual sales were in the 10-plus million autos range. What changed the course of that seemingly inexorable train of events?

Innovation was the central force in how things turned around for the auto industry. This is the same factor that appears at the bottom of Table-1. Innovation led us to the boom years of the late 1980s and the entire decade of

1990. In fact, the same boom ushered in the new Millennium. Japan is now nowhere on the scene, certainly not as an invincible economic superpower as most had then predicted. The lesson here is that *ongoing* innovation always comes to the rescue of any spiraling course of actions that cause short-term disruptions as most paradigm shifts do.

Going further back in time, it was predicted that computers would lead to mass automation, causing widespread unemployment. That, too, never happened. Rules-based jobs were taken over by computers; freeing people to do high-end jobs (knowledge jobs) that required sophisticated thought. This sea change spawned new opportunities with higher wages in the process. This rather simplistic model, however, needs to be tempered with population growth of the past few decades, dramatic increases in productivity, and redistribution of work itself, which make this discussion more interesting.

Off shoring is helping U.S. companies stay competitive and profitable. If they do not fritter away that profit and wisely invest in innovation, the domestic economy will, once again, lead its way to health and yet higher-end jobs will still be created. This cycle will continue, perhaps at an even increasing pace. What does this mean to an average employee? The implications are both obvious and subtle from a career-management standpoint.

Let us take a closer look.

Forces that Changed the Workplace

Over the past couple of decades a number of forces helped shape the way today's workplace evolved. Although these forces shaped today's workplace, not all factors shaped made equal contributions in the process. Some contributed more than the others. Some caused a dramatic shift and others evolved in the way that they created a workplace we see today. The following list will help shed some light on these forces and how they changed the way we view our workplace.

- ✓ Information Ubiquity
- ✓ Flattened Hierarchies
- ✓ Core Vs. Context
- ✓ Sourcing and outsourcing
- ✓ Off shoring
- ✓ Client-server networks

✓ Focus on value creation

✓ Managing virtual teams

✓ Common understanding of the management process

✓ The concept of leadership process

Each will be discussed briefly below:

Information Ubiquity

Running any organization entails information flowing up and down the chain of command and throughout an organization. Information is the lifeblood of an organization. Access to information was at the heart of effective management and in the days before computers became so ubiquitous. Before then, only the top managers held all the information and rationed it depending on their management style and what objectives they wanted to achieve with it.

Ubiquitous computing changed the entire equation of information management. What was previously exchanged on paper in the form of memos, notes, letters, and statements, is today created, stored, and exchanged as digital signals that reside deep in the infrastructure of an organization's network. Immediate and uniform information availability throughout has flattened an organization in ways that are hard to express.

As a result, the focus has now shifted to what actions are taken on the information and what information is critical to the decision-making process inside an organization. It has taken nearly 30 years for the information revolution to make the organization information-transparent.

Flattened Hierarchies

The concept of organizational hierarchy came from the command and control structure of the armed forces. Historically, hierarchies came into effect to maintain the command structure in a group of people who shared common purpose and goals. This was an efficient way to make sure that those working in an organization followed a certain direction and had a common understanding of how to pursue objectives that an organization considered worthy.

Information was central to the hierarchy to function and when it became a commodity, hierarchies disappeared. Today's organization reflects flattened hierarchies stemming from democratization of information and the empowerment of those working inside an organization. Flattened hierarchies resulted in less bureaucracy and increased speed with which an organization functioned.

Core Vs. Context

As technology became more easily available, it was possible to focus on a specific function that was performed inside an organization and achieve economies of scale, by providing that function to multiple organizations. One of the first such activities to be sourced was perhaps payroll. Originally, many organizations held that payroll was their own little secret that they did not want anyone else to know about. But, once companies realized that often this mundane function required much ongoing knowledge of tax and compliance laws and that there was no competitive or strategic advantage to doing this in-house, they started sourcing this task to bureaus that do this efficiently and effectively. Other tasks as mailroom activities, security, travel, maintenance followed.

The next wave of sourcing expanded to many other functions that were once considered "core" in a company's charter. Companies came to realize that the "context," which defined the ecosystem in which they operate is the requirement for staying in the business that they were in. The "core," on the other hand, provided the competitive advantage that defined their unique position in the market. The context increasingly included manufacturing, testing, logistics, and invoicing. In the process, companies clarified what they were unique at—their core. This led to the evolution of their core competencies. The sourcing alternative allowed companies to focus on their core competencies and create a competitive advantage in the process. See the 7-S model in the next chapter and how this came about. Sourcing and focusing on its core competencies changed the landscape of how companies functioned.

Sourcing and Outsourcing

As discussed under the previous heading, sourcing and outsourcing changed how a company shaped its mission. As more and more functions became commodities, technology more available, and the supply chain more efficient, companies started farming out more and more of their context or "infrastructure" activities to those who could provide them more efficiently. In today's business ecosystems, data centers, computing, information handling (emails), and even competitive analyses are being farmed out to those who can do them more efficiently. Many companies considered these activities sacred cows and would not even imagine sourcing them out to anyone else, merely a few years back!

Continued trends on sourcing and outsourcing have dramatically changed how an organization is structured and how it manages itself in a given ecosystem.

Off-shoring

Although off-shoring became a more visible—and dreaded—term during the past five or so years, it has been an important part of the business ecosystem since the mid '80s. The rapid spread of the Internet, accelerating globalization, and the availability of highly skilled labor overseas catalyzed the spread of off shoring. If there was just one factor that precipitated the rampant growth of off shoring it was the infamous Y-2K episode in the late '90s. The need for skilled labor to change the computer code to accommodate the turning of the clock to the new century resulted in many companies going after the labor pools of countries such as India and China that had the skilled workforce to do the job. In the process many companies realized that the capabilities offered by these countries went far beyond the mere Y-2K patches. As a result, a whole new sourcing alternative was born, almost overnight.

The impact this single factor has had in the corporate world has sent shock waves in the U.S. work force. It is estimated that in 2004 nearly 450,000 jobs were lost to off shoring. By 2015 this number is estimated to swell to nearly three million. What this means is that how companies manage their projects and how they operate is going to change in the future; that change has already begun.

♠ Off-shoring and Outsourcing: An outlook

The practice of outsourcing and off shoring has come into sharper focus during the past few years, particularly starting with the incidental dotcom implosion in early 2001. During 2003 about 250,000 jobs, mostly high-tech and knowledge jobs, were "off-shored" to India and other countries as China, Indonesia, and the Philippines. Exactly how many jobs were lost to off-shoring is a matter of debate. Some jobs have even gone to Russia and the Eastern European countries. Unbeknownst to many, off-shoring to India began in the early '80s, with many manual computer tasks—the digital toil—being shipped there for low-cost processing. Only in the past few years has this trend taken on an exponential trajectory, brought into sharper focus by the intense media interest and rampant job losses that go well beyond those lost to off-shoring. See below, the "Hype" phase!

The off-shoring and outsourcing of jobs are two somewhat different practices that an organization can adopt. Outsourcing is where an organization decides to stay focused on its core competencies and farms out its more routine functions to those who can do them more efficiently, *regardless* of the geography. Typically these functions include payroll, security, front lobby administration, mailroom, and other routines. Outsourcing practice has been a management alternative since the late '80s and it accelerated in the '90s. This trend is not going to change. More and more companies are going to find ways of consolidating their routine tasks and finding ways to cut costs to become more efficient in what they do. This cost advantage is what keeps them competitive; they are not so much strategic practices, as they are survival tactics. As we discussed previously they represent the "context" in which a company stays viable in a given ecosystem.

Off-shoring is a different matter: companies have found that some functions, even core functions, can be "off-shored" by keeping a pool of labor forces overseas that can do many jobs more efficiently, allowing them to develop an ongoing capability to perform critical tasks competitively. India has emerged as one country with resources that can support many such initiatives. Major Fortune-500 companies, in the past few years, have "off-shored" many white-collar jobs to India and other countries. This practice is not limited to call centers and administrative functions; it has pervaded today's almost all knowledge work, which now includes even radiological diagnostics, using some of the physicians trained to interpret medical tests and MRIs. This trend will not reverse; it is, in fact, going to accelerate.

Many complain about the low cost of knowledge work in India. By some estimates there is a 6-10:1 salary advantage for comparable skill between India and the U.S. Considering the overhead and other costs, the net saving can easily be 4:1. But this is not the whole story, particularly in software. Not only is the salary of comparable software professional less by a significant factor in India (compared to the U.S.), the efficiency of production is much higher to boot! How is this possible?

One reason is that while the U.S. software industry focused on cranking out constantly revised, complex, and functionally cumbersome software during the pioneering phase of the software and the personal computer industry, India focused on streamlining software development methodology by adopting a disciplined approach. This is much analogous to what happened to the automotive industry in the '70s when the Japanese ate Detroit's lunch by beating them on the quality of their automobiles at a lower cost. This is a race between invention and innovation. While both are central to success how they are practiced can greatly influence the long-term scenario.

In software there is a methodology for improving the effectiveness of how it is developed. In this methodology there are five levels at which this development can take place and it is called Capability Maturity Model (CMM). In this model, Level-I represents the most rudimentary approach to software development methodology, and Level-V, the most evolved. The ratio of the outputs between the two levels is typically tenfold. Marching through these levels and attaining a Level-V capability requires continuous innovation.

Much of the U.S. software development process, on average, operates at Level-II or just above it, according to experts. India produces software at Level-IV or even Level-V. Many prominent software sources operate at Level-V and that is their selling point. This means that the output difference, *not* accounting for quality issues, is two to five times what is produced here! This is a significant factor to combat. This is why software and IT projects will continue to gravitate to India in the future, despite any political backlash from the migration. The force is economic and compelling for software.

The rate at which the off-shoring trend across a broad skill set, not just software development, is going to accelerate will depend on a variety of factors. When an initiative captures public attention, as off-shoring has, since the early Millennium, it is usually in its early stages of "hype." As a result, many perceptions about the advantage of off-shoring are distorted. Why? Let us take a closer look.

Any major "new" idea or fad evolves before it is adopted as a valid and accepted business practice across a wide range of industries. There are four stages in this evolution:

➢ Hype

➢ Disillusionment

➢ Redeployment

➢ Integration

The first phase "hype" is when there is much public focus on the issue and there are constant media reports about the initiative, including its political ramifications. Many companies jump on the bandwagon and follow those who are "successful" adopting the new fad. Soon there is a backlash as a result of the hyped activity. The gains are not what they expected, there is political backlash, there are hidden costs, and there are social pressures and so on.

Enter disillusionment, the next stage! During this stage many companies back peddle the initiative and retract their positions. On the off-shoring front, recently Dell and IBM have backed off and pulled some of their functions back into their U.S. operations. This trend will continue as will the trend to outsource, as more and more tasks and functions are identified during this shakedown.

Redeployment is where organizations learn the true cost of implementing an initiative and use that learning and other factors to develop their long-term plan on how to stabilize their operations and benefit from the positive aspects of the trend. During this stage, the initiative loses its media interest and pure economic rationality and organizational considerations drive their fate. The off-shoring trend is not yet seen this stage, but is expected to see it within the next year or so. The off-shoring initiative is one of those inevitable economic forces resulting from the global economy spawned by the Internet. The irony here is that those who made the Internet a commercial success have been hit the hardest by its emergence!

The final stage is integration, where the initiative matures and so do people's perspective on it. Their long-term benefits tend to become visible. This horizon is a few years away for the off-shoring trend.

The idea presented here validates the concept of the Change Curve of Figure-4 in Chapter-4.

High-tech has suffered the most impact by the off-shoring trend. It is estimated that in the coming years, about one in seven jobs in this industry (mostly in the Silicon Valley) is going to be off-shored, mostly to India. In 2003 about 250,000 jobs were lost to India as mentioned before. Even though there were some three million in the U.S. labor pool who had lost their jobs (and nearly 15 million out of work or underemployed!) in the past three years, each one of them thought that *their* job had gone to India. This is called perceptual amplification!

The reality, though, is that as companies find better ways to manage global resources, more and more jobs are going to go overseas. It is estimated that by 2015 about three million jobs are going overseas. But by the same token, new jobs are going to be *defined* right here. Typically those jobs are more "upstream" in the value chain. This means getting closer to the customer and developing business models that are more service based. This trend has implications that are worth considering for the future well being and management of one's career.

♠ Career Implications

The factors listed have now resulted in an inescapable shift in the way organizations are considering how to fill open positions. Some are using a conscious effort to take the emerging trends into account; others have to be reminded by those looking for opportunities in these organizations. In a bear market employers are selective. It is no longer enough to be the best at what one once did; but what they now need to demonstrate clearly is that the skills presented in their résumé will benefit the target organization's *future* needs. Being aware of the emerging trends and the way future job competencies are shaping up will give job applicants an edge in their search. Table-2 is a partial list of traditional and emerging job competencies for some job families. Using this map of forward-looking competencies, job seekers must now position themselves for a favorable consideration—even an edge—during the hiring process. If they are already inside and working, they can also use this trend to fortify their own job by suggesting a job description that reflects this knowledge.

♠ Integrating Job Trends in Your Message

Integrating job trends in a message is an advantage that must be exploited in each opportunity during a job search. Such an opportunity exists even as you are engaged in your current job. Why? There are three reasons:

Most posted jobs do not reflect today's reality. They're often constructed by "copy and paste" of the past ones, often dating back a few years!

Most applicants responding to job openings try to match what is already described in the job posting. Having a message that goes beyond this description and the one that captures an employer's imagination gives an edge!

Demonstrating an understanding of how a position can create greater value by integrating broader aspects of a job can create a competitive advantage. This holds true for open jobs as well as jobs currently filled.

Job trends are an important element of the overall message of a job-search campaign as well as success strategy in a current job. For example, for a software developer, especially in high-tech, the very nature of the development process has changed dramatically in the U.S. Much of the work is now parceled out to India and overseas. No matter how great you are at developing software, unless you understand how this trend of off-shoring is going to affect the potential employer, you are not going to have a long-term job there. Even if a company does not have any language in the job opening about off-shoring now, responding to an opportunity with the knowledge of this trend is an advantage. This insight can be presented in the following way in a Career Objective:

Before

Career Objective: A position as a software development lead

After

Career Objective: A hands-on technical lead in software responsible for: collaborating with customers to capture their requirements, organizing teams and setting up projects that include off-shore resources, managing overall projects to ensure that the final solution is delivered to delight the customer, and managing the entire product life-cycle for a profitable revenue stream.

For someone already doing a job in software development, presenting this expanded version of what you can now do can make a difference between keeping your job and getting laid-off.

Creating a résumé for a job with an employer that supports outsourcing or off-shoring requires specific messages. One cannot present a message without awareness of the needs. For example, if someone is looking to migrate from a traditional manufacturing organization, an OEM, to a company that does contract manufacturing, even for the same OEM, the skill set now required in the new position is different. Why? This is mainly because the focus of value creation in the two organizations is different. The OEM, typically, requires a broad skills set to realize its manufacturing operations, as a part of an integrated capability. Working across a broad cross-functional organization is critical for the OEM. For the outsourced manufacturing organization, however, the focus is the depth of a given function more than the broad knowledge, because this is how the outsourced business achieves cost benefits: doing repetitive operations at minimal cost. The résumé and the cover letter must incorporate this awareness in unambiguous messages.

♠ Differentiating Yourself

Throughout this discussion we have and will continue to emphasize that differentiating is a key strategy for career success, not just job search. Differentiation does not just start during the marketing process; it goes way back with the first piece of a message—the résumé! Even before the résumé is written, how one thinks has much to do with how it all ends up being differentiated. Once at a job, the differentiation that got you in can be continued to sustain and even secure your job, as you advance in your position.

Notes:

Table-2: Emerging Job Trends in Today's Economy: A Sampling

#	Traditional Job	Traditional Role	Emerging Job	New Role	Drivers	Opportunities
1	Account Manager	Sell to generate revenues, protect accounts/revenue streams standing	Relationship Manager	Understand customer drivers, value transfer equation, long-term relationships, alliances	Customer loyalty, cost of landing new accounts, cost of defections	Customer intimacy
2	Business Development Manager	Promote business, create new revenues, make profits, and expand	Opportunities Seeker	Explore what is NOT happening and ID avenues to catalyze it	Current value creation not supporting expectations competition, commoditization	Alliances, value loops with suppliers, consolidation
3	Component Engineer	Define and specify components / vendors	Applications Engineering	Define new applications for components, creative single source	Simplicity, reliability, alliances, partnership	Alliance creation in value chain
4	Customer Support	Post-sale customer support	Customer Experience Champion	Understand customer needs, use, issues, and know how to close	Product complexity, customer impatience and expectations	
5	Does Not Exist	N/A	Account Executive Process Steward	Promote organization-wide process to match large accounts with senior execs to manage discovery, relationship, and growth.	Large accounts are orphans left to the will of the Account Managers; account defections, lack of long-term visibility	Global and strategic accounts

#	Traditional Job	Traditional Role	Emerging Job	New Role	Drivers	Opportunities
6	Facilities Manager	Construction, utilities, services, space allocation, special facilities, regulatory	Facilities Overseer	Real-Estate Custodian, strategic planning, Hoshin, energy incentives, subcontracts	Cost, globalization, work habits, virtual orgs, regulatory compliance incentives	Subcontracting services
7	IT Specialist	Design and support IT infrastructure with the latest and the greatest	IT Resource	Make available what is installed, increase investment effectiveness	Installed capacity, low availability, utilization, and capital, increased hurdle rates, IT as a business partner	IT effectiveness; welding business ops to IT
8	Maintainability Engineer	Product life-cycle, downstream costs, logistics	Revenue protection engineer	Find creative ways to enhance product's overall appeal in its long-term life	Throwaway designs of the past, environmentalist, back-to-basics	New models of maintenance logistics, self-help diagnostics
9	Marcom Specialist	Develop product/service communications and collaterals	Marcom Generalist	Guerilla approaches to reaching end users, creating product excitement/demand vacuum	Limited budgets, multiple avenues, savvy but time-constrained end user, highly customized real-time collaterals	Customer-intimate campaign, HP's new INDIGO is on point Print-on-Demand Collateral
10	OD Specialist	Organizational development, teams, training, leadership development	OE Catalyst	Project Teams, PM Methodology, Career Ladders, reward structures, Operating Protocols, Six Sigma	New Team Paradigms, Structure (PMOs), Alignment, Cycle Times	Organizational effective initiatives

#	Traditional Job	Traditional Role	Emerging Job	New Role	Drivers	Opportunities
11	Reliability/Maintain-ability	Predict performance	Product Experience Engineer	Technology life, value alternatives, availability, value experience	Emerging technologies; value alternatives	New approaches to Product Design; manufacturability.
12	Software Developer	Translate requirements into code, then rework as needed; keep doing version iterations to create complex, hard-to-use s/w	Product Developer	Translate Customer Needs to Requirements, liaison, teaming, validation, customer champion, disciplined development	Process integration, accountability, cost, schedule, customer experience, and globalization.	Extreme programming, Capability Maturity Model (CMM); S/W Reuse Coaching/Mentoring. Off-shoring integration.
13	Software QA	Validate code, document, Configuration Management	Product Assurance/ Support	Liaise between customer and developer, strategic testing, life cycle, customer experience	Process integration, Outsourcing, India connection, CMM,	Extreme Programming, Software Reuse
14	Technical Writer	Develop materials to help customers with product use.	Product-use facilitator	Create print, Web and other deliverables with interactive capabilities; up-to-date materials	Web, complex products, Limited training, language barriers, product changes.	Multi-media skills, knowing how users need information managed/delivered

#	Traditional Job	Traditional Role	Emerging Job	New Role	Drivers	Opportunities
15	Procurement Manager	JIT, quality, multiple sources, vendor ship.	Supply Network Catalyst	Supply chain integration value capture, ecosystem dynamics, transform resources to provide package goods.	Complex ecosystems, dynamic world economy, M&As, cheap labor	Cultural training, values, supply network dynamics value exchanges
16	Project Manager	Lead product/service development, deliver against set objectives	Profit Center, autonomous units, line of business, accountable to customers/suppli er	Value-chain network, team leadership, cross-functional cooperation, subcontract management, customer experience	Web capability, team dynamics, life-cycle, Earned Value, Global workforce	New team paradigms; PMO and benchmarking
17	Product Development Engineer	Translate inventions into profitable product suites, platforms and derivatives	ODM Specifier	Liaise between R&D, emerging component technologies, capabilities, and ODMs for differentiated products	Major players are now brand promoters, not operational participants, techno-logy commoditization	Prototype capabilities in-house and ODM development
18	Production Planner	Develop detailed work/material flow /logistics, inventory	Production Overseer	Align demand with capacity, shift loads, global cost awareness	Global resources, ODM	Integrated planning
19	R&D Manager	Lead creative teams to generate new product stream, new platforms, future revenue streams	Innovations Catalyst	Establish a new core competency for innovation. Establish organization-wide process for innovation	Slow inventions, lack of continuity of new platforms, future value and competitive advantage	Leveraging innovations across entire organization not just in R&D.

#	Traditional Job	Traditional Role	Emerging Job	New Role	Drivers	Opportunities
20	Test Engineer	Design test scenarios to validate new products, assure compliance, support complaints.	Test Champions	Participate early in design process; help create test simulations, test as an ongoing process and then final testing.	Cycle times, test capabilities, Automated testing; computerized simulations, test costs and time.	Outsourced testing.
21	Training & Development	ID Needs, develop content, deliver training	Training Management	ID opportunities, find resources, TTT Line managers, monitor how it impacts bottom line	Emphasis away from Level-1 measurements,	Developing training to affect the bottom line Level-5 not just Level-1
22	Usability Engineer	Product use; User interface	Customer Experience Engineer	Ease of use, post-purchase experience, clever/creative applications	Consumer disillusionment value expectations, innovation	Speaking customer and user language in final deliverables.

Client-server Networks

Client server networks have replaced mainframe architecture. This "new" architecture, which has become into increasing prominence since the mid '90s, has displaced the central node of information hub. Information is now more uniformly spread and its management has also spread across an enterprise. This is very similar to what happened when hierarchies got flattened as described earlier.

Focus on Value Creation

As competition became global and the workforce boundaryless, companies realized that unless every activity in which it engages creates value, it is going to lose its edge to its competitor. During the past decade, companies have focused relentlessly on differentiating themselves and creating value at every step of their operational existence. So, if an employee does not create value that provided the company a competitive edge, that employee would no longer be considered vital to the company's survival.

This relentless focus on value creation has changed how companies look at their labor pool and how they carry out their activities in today's global economy.

Managing Virtual Teams

With the geographically dispersed workforce, companies had to develop capabilities to manage their teams that were engaged in projects throughout the world. Outsourcing and off shoring accelerated this need.

Respect for the Management Process

To many, "management" is a mystery. Some think that good managers are born and not made. What changed the view of management is the work of many authors and pioneers who defined the management process over the past four decades and identified a framework that makes management a process that can be learned, practiced, and improved. Using scientific approach to information gathering, understanding how people and resources contribute to a common cause and using a framework of rules, tools, and concepts management has now become a common practice that has changed how employees look at their company.

The Concept of Leadership

Closely aligned with the evolution of the management process, is the concept of leadership. Leadership is defined as a process that results in people following the leader's vision. It does not take someone to be a manager to be a leader. Leadership is one of those topics on which thousands of books have been written since the early days, beginning with Confucius and Plato. There are different perspectives on what leadership means, how it comes about, and what it does to an organization. Leadership is not an act but a process; it is also a choice in the way one decided to act in a given situation.

Regardless, leadership is seen as a force that comes from within that allows a person to lead the activities of others to achieve a purpose, common and uncommon. Leadership is both a natural and nurtured attribute.

Implications of the Changed Workplace

The forces that have shaped today's workplace continue to shape its evolution. What the changes mean to those working at these places of employment is what this book is about. It is not what the change is but how it results in the way employees need to behave at their place of work to be productive, derive some measure of purpose in their engagement, and get a reward in the way they are compensated for the value they bring and create.

Over the past 50 years the perception of a workplace has moved away from being thought of as something that provides an altruistic benefit to those who work there, to something that brings people together for a common cause to create ongoing value. This shift may sound obvious but how this has affected both the employer and the employee has profound implications on how expectations are being managed on both sides.

What did not Change

Despite the sea change in the way organizations have evolved and how they are managed, a few things have *not* changed. For one, the way an enterprise looks at its value-creation process. Creating economic value is at the heart of any enterprise. This is even true of the government or charitable organizations. This latter allusion may seem farfetched, but if one looks at the long-term horizon of the purpose of such institutions they fit this bill. Social organizations create similar value at a more human level, whose long term effect is economic, but which is difficult to measure in a transactional context.

In this context, then, the other aspect of what remains unchanged of an organization is its human ethos. No matter how much technology drives an organization's mission and no matter how fast a technology is being assimilated in an organization to "automate" its operations, it has a basic purpose. This purpose is the final outcome it provides as a human experience. It is this purpose that will determine the ultimate fate of a business. This human dimension is the overriding factor that will ultimately dictate how an organization succeeds.

Looking Ahead

What lies ahead is anyone's guess. But despite all the changes that have taken place since the early days of the human race, what has remained unchanged is the human condition. As long as the humans dominate this planet, their primordial needs are going to override any other factors that influence the endeavors that they undertake. So, as difficult as it is to predict what lies ahead that is specific it is also not that difficult to project that little is going to change in an overall sense. Humans are going to remain humans for eons and they are going to create conditions that define their survival.

Surviving Today's Workplace

Today's workplace is vastly different from the one merely a decade ago. Why? There are many reasons for this difference. For one, the layoffs, job consolidations, and the continued uncertainty of what is going to be off shored, outsourced, and cut back have created a level of unprecedented uncertainty and resultant anxiety in today's workplace. Many seasoned workers, who have changed jobs in the past few years, have suddenly realized that the place they are entering today is unfriendly to a new employee. Their peers are less willing to accept them as a part of the team and cooperate with them in ways that will give them some level of comfort to settle into the new place.

This paranoia is not limited to those entering a new place of work, it is apparent to them even in their own place of work. So, how does one deal with this ratcheting anxiety, paranoia, and uncertainty? The following guidelines may help:

1. Be clear about your role, responsibilities, and accountabilities within your own group. Know your manager and understand what their priorities are.

2. In a matrix organization, where you may have two bosses to report to, be clear about your role and how you will be measured.

3. Do great work. Merely doing great work is, however, not enough in today's climate. You must make sure that your work is known to others, especially your chain of command. Write emails, memos, or otherwise communicate to all those who matter in your immediate welfare. Do not assume anything.

4. Often, out of sight is out of mind. Those who telecommute and are mostly invisible to the rest of the organization must keep their visibility through adopting some suggestion from # 3.

5. Even though you may feel removed from the customer, make sure that you take care of the customer in ways that is consistent with your current role. Publish stories about your customer encounters in memos, emails, and other communications.

6. Develop good relationships with others and communicate well with those who can help you advance your agenda.

7. Do not gossip or spread rumors

8. Under promise and over deliver

9. Learn something new every day

10. Be good to yourself

11. Have a concerted development plan for your own growth

12. Ask, do not assume

13. Be confident and look powerful

14. Determine what your emotional tonic is and have it at least once a day

15. Don't let others bring you down

16. If in doubt, read the quote at the head of this chapter

Summary Chapter-1: Today's Workplace

The chapter begins with the historical perspective on how today's workplace evolved, especially over the past 50-plus years. Because of the rapid globalization, the changes—shifts—in the workplace accelerated. This discussion then leads to the enumeration of the 10 factors that cause today's workplace to be what it is:

- ✓ Information Ubiquity
- ✓ Flattened Hierarchies
- ✓ Core and Context
- ✓ Sourcing and outsourcing
- ✓ Off shoring
- ✓ Client-server networks
- ✓ Focus on value creation
- ✓ Managing virtual teams
- ✓ Common understanding of the management process
- ✓ The concept of leadership process

Although off shoring has created an acute problem in the U.S. labor market, its long term effects have to be dealt with by developing job skill strategies that accommodate how the jobs are shifting as a result of this off shoring. There are many hidden opportunities, as a result, that are not visible to most. To those looking for jobs this insight—Table-5—provides an avenue on how to structure your job search or stay competitive in your current job. To those who are already working, this insight provides a way to fortify their current job in ways that gives them a competitive advantage. To survive and even thrive in today's workplace, having a good handle on the last two items listed above is critical: the concept of the management and leadership process. Later in this book, both concepts are presented to help the reader understand this.

To survive in today's workplace each employee must develop their own survival guide. Some of these survival strategies are presented at the end of the chapter.

CHAPTER 2

Organizational Basics

> *"Organization is not an organizational chart, but a complex pattern or communication and other relationships in a group of human beings."*
> —Herbert Simon in *Administrative Behavior*

This chapter is presented to help readers understand how an organization came into existence and describe some fundamental concepts that shaped the modern organization. This chapter is not meant to provide an academic perspective of organizational theory—there are many excellent books written on this topic—but is presented to provide a practical perspective of how organizations came into being and how they evolved to their state today. The chapter also provides some basic rules of survival in today's organization.

What is an Organization?

An organization is a place where two or more people work together for a common purpose. The "place" does not have to be a physical entity. People could be connected in cyberspace forming a virtual organization and still share an organizational purpose. Often, some never even meet face-to-face to achieve what they set out to do, but nevertheless are brought together with a shared purpose that creates an organization. Thus, an organization creates a forum for socializing a purpose by virtue of its ability to bring people together.

The purpose of an organization is to provide a means to achieving performance and results for the business to which it belongs. The *purpose* of a business itself is to create customers and deliver value to them. The *function* of a business is twofold: marketing its value and engaging in meaningful innovation that creates a stream of ongoing value for the customer. At the epicenter of an organization is management and managers. This topic is discussed more fully in the next chapter.

Although an organization may have a single purpose, not everyone in it sees it the same way. Having a supportive purpose is enough for an organization to function. The closer the different views of those who work in the organization the more effective the organization becomes. Misaligned objectives and differences in peoples' views, of what the purpose is, can cause misalignment resulting in the organization becoming dysfunctional. This does not mean or imply that everyone in an organization must think alike. This, too, can cause dysfunction. Certain amount of dissent and differing perspectives can create a healthy tension in an organization because of the debate that they create and force leaders to think more clearly about the right way to move forward.

Being a social entity with a purpose, an organization has two elements: The human side and the purpose side. When the purpose side has an economic motive an organization becomes a business. In all other cases an organization remains a collection of people with an end objective.

In order to understand the human aspects of the organization, it is important to understand the human behavior in the following scenarios:

> Individual behavior

> Interpersonal behavior

> Group/Team dynamics

> Intragroup behavior

> Intergroup behavior

> Interorganizational behavior

In the absence of strong leadership (to be discussed in the next chapter) human behavior, in any setting, tends to regress to maximizing individual benefit. In a social environment, where multiple individuals are involved, a particular point of view will drive the agenda to attain the given mission at hand. In such cases, the individual agenda becomes a hidden agenda, when there is an open conflict between the agreed mission and the individual's view of it.

According to management science, most organizations fall roughly into five types:

> Pyramids or Hierarchies

> Committees or Juries

> Staff Organization or Cross-functional Team

> ➢ Matrix Organizations

> ➢ Ecologies

> ➢ Composite Organizations

> ➢ "Chaordic" Organizations

Pyramids or Hierarchies

A hierarchy exemplifies an arrangement with a leader who leads leaders. This is the classic bureaucracy. Usually one "rises" by seniority, or by acquiring authority over more people.

Pyramids are an effective way to achieve repeatable results because they have the shortest path from the standard-setter to the worker. They suffer from communication and supervisory faults because the organization is only as good as its weakest link. They lack creativity because they have poor communications. The classic fix for the communication problem is a magazine that reviews the whole hierarchy's business, perhaps daily or weekly. One good scheme has each person send e-mail up each week, telling what they did, their plans, and problems. Each boss makes a summary and sends it up. Then all the bosses send their summary down, appended to the summary from their boss.

Hierarchies were satirized in *The Peter Principle* (1969), a book that introduced the term *hierarchiology* and the saying that "in a hierarchy, every employee tends to rise to their level of incompetence."

Committees or Juries

These consist of a group of peers, who decide as a group, perhaps by voting. The difference between a jury and a committee is that the members of the committee are usually assigned to perform or lead further actions, after the group comes to a decision, whereas members of a jury merely come to a decision. In common law countries, legal juries render decisions of guilt, liability, and quantify damages. Juries are also used in athletic contests, book awards, and similar activities. Sometimes a selection committee functions like a jury. In the middle ages, juries in continental Europe were used to determine the law according to consensus amongst local notables.

Committees are often the most reliable way to make decisions. Condorcet's jury theorem proved that if the average member votes better than a roll of dice, then adding more members increases the number of majorities that can come to a correct vote (however correctness is defined). The problem is that if the average member is *worse* than a roll of dice, the committee's decisions grow worse, not better! Staffing is crucial in such memberships.

Famously, unstructured committees can dither without making decisions. Parliamentary procedure, such as Robert's Rules of Order, helps prevent dithering.

Staff Organization or Cross-functional Team

A staff helps an expert get all their work done. To this end, a "chief of staff" decides whether an assignment is routine or not. If it's routine, he assigns it to a staff member, who is a sort of junior expert. The chief of staff schedules the routine problems and checks that they are completed.

If a problem is not routine, the chief of staff notices. He passes it to the expert, who solves the problem, and educates the staff—converting the problem into a routine problem.

Staffs make decisions quickly, and carry out assignments efficiently, though less reliably than committees or matrices. For this reason businesses often prefer to use this method.

Staffs break down easily, usually from bad selection of people. Dilbert's boss is a non-expert trying to run a staff. In a "cross functional team," like an executive committee, the boss *has* to be a non-expert, because so many kinds of expertise are required. Also: chiefs of staff can be disorganized, play favorites, or can't tell what should go to the expert.

Matrix Organization

On the face of it, this is the perfect organization. One hierarchy is "functional" and assures that each type of expert in the organization is well-trained, and measured by a boss who is a super-expert in the same field. The other dimension is "executive" and tries to get projects completed using the experts.

Matrices are the only known organizations that can consistently create complex technical products like airplanes and engines. The problem is that going through channels takes too long. Getting approval to actually *do* anything often needs the approval of each type of expert, and both of each expert's bosses! The trick is to speed approvals: make approval everybody's number one job, and simplify sign-offs. The other problem a matrix organization faces is lack of control of resources. The "executive" who runs the project is at the mercy of the line manager who furnishes the resources to complete the project. Often, the "executive" is helpless when resources are yanked away at critical times and the projects are left to languish, awaiting resources. From a customer view point this resource allocation can be less than optimal.

Ecologies

This organization has intense competition. Bad parts of the organization starve. Good ones get more work. Everybody is paid for what they actually do, and runs a tiny business that has to show a profit or they get canned. For example: upper managers invest, and if they make bad investments, there's no profit. Engineers rent their designs out to manufacturing. Facilities people rent space, etc.

This is a really effective organization. But it's wasteful because all those dead pieces of organization have valuable training, and are very hard to recycle. They're bitter and they will stop taking it after a while. Reorganization follows.

Composite Organizations

These try to use each of the above types of organization in the right places. Very occasionally, a true organizational genius can make this work, for a while. Don't bet on it in the long term. Success outgrows the ability of the genius.

"Chaordic" Organizations

An emerging model of organizing human endeavors, based on a blending of chaos and order (hence "chaordic"), comes out of the work of Dee Hock and the creation of the VISA, a now ubiquitous credit card franchise. The organizational concept behind it is based on the loose collection of member entities that subscribe to the common principles of the brand that went on to become one the most recognized symbols of the modern business world.

Faulty Assumptions about Organizations

Leadership vs. Management: Many assume that leadership has to come from the top. This is not true, because leadership does not require authority derived from a position. Anyone can be a leader and provide leadership in thought, action, or results. Management, however, requires position of authority. For someone to manage they must have an organizational position that allows them to implement changes to the system and enforce their will on the rest of the organization. Leadership can be challenged but management cannot be, at least without serious repercussions.

Coordinating vs. Managing: There is yet another assumption many make that involves coordinating a function. They assume that it requires management authority. Coordinating entails merely making sure that various elements of an organization, assigned for the task for coordination, do what they set out to do. Coordinators usually work on exercising their ability to persuade others rather than using any authority, which they may or may not have, to make things happen.

There Is One Best Way: If one considers an organization as a system, then to achieve the end, many approaches can be considered equally viable. In the parlance of systems thinking this is called equifinality. Whatever works is the best way, rather than a specific way someone may consider to be best for their purposes. Unless experience has proven one way of doing something produces better results than others, all avenues are equally fruitful. With many personal agendas and many perspectives on any given topic, the best approach to achieving the ends is to set the objectives and leave the driving to those on the front lines, with some guidance and guidelines as appropriate.

Agreement vs. Disagreement: Many in an organization believe that disagreement is detrimental to an organization's success. Nothing could be further from the reality. Disagreement is healthy in an organization. Disagreement spawns debate and debate often leads to clarity, agreement, and respect for the thought leadership. If everyone agrees, on the other hand, to the top decision makers, who are often removed from the realities of the front lines and are even insulated from it, the organization often becomes unrealistic in its expectations and things start going wrong. Morale tanks and the whole organization loses its purpose. Although disagreement is good, once a decision is made, all those who disagreed initially and participated in the debate must then give their wholehearted support to the final course of action, even though they may not have endorsed the final decision.

Resistance Vs. Fear of the Unknown: Any change in an organization meets with resistance. Often this resistance comes from lack of clarity surrounding a change and how it may affect those who are participating in it. As a result of the change, some may lose their organizational position or power and that creates apprehension. Any time a change or an idea meets with resistance, it is incumbent upon the leaders and particularly the management to understand the reason for the fear and then allay it so that everyone participates in the process.

Fear of the unknown is existential. Everyone deals with existential fear and no one can claim immunity from it. The best avenue for those in the position of power is to dispel the fear among the rank and file by modeling behavior that encourages risk taking.

Optimizing Vs. Doing the Best: For an organization to succeed, it is required that each of the component sections do its part in ways that the sum total of their contributions produces the optimal outcome. If, on the other hand, each one did their best, the overall effect may not be having the best outcome. An organization is a system and, as stated in optimization, having only one part of the organization do its best does not produce the best overall outcome. In fact, it requires that everyone perform sub optimally to produce an optimal outcome. This is counter-intuitive to most. The best metaphor, in this context, is that of an athlete, who is practicing for a decathlon event. For winning in this event, the champion does not have to be tops in any one of the ten events, yet overall winning is possible!

Faulty Assumptions about People

Just as there are faulty assumptions many make about how an organization functions, there are faulty assumptions about people who work in them. Often, these assumptions are held out by managers and executives, who manage the activities of people reporting to them with the hope that they will do well by them. They are often surprised when the decisions they make and the resulting actions they take and what they expect as a result do not comport with their expectations. Often, they do not bother to investigate deeper and dismiss their experience as something anomalous with the particular employee or a group of them. When they repeat a similar mistake, in a different context, there, too, they rationalize.

Everyone wants to learn and grow: This is one of the most common assumptions made by managers, who often take it for granted in making decisions that affect those working under them. It is often that people make assumptions about others based on what drives them. It is likely that a manager assumes that those who work for them are after their job and want to climb the corporate ladder as they did. Many employees are doing what they do for a mere paycheck and nothing more. Many see their managers struggling in their roles and vow never themselves to become one! Although everyone wants to grow, they may choose to grow at their own pace. Managers often make a mistake, in such cases, by rewarding employees for good work by sending them to workshops and training camps to improve their skills. Unless such junkets result in an employee's increased performance on the job, a manager may be surprised to know that the employee did not particularly appreciate the gesture. The best approach is to ask each employee what they see as a good reward for their special act.

One pay system satisfies everyone: Although it is easier for an organization to have a single model for compensating its employees, more is not always better. Some may chose to defer some of their compensation to later. Some may want a different structure of how they are rewarded and so on. Also, with age employees' priorities shift in the way they see their rewards and compensation.

Better teams for better results: Teams are an organizational design that has its place. Some tasks lend themselves to a team setting while others can only be done by individuals, without anyone else interfering in the process of how it is done. Also, not all teams are created equal. A football team functions very differently from a team that supports a race car driver and that again differently from a tennis duo. The need for how a given task is carried out in an organization must drive how the organization is designed. Often, teams are formed just because everyone thinks that teams are the way to go in all their activities. This was amply demonstrated by the egregious failure at Levi Strauss, the famous jeans manufacturer. In their design they forced people to perform in a team setting, where individuals far outpaced team norms. Levi Strauss finally shut down most of its manufacturing in the U.S.

All technologies require teams: This is yet another faulty assumption about teams and teaming. Once again, organizational design is what is behind how work gets done. Later on in this chapter the seven factors that make an organizational system will be presented. In that model, technology is one of the seven factors that make the organizational system. Some technologies support teaming better and create an environment where work gets done more efficiently, but in other cases some technologies do not support that design. For example, before the advent of the personal computer, it was not easy for each author to make overheads on their own. In the bygone era, before the advent of computers, a team of professionals was needed to manually prepare each overhead and it took time to produce such visuals. To maintain such a team in today's organization would be suicidal. Yet another example is how the steam locomotives were operated. They required three operators: a fireman, an assistant, and an engineer. When electric locomotives came, only one engineer was needed. Unions fought this to protect their ranks, despite the irrelevance of the old team design. Many railroads were forced to go out of business as a result of such practices, which they had to comply with, merely to keep the unions happy.

Job satisfaction means productivity: This is yet another false assumption managers make about how jobs are designed and how people are assigned to the jobs. It is true that a happy employee is a good employee, how they perform their job and what they produce is more a matter of the system they are using to carry out their work. Setting up such a system is a managers' job. The managers work on a system and the employees work in it.

Motivation comes from challenging work: Just as we dispelled the myth of everyone wanting to learn and grow, not everyone wants to be challenged in what they do. Some look forward to a challenge in what they do while others do not. In fact, it should not be a surprise to managers that given a challenging task, some will become conscious of being watched and do poorly in their tasks. The best policy, once again, is to ask before assigning a challenge to someone, in the hope that they will rise to it. Also, looking at the track record provides a good sense of what the employee expects.

Smart employees speak up: Yet another fallacious assumption managers often make is that those with something worthwhile to say, about how things could be better, will speak up and communicate what is on their mind. Often, those who are good at what they do and especially in the individual contributor group, do not speak up, even when their idea may be better than those more vociferous and aggressive in how they present themselves. In staff and other meetings, those who speak up are typically uninhibited about expressing what is on their minds and it is they who take most of the air time in such meetings. There are many who have great ideas, but lack the confidence to articulate them and to defend their stance in a group, where they may be challenged. Good managers have the ability to seek inputs from everyone in a variety of ways, not in just staff meetings, to allow them to get a broad perspective on what is possible and what can be different. See Appendix-III: How to Manage Meetings.

The desire and willingness to openly speak up is particularly an inhibition for those who are first-generation immigrants. Many have language and cultural barriers to overcome. Many think that to suggest something different than the status quo is tantamount to challenging their manager or management, an act perhaps unthinkable in their native country.

The other side of the coin, too, is that this perception of leadership, where those who speak up are perceived as good leaders, is not going to change in the corporate world. So, it is worth considering for those, immigrants or not, who feel inhibited in voicing their opinions in meetings—a common forum for such opportunities—to develop the skill to be able to do this effectively. This is a learned and acquired skill.

The Evolution of the Modern Organization

To appreciate how far we have come in a short time in the context of organizational thought, it is instructive to look back and see the starting point. The modern industrial enterprise is not that old, although the concept of an organization dates back to the armies of the Romans and the Greek empires. The first industrial enterprise was the weaving mills started by Frederick Engles in England in 1834, which had about 200 laborers. In fact, it was Karl Marx, a friend of Engles, who wrote his first white paper about communism based on his observations about that enterprise. The graphic in Figure-1 illustrates the evolution of the modern organization.

A brief discussion of each stage follows to provide a perspective to the reader.

Feudal Management

Until about the early 1800s the largest enterprises were farming or the armed services. There were some industrial establishments coming into existence at that time as a result of the industrial revolution but they were, by far, in minority and were small in size.

Most farming was done for landowners—lords—by their vassals. Feudalism was the system of political organization prevailing in Europe from the 9th to about the 15th centuries. In that system, the lord held the land in fee. When a land or property is held in fee, it meant that the owner had absolute right to the property and the vassals owed their existence to the owner of the land. This arrangement was prevalent in most of Europe, Asia, and the Middle East.

The same arrangement was also true—and is true today—of the organizations based on the needs of the military. In these organizations, the authority of the chain of command is absolute, where those working under them can lose their life in carrying out the orders from the top. By virtue of the mission of such organizations, this is not likely to change.

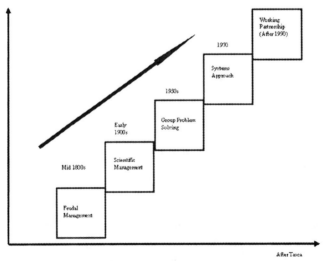

Figure-1: The Evolution of Organizational Management

As the industrial age exploded into the civilization in the mid 1800s, organizations came into being with the seed of the modern-day enterprise. People came to a place of work, which was organized along functional lines. There was structure to the work that was done and there was also structure to how the organization carried out its mission. Although there was the separation between the management and labor, the arrangement was vastly different from the one where the land was in fee for the vassals in the farming economy.

Scientific Management

As the industrial revolution came into being, larger and larger industrial organizations came into existence. Towards the end of the 19th century, textile, steel, railroad, bicycle, and consumer goods began their industrial existence, as we know it today, in its infancy. As a result, larger and larger organizations began to form. As the process of mass production began to take shape, a leading figure then, Frederick Winslow Taylor, an industrial engineer, began the study of how humans carry out their tasks using scientific methods. What Taylor found in 1929, was that to extract the maximum output from each worker, if the workload and how it is carried out were methodized, then the productivity could be dramatically improved. He demonstrated that using counterintuitive approaches to how work was carried out.

For example, Taylor showed that instead of giving each worker the maximum load to carry on each trip, if an optimal load were identified and if the worker were given frequent rest periods, the throughput could increase. He demonstrated this by his time-and-motion studies. His methods are still in use today wherever mass production methods are used, as in automobile manufacturing and even fast food restaurants. In today's context, the word Taylorism is used disparagingly to express dehumanizing work.

Taylor's methods were in vogue in the industrialized world, until the early part of the 20th century.

Group Problem Solving

As the population of the blue collar and white collar workforce began to equal in most organizations, the working arrangement became more and more fluid, less rigid. Management began to realize that workers, at all levels, had ideas that were worthy of consideration to improve work and productivity. As a result, groups of workers, on both sides, began to collaborate to find better ways to do things and carry out decision making.

Manifestation of such thinking emerged into what came to be known as the Quality Circles in Japan and later adopted in the U.S. in the 1960s. Quality Circles were an organizational design, albeit informal, responsible for providing an oversight to improve the quality of the goods, services, and work life. In a typical design, a group of workers from different functional areas formally got together on a regular basis. In their group, they discussed production and process problems that got in the way of the smooth workflow and identified solutions to these problems. The management then prioritized these solutions and implemented them.

Systems Approach

Even in the group problem solving model an organization was viewed as a discrete entity of various functions collaborating to achieve the desired outcome. It was not until the mid 60s that leading organizational thinkers started modeling an organization as a system of components tied together to perform as an integrated whole. This approach to looking at an organization as a whole, resulted in a systems perspective being applied to how organizations behave, produce results, and can be managed resulted in breakthroughs that helped improved understanding of how things get done and how they can be improved. In this context an organization was viewed as a social system.

As the systems perspective became in vogue, managers began to realize that:

- To understand how different parts of an organization behave, merely cause-and-effect relationships, a product of linear thinking, were not enough. One needed to understand the *relationships* between all elements with each other.

- To optimize the functioning of the overall organization, all contributing elements needed to understand that they each did not need to operate optimally

- Cause and effect in a complex system were not related in nearness of time and space.

These insights were breakthroughs in developing an understanding of how organizations behave, how to solve problems to eliminate the root cause, and how to optimize an organization's capability.

Working Partnerships

In today's organization, boundaries have disappeared across functions, levels, and participants that help it create economic value in a global context. Supply chains have gone global. The workforce has become virtual and the supplier and the customer have become partners in an increasingly collaborative way. This thinking has created a business ecosystem that has global tentacles.

Looking ahead, as relationships between different constituencies that make an organization or that support it get more and more complex, the structures that bind them have to become more fluid. Also, the formal relationships among different entities have to be somewhat based on *ad hoc* understanding than a one cast in stone. Such rigidity can only hamper an organization's ability to support a business that relies on it to provide the lifeblood for its success. In this context, an organization can be seen as the soul of the business that benefits from its existence. At the same time, the business drives the organization and not the other way around.

The "7-S" Model

To describe how organizations work (should work), organizational theorists have posited models. These models have evolved over time and are of different flavors, offering different views. One model proposed by Tom Peters and Allen Waterman of McKinsey Consulting has evolved and endured over the past fifty years or so and is still used to explain, predict, and diagnose organizations. In today's "Chaordic" organizations this model has limitations as we shall see in this discussion, but it still provides a good basis for thinking of how organizations must be led.

The 7-S model is a systems model in that it views an organization as a system, an assemblage of interconnected "components" that behave as a whole. In a systems context, we often talk of relationships among the components or elements, than about cause and effect. Cause-and-effect reflects linear thinking, not systems thinking. In view of this model, it is difficult to change one element and not expect to have its ramifications to the other parts of the organization. This is analogous to any system that is well put together. For example, when a person has a vision problem and it starts getting worse, the rest of the senses come to the aid of this sense by increasing their role in how they function to compensate for the failing vision. Those visually impaired often exhibit keen application of other senses where they are able to use their heightened senses to "see" what others cannot.

The following is a brief description of the elements of the 7-S model shown graphically in Figure-2:

Shared Values: There are various names for this element of the model: Super Ordinate Goals, Vision, and Purpose, just to name a few. A shared value is what everyone in an organization comes together for, to achieve a vision that the organization holds. One way to get a sense of this shared value for an organization is to ask anyone, especially the top managers, what the company's mission is. If all the responses are in synch, then there *is* a common shared value.

Strategy: Strategy is the single factor that differentiates one organization (or business) from another. Strategy is doing different things from what the competitors are doing or doing the same things as competitors', but doing them differently. Once a strategy is chosen, it should not be changed based on everyday changes that happen around the business ecosystem. Steadfastly applying a strategy, once it has been carefully thought out and implemented, is one of the hallmarks of success of an organization or business and its leadership.

Structure: Structure refers to how an organization is put together to carry out the various functions that are required to deliver what it sets out to deliver. Structure follows strategy. In other words, unless an organization has a clear strategy, it cannot organize itself to execute its mission. No amount of shuffling can compensate for a sound strategy and a well executed structure that supports that strategy.

Classically, there is a functional organization, where each function is represented by a department that executed that function. Another design is a product organization where each product has its own organization that is responsible for its own product line. A third design is a matrix organization that entails a functional organization assigning its experts to a business or product organization on a project basis. Each design has its pros and cons. Of all designs, the functional organization is the most efficient (although not always customer friendly!).

Systems: These refer to the infrastructure of an organization. There are information systems, communication systems, payroll systems, management systems, scheduling systems, etc. Collectively these systems form the backbone of an organization and are considered the 'background" on which everyone relies on to carry out their everyday roles. When these systems fail the "background" becomes the "foreground" and those affected, suffer greatly by focusing on something other than their job!

Staff: Staff is the lifeblood of an organization. It is the organization's soul. No organization is stronger than the people who are in it. Creating a balanced staff in terms of their strengths weaknesses and values is one of most critical leadership challenges.

Skills: Skills or knowledge are the competencies of the people who work in an organization. Each organization builds its capability based on the needs and then hiring those who bring the skills to produce results that meet these needs (See "Needs, Work, and Results) in Chapter-4: Management Basics.

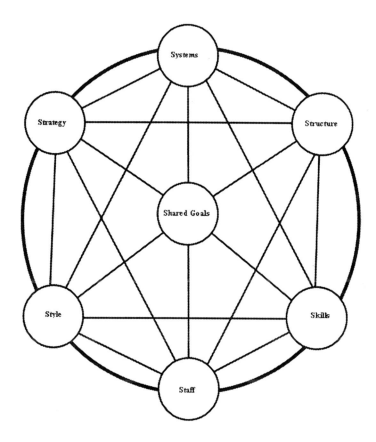

Figure-2: The "7-S" Model of Organization

Style: Style is the invisible that governs an organization. It is also a major component of an organizations' culture. This refers to how the important decisions are made and how the top management communicates these decisions. Style is also what the management does on a day-to-day basis to:

- Reinforce standards

- Deal with the customer

- Emphasize quality

- Encourage risk taking

- Clarify goals, roles, and responsibilities

- Reward those who perform well

- Discover why employees should give their long-term commitment to the organization

These are some of the factors that govern an organization's style.

Limitations of the 7-S Model

The power of the 7-S model comes from the fact that it helps people assess their organization in terms that others understand. It also helps people diagnose problems and figure out ways to solve them so that the organization becomes stronger and healthier. Most recognize that purposeful and efficient organizational action cannot take place unless all the seven elements are in alignment. Dysfunctional organizations result from having these elements at cross-purposes with each other.

One limitation of this model comes from the fact that, to gain competitive advantage, an organization must learn faster than its competitors. This capacity to learn comes from fluidity, flexibility, and openness. A well-aligned organization has these links (see Figure-2) more and more crystallized, hence rigid and even brittle. The dilemma is that when unaligned, they work at cross-purposes from an organization where the alignment is perfect. A fluid organization is what is needed in a rapidly changing business ecosystem.

For an organization to be competitive—a key ingredient for success, not just survival—it must constantly re-examine itself. Adaptability is the basis for a learning organization.

Where Do We Go from Here?

Organizations are the backbone of a business. Its structure is the basis on which it is organized. From a management standpoint, the way an organization is structured says much about what is expected of an organization and how it functions. Its mission is integral to its structure. This is why a military organization will not change in its design, whereas a business that is expected to function in a fluid economy will evolve to succeed in a changing environment. The dictum that business must change to succeed (and, not *grow* to succeed, as is commonly misquoted) aptly puts into perspective, its survival mantra.

As has happened in the past few hundred years, organizations have undergone metamorphoses. Whereas the basic premise of a business has not changed. And, so it will continue. The basic purpose of a business is to create value (economic, social, political, or spiritual), but the basic purpose of an organization is to make sure that as conditions change, the purpose it serves is always in harmony with how the business must function to create that value. So, as conditions change that require the business to stay its course, the way an organization is managed and put together must make that eminently possible. To make sure that this happens, with accelerating economic and political changes, it should not be a surprise that the way an organization is brought about will also bring changes.

Summary Chapter-2: Organizational Basics

The chapter begins with the definition of what an organization is and describes it as two or more people working together to attain a common business objective. Behaviors in an organization can be identified as those belonging to any of the following categories:

- Individual behavior

- Interpersonal behavior

- Group/Team dynamics

- Intragroup behavior

- Intergroup behavior

- Interorganizational behavior

According to the existing theories most organizations can be classified into the following categories:

➢ Pyramids or Hierarchies

➢ Committees or Juries

➢ Staff Organization or Cross-functional Team

➢ Matrix Organizations

➢ Ecologies

➢ Composite Organizations

➢ "Chaordic" Organizations

A discussion on faulty assumptions (six) about organizations is presented, followed by faulty assumptions (seven) about the people who work in them.

How the modern organization evolved, starting from its early stages in the 1800s is depicted in Figure-1, which shows the five stages bringing us to today's reality.

A commonly accepted model, of how an organization as a system behaves, is presented in a graphic that shows the classical "7-S" model:

- Shared Goals

- Systems

- Structure

- Strategy

- Skills

- Style

- Staff

Using the current velocity of how organizations are emerging, the chapter ends with where this may all lead in tomorrow's organization.

CHAPTER 3

Management Basics

"Leaders are not just scorekeepers. They are responsible for creating something better."
— Bill Creech, author, management consultant.

Organizations have been around for as long as humans have got together for a common purpose. To run an efficient organization it must be *managed* well. As organizations grew and evolved over the centuries, how they were managed also changed. The purpose of managing was to make sure that the organization that was created to drive a business towards its goal met its objectives and served its purpose. This is true of all organizations. Even armed forces, whose mission is to defend their country, are driven by these principles. Their business is to project defensive and offensive powers, so that a nation achieves what it sets out to achieve.

In the context of this chapter, the word management means directing businesses, government agencies, foundations, and many other organizations and activities. The central idea of management is to help achieve a carefully chosen goal. The word management also refers to the group of people—executives— who perform management activities. In the context of this chapter, the word implies the directing of organizations, and not the people who do the directing.

The purpose of management is to marshal resources it has at its disposal to achieve the objectives of the business it manages. Although the concept of management involves resources, its focus is always how the people, who staff different functions, carry out their duties so that the resources for which they are responsible and the outcomes for which they are accountable are clearly delineated. The challenge of management, then, has been how best to carry out this duty. Over the centuries, this single mission has been central to the way the management theory and practice have evolved. This chapter is presented so that the role of management and how it comes about in the modern-day organization and business are clear.

The Management Challenge: Leadership

Not many distinguish between management and leadership. In fact, many assume that once you have "manager" in your title—or something similar—you are a leader. Nothing could be further from the truth! In this chapter, we define both and clarify key concepts around these terms. In this section we define terms in the context of their historical evolution and how they should be viewed in today's organizations.

Let us first define the meaning of leader. A leader attracts followers. Leadership does not require a position or a title. It comes from within, and it radiates in the direction of those who see its power.

Although being a leader does not require a position within an organization, having a position of power amplifies its effects. For example, an individual contributor can be a leader if the person's idea appeals to many colleagues and they embrace it. Whether their followers are able to implement the idea and make it work depends on the support they derive from the rest of the organization. If the CEO gets behind this idea, it has an entirely different gravitas; very soon, the entire organization would be rallying around the idea to make it work and to implement it.

This is why open communication and a process where such ideas permeate an organization, regardless of their origin and pedigree, are so important for its success.

Thus, regardless of one's position inside a hierarchy, the power of a leader is derived from their ideas. How manifest those ideas are and what happens to them, once articulated, is a matter of how many must follow those ideas to further their interests. And, this clearly depends on the legal authority and positional power a leader wields. This is a position-based proposition. A simple implication of this discussion is that anyone can be a leader, regardless of where they are inside an organization!

Managers, on the other had, derive their power from the positions they hold. There is no concept of followership here, only that of obeying the chain of command. The power of their decisions and actions come from their hierarchical authority, which is derived from their "legal" status. If this manager also happens to be leader, then there is also a moral force that is integral to the power that they hold. Having both makes them a great manager.

How many managers do you know who are also great leaders?

So, the management challenge is building leaders. In this chapter we will explore how, using some concepts of the functions of managing and defining some key terms, easy it is to articulate a framework for defining leadership and management. In this discussion it is easy to also show how they flow from each other and how they can be developed as a capability.

What's a Manager

As employees get promoted from their positions as individual contributors, they soon reach the first level of management. Typically, this level is called a supervisor. A supervisor is responsible for a group of individual contributors who work under them. As the supervisor gets promoted, they go on to achieve higher levels of titles based on how the organization is structured.

One of the greatest ironies, in this evolution, is that as an individual contributor gets promoted to a managerial position, the relationship of the two roles this person is expected to play is not well understood by many. This is particularly true for those in this new role. In simple terms the two roles are at cross purposes. As an individual contributor, the person was responsible for producing an outcome on their own. In today's organizational context they may be required to collaborate as team members with others, but even there the role remains focused on producing individual outcomes. As a manager, however, they are expected to get others to produce an outcome using the resources for which they are responsible, including themselves, as needed.

This shift in expectations is very difficult for many to understand. Their interpretation of the promotion they just received is that they must do more of what they did to secure that promotion—doing good hands-on work! To get others, who are now reporting to the new manager to carry out their work, this manager must use a different approach to create the outcomes. Newly minted managers believe that, since they got promoted for doing the work that they did and the way they did it, others must follow them and their methods. This is *not* the role of a manger. So, there must be a framework that shows these newly minted managers, what they must now do differently, to be effective in their new role.

Gunning for the Manager Role

Individual contributors often expect to be promoted to a manager's role, after they have been in that role for a while. They continue to do a good—even a great—job as an individual contributor and are often disappointed and surprised when another peer becomes their new manager. Their disappointment multiplies when this appointee is relatively new to the organization. The seed of this discontent stems from what is presented in the previous paragraph. It is repeated here for emphasis: the functions of a manager and an individual contributor are disparate. So, for an individual contributor to be viewed as a manager, they must start behaving like one, well before they expect to get the promotion for themselves. Merely doing more hands-on work and producing great results may lead to disappointment. See the author's *Pathways to Career Nirvana: An Ultimate Success Sourcebook!*, Chapter-2: Career History, specifically, making transition from Stage-II to Stage-III. Those, who continue to look at their seniority and technical contribution, to lead them to be appointed managers, will have a long wait.

Functions of a Manager

In the new role, the manager must understand the functions of managing. There are four functions that a manager must perform to be effective:

- **Lead**

- **Plan**

- **Organize**

- **Set up Controls**

The division of a manager's function dates back to Plato's writings of circa 400 B.C. In his famous book, *The Republic*, Plato outlines five "causes" that are central to the effective functioning of an organization or a society. The four functions above are a variant of the original five that Plato proposed.

Below is a brief description of each of the four functions for which a manager is responsible.

Lead

To Lead is what managers must do, although few do it well. Leadership is a process and leading is what leaders must do. Both words derive their origin from the verb *lead*. Lead means, in its dictionary sense, to guide in a way by going in advance. This going in advance can refer to anything, from providing thought leadership to directing a platoon's charge to attack an enemy camp. Every act of leadership creates followership; without followership there is no leadership.

Leading can be defined as getting people to work together and influencing them to take effective action that takes an organization to the goal it seeks to achieve. For a leader to succeed, they may not need people to work in teams. A good leader will let those who are more productive in teams, work in such a setting and simultaneously provide the right environment for those who prefer to work alone. Good leaders do not impose any particular design, to achieve their goals. They are not hidebound. Rather, they have conquered the art of providing the right and fluid environment for all those whom they respect, so that, together, they produce the desired outcome.

The leading *function* comprises many *activities* that flesh out what is involved in executing this function as a leader. A partial list of the most key activities, in which a leader must engage follows:

Envision new possibilities and make them achievable, by socializing the ideas and communicating them to others. Create excitement and energy around their vision and make their vision the mission of each individual for whom they have responsibility.

Change the status quo. Being a change agent, is one of key roles of a leader. Change is hard because of the inertia that sets in an organization and then people get comfortable with the status quo. Metaphorically, a leader is like a grain of sand in an oyster to create discomfort so that people build something valuable as a result. The leader must become a change agent, and not just someone who proclaims an initiative and goes about doing things without *leading* the change.

Select People to staff the organization is one of the key activities of a leader. Selecting the right people who, in turn, can provide the ongoing leadership to the organization, and who can follow a leader's path, is critical to an organization's success.

Communicate to others how a leader envisions goals and how the followers carry them out is central to a leader's success. Communication plays a central role in today's organization. Some of the importance of this activity is masked by the over communication that takes place in today's technology-ridden organization. Over communication, as can result from emails, web conferences, cyber channels, and surveys, can actually block learning by how these channels are used to carry out everyday communication that is vital to an organization's functioning.

Make Decisions that cause the change to happen involves the culmination of a process of facts gathering, intuiting, and getting the sense of what is the best course of action for the organization to follow.

To **Galvanize** their followers, leaders use their natural powers to energize action in their organization to achieve things that they get excited about. A leader must provide the impetus for their followers to act in ways that takes them closer to the vision that the leader espouses. Motivation to act must come from within and can be provided through *inspiration, encouragement,* or by *impelling* others to take action. How this motivation is provided has much to do with how it sustains itself. For example, if a leader *inspires* their followers to act in a certain way, the followers are likely to sustain that effort far more diligently than if the leader were to *encourage* the followers to act. To have to impel others to act is the weakest form of motivating followers.

Development of people is the final activity that a leader must engage in, to make sure that those under them grow and become more confident in their own ability to lead in turn. Coaching and mentoring are some of the ways a leader can develop people.

Plan

Plans are the outcomes of the planning process. Planning entails evaluating available options, methods, and approaches and then choosing a course of action that takes the organization to the destination it is seeking. Planning a trip is good example of this. The function of planning involves the following activities:

Understanding the Ecosystem is the starting point for any planning process. A leader must understand the environment in which they must navigate their organization, to take it where they wish. This includes the markets, customers, competitors, suppliers, and all the emerging options available that can drive an organization and the business that it supports. As a result of this understanding, a leader must continually decide what the context is and the core that creates unique value for their customers. A more detailed discussion of the difference between the context and the core is presented in chapter-10: Managing the Customer.

Developing Strategies entails identifying the best way to achieve an objective with the existing resources. Strategy has to do with doing things differently from the competitors or doing the same things, but differently. Once a strategy is developed and chosen, it should not be casually changed, because it takes time for a strategy to produce results.

Forecasting involves estimating and predicting future conditions and events and the forces that shape these events. Developing specific actions to deal with these forces and protecting the intended outcomes is what forecasting is about.

Developing objectives deals with clearly identifying results that are intended as measurable outcomes from the overall leadership process.

Budgeting is yet another planning activity that deals with resource allocation in a studied way to achieve the set objectives. Capitalism refers to the best use of available resources to create unique value. Budgeting is a process to achieve this optimization and is, hence, central to the planning process.

Scheduling is establishing a time sequence for creating the desired outcomes. When the milestones and actions are complex, the activities are called a program and the process of managing the schedule (and budget and deliverables) on such a set of activities is called program management.

Program Management involves setting a sequence of work steps to be followed to achieve the objective.

Developing Policies establishes standing decisions to apply for recurring issues and problems of concern to the organization

Developing Procedures and Processes allows standardizing work and methods that must be done uniformly.

Organize

To organize refers to the function of using available resources in a disciplined way. The function of organizing relates to arranging and relating the work to be done, so that people can perform it most efficiently. Structuring an organization, to organize the employees in different functional areas and then assigning them their tasks, falls under this function.

Some key activities in this function are listed below:

Translating Strategy is an important activity. It must be done so that it is executed in the most effective way. Structure follows strategy is the organizational dictum, and it means that unless the leader understands the strategy and how to make it work, forming an organizational structure is premature.

Developing Organizational Structure entails identifying and grouping the work to be done so that it can be accomplished effectively.

Delegating involves assigning responsibility and authority to others and setting up accountability so that results can be achieved through people.

Developing Teams is an integral part of Organizing, in that, in this era of off shoring and outsourcing, how these teams deliver on their mission is very much at the heart of this activity.

Set up Controls

In today's politically correct environment, this word is likely to have connotations that go beyond its original intent in this context. Here, Control implies setting up mechanisms so that a functioning organization lets the managers monitor its vital signs and takes actions when preset conditions are met in the way events are happening. Setting up controls involves assessing how work gets done and interjecting mechanisms for setting up standards, measuring, evaluating, and correcting the work done, so that it can be regulated. Control is an anticipatory concept in this context, much like the controls of an automobile or an airplane. The four activities of setting up controls are summarized below:

Assessing the degree of control needed is the first order of business. Different organizations require different degrees of monitoring and control. An organization's culture and what it aims for has much to do with the kinds of controls it espouses to implement. This activity is central to how the culture of an organization grows and hence critical to this function.

Developing Performance Standards allows establishing the criteria by which work and results get evaluated.

Measuring Performance entails documenting and reporting the work being done and the results of this work.

Evaluating Performance is the logical next step of analyzing, interpreting, and determining the quality of the work produced and its value in terms of results.

Correcting Performance entails rectifying or improving the work being done and the results secured.

Evaluating Controls entails assessing how well the set up controls work and drive the organization in the direction the leader intends to take it. Changing these points and measures of control is an important ongoing activity.

The four management functions and the associated activities comprise an articulated system of management. The reason this assemblage is called a system, is that each function and its associated activity is related to the other functions and activities, in ways that create a composite effect that cannot be isolated to just one of the elements. The word articulated implies that the elements of the entire system are all affected by each other. In other words, you cannot change one element without making an impact on the others. In a system, all parts contribute to producing an outcome. Changing one element affects the other in time and space. Thus, if the strategy for doing something changes, the organization structure changes (structure follows strategy). Similarly, if the method of measuring performance is revised, so does the way employees get measured, evaluated, and compensated. In understanding the behavior of an organization—certainly its people—it is imperative to understand this systemic relationship.

Accountability Agreement

As an example of how to use all that we have so far posited, into an operational reality, is shown here. In a typical organization, one of the challenges managers face is, clearly defining a task, assigning it to the right group of individuals, and then setting up mechanisms, so that the task gets accomplished with full visibility to how it is being executed. Managers lack tools and knowledge, of how to hold people under them accountable for actions and reward them for success. It is often done anecdotally, by *ad hoc* means, and sometimes, by political expediency. This is why proper accountability—or its lack thereof—is at the root of much unhappiness for many.

Setting up accountabilities is hard work. Both for managers and workers, who report to them, this is somewhat elusive. Both, managers and the direct reports often embark on tasks that are ill defined, poorly resourced, and improperly measured. For the past 20 years, the word "empowerment" has been thrown in the mix to point fingers in any direction possible, when ill-defined tasks are inadequately resourced, poorly planned, and launched on a hopeless schedule. Managers often tell their teams that they should feel empowered to do whatever necessary to complete the task. This is not empowerment, but a cop out. Neither the manger nor the team responsible for carrying out the task are fully committed to it, in the absence of the most basic requirements for a job to be done correctly. Often, people inside an organization take the "empowerment route" and hope for the best, by keeping their figures crossed!

Enter Accountability Agreement. An Accountability Agreement is a single management tool that emerged from the framework just outlined, on how management does its work. It allows both, the manager, and the team carrying out the task, to define all parameters of the work, how it will be resourced, scheduled, and measured upon completion. This is done, so that it leaves no doubt in the minds of all involved. As can be seen from the sample provided for a typical task at hand, an Accountability Agreement can nail down many aspects of what must be done so that there is no doubt in anyone's mind about what is expected. Implementing an Accountability Agreement in major undertakings or projects eliminates finger pointing and blame when things go wrong. It, however, does not guarantee success in an undertaking!

Typically, in project settings, an Accountability Agreement can take the place of a project plan or vice versa. In a functional setting, the annual performance review and plan can be a good substitute. Even in a functional organization, it is a good idea to have such an agreement, when undertaking major initiatives.

Accountability Agreement (Illustrative Example)

Mission: To change the inspection process and methodology for the incoming material, so that the overall scrap, return, and in-process assembly product failure that is material related is reduced by 50 percent. Reduce cost of material-related quality by $4 million annually.

Strategy: The key strategy to accomplish the mission is to identify where the losses are and prioritize them. Using the Pareto principle (The 80:20 Rule), prioritize the areas that will provide the most benefits. Eliminate the root cause, for each identified symptoms to achieve the set target of 50 percent reduction.

Duration: The project will start on January 4, 2005 and end on December 20, 2006, with final measurement on December 20, 2007.

Leader: The project lead is Jim Hicks (full time) and will report to Sally Smith, his manager.

Resources: Jim will be provided help, throughout the organization, in the areas of activities that affect the material quality, including assembly line personnel and operations. Although none of these employees will be assigned to Jim, he will have access to them as required. Jim is to identify names and duration of those needed on the project and give that list to Sally by March 1, 2005. Additional resources may be provided based on the review of the needs.

Measurement: The current material quality cost is estimated at nearly $8 million annually. This must be documented as a baseline. This includes the labor associated with inspection, administrative, and shipping costs. The same measurement will be used to determine the results of the project on an ongoing basis, and, finally, by December 2007.

Contingency: If there is a major change in the organization, the project will be redefined.

Management Role: Sally will communicate the initiative to the organization and request support from affected departments by January 20, 2005. Sally will also provide her support on an ongoing basis, to ensure that the entire organization is supportive of the initiative, and that Jim is provided unfettered access to operations that are central to the success of this project.

Milestones: The following major milestones are agreed to:

1. Complete project plan   March 1, 2005

2. Initial measurement benchmark   June 1, 2005

3. Prioritized loss costs (ranked loss centers)   August 1, 2005

4. Initial quality improvement milestone (25%)   December 21, 2005

5. Management presentation   March 1, 2006

6. Updated quality improvement milestone (40%)   December 20, 2006

7. Final measurement milestone   (50%)   December 20, 2007

Reward: Upon meeting of all the parameters, stated here, Jim will be paid $10,000 in recognition of his success, half of this amount on December 31, 2005 and the remainder on December 31, 2007. Reward will be prorated in case of milestone shortfall.

Changes: Any changes to Jim's roles and responsibilities during the above period will be documented in this agreement as they occur.

Jim Hicks   Sally Smith

January 4, 2005

Management Work Gap

The management work gap refers to the difference between the manager's work (lead, plan, organize, and set up controls) they should perform and the amount of management work they actually perform. Most managers spend too much time performing inappropriate management work and meddling in technical work, which does not belong to their positions. This results in their spending less time *doing the management work that only they can do.*

There are reasons why managers spend too much time doing things that do not need to be done or doing technical work that others can do at a much lower level. One reason managers revert back to doing technical work, beyond their need to do it, is their *desire* to do technical work. Some rationalize this by convincing themselves that keeping up with technical development is good for their careers. Others do it to show their direct reports, peers, and bosses that they have not lost touch with their core skill that got them where they now function as managers. Others do it merely to satisfy their own ego. Whatever the reason is, the effect of a manager doing technical work, beyond the appropriate level, reverberates down the chain inside their own organization and creates gross inefficiencies. As a manager does more technical work their subordinates, then, end up doing even more just to keep up. The reverberations of pushing technical work down the chain of command have long-term effects on an organization that are often difficult to measure. Undone management work often has long-term detrimental effects.

Another reason why managers choose to do technical work, in preference to management work is that, often, technical work has an urgency that is hard to ignore. This constant firefighting promotes a culture of crisis management and, as a result, the organization is unable to attain its true potential.

To understand the implications of the management work gap, Table-3 provides some insights. From that table, a first-level manager is expected to spend 50 percent of their time doing management work (lead, plan, organize, and set up controls). Most do only about 10 percent and, spend the remainder of their time on technical work or doing inappropriate management work. For someone at this level, inappropriate management work entails micromanaging or looking over someone, reporting to them, when there is no reason to do so. As one moves up the organization, a middle manager spends about 30 percent of their time doing management work, whereas they are expected to spend about 70 percent in that activity. A CEO should not spend more than about 10 percent of their time doing technical work, or inappropriate management work; whereas they are known to spend as much as 50 percent of their time dong such work. Thus, half of a CEO's time goes into doing a combination of technical work and inappropriate management work. An inappropriate management work entails doing the work that *someone else* can do. Managers must spend their time doing work that *only* they can do. Even if a manager does not do as much technical work, as may be represented by numbers suggested in the table, their doing inappropriate management work—not delegating enough—has a similar effect. When a manager repeats the work of his subordinates or does not let go of its control, overall, long-term management work suffers and the organization mortgages its future.

The price an organization pays, in dealing with the management gap in terms of lost opportunities, morale, unattained potentialities, and stifling creativity, is incalculable.

An Antidote

An antidote for the management gap is not just one, but many. The following list is self explanatory, once the concept of the management gap is clear:

- Understand the difference between management work and technical work

- Set a threshold for the level of technical work that you must do; do not exceed it

- Identify the management work that *only* you can do

- Delegate all other management work to your direct reports

- Develop value consciousness for the work that you do as a manager

- Create a circumfluent awareness of how management work gets done

- Alert your peers and subordinates to catch you when you do inappropriate management work

- When tempted to do technical work, defer it as a reward

- Keep a daily log of how you spend your time

- On major projects and initiatives establish Accountability Contracts

- Clear the backlog of all management work (Performance Reviews constitute the worst backlogs)

- When technical work is likely to suck you in, delegate that to someone who works for you

- Do not solve management problems using technical approaches; management problem must be solved using management functions (lead, plan, organize, and set up controls)

When someone at higher levels of management gets involved in taking calls from irate customers, they must discipline themselves from not getting involved in solving the root cause of the problem. This must be done by a disciplined organizational process that is owned throughout the organization.

The following table represents how employees, at different levels, spend their time in a typical environment. This data came from the manufacturing in which 1200 individuals were polled.

Although the data in Table-3 comes from those working in the manufacturing sector, it is easy to see that the pattern of how managers spend their time is independent of industry. The primary reason for this dysfunction is that management work does not present itself as something requiring urgent attention until it is too late. Technical work, on the other hand, screams out for attention and must be addressed immediately, otherwise things immediately deteriorate.

#	Title	Mgmnt	Work	Technical	Work	Admn Work	Comments
	(Percentage time spent)	Ideal	Actual	Ideal	Actual	Ideal	Actual time from Research data
1	Individual Contributor	0	0	90	90	10	
2	Team Leader	20	10	70	80	10	No line authority
3	Supervisor	40	15	45	70	15	
4	Manager	50	20	30	60	20	
5	Director	60	25	20	55	20	
6	Vice President	70	50	15	35	15	
7	Sr./Exec. VP	80	55	12	30	8	
8	CEO	90	60	10	40	0	Here technical Work includes Inappropriate Management work

Notes:
1. Technical work implies all work other than management and administrative work
2. At levels above director, administrative work is done by their assistants
3. Inappropriate management work refers to what can be delegated downwards
4. Individual Contributors may have to start undertaking management tasks *before* getting their promotion

Table-3: The Management Work Gap

Managers Doing Technical Work

The question that jumps out from this discussion of the management work gap is why do managers spend so much time doing technical work, or doing inappropriate management work. The following list may be helpful in under-standing the answer to this question:

1. Their fear that removing themselves from day-to-day technical work will make them obsolete. An antidote for this is that if you continue to feel this way then you are headed in the wrong direc-tion. A manager must develop conceptual skills, as they grow in their role so that detailed technical work becomes less relevant in how they generate value.

2. A sense of loss of control when they delegate appropriate management work. Since management work does not scream for attention—it quietly piles up—managers are likely to feel that they are not being kept busy by their "workload." This sense of "idling" prompts them to get involved in doing things that are inappropriate.

3. Most technical work that managers do involves checking the work someone is doing or has already done. If the person doing that task is not competent, then the manager must reassign them or terminate them. Many managers find it painful to take that step. Many lack the confidence, in their own style, to hold others accountable for their output. This habit has an opposite effect on how the people resource gets managed: those who are marginal get the most management attention!

4. Many managers think that since they got promoted for doing superior technical work, they must be better at it than anyone who works for them. This often results in their doing or redoing the work of others. This practice results in thwarted development of people.

Effects of the Management-Work Gap

The Management-Work Gap is a symptom of how managers, at all levels, fail to see their proper role in the management process that drives an organization and the business it supports. The effects of the Management-Work Gap are at many levels, the most important of which is at a personal level for everyone in an organization. It creates a pervasive culture of everyone working well below their potential and capability, frustrating those who can see what needs to be done, but are unable to articulate the syndrome or its cause. At a personal level, those who fall victim to the pernicious effects of the Management-Work Gap, suffer from stress that accelerates their health-related problems, including mental health.

Cardiovascular disease is a leading cause of death. Annually, about 500,000 deaths due to heart attacks alone are attributed in the U.S. Additionally, $400 billion is estimated to be lost to the economy, due to the costs associated with this affliction, a staggering amount even in a $12 Trillion economy.

Managers seem to have an abnormally high rate of both morbidity and mortality, when it comes to cardiovascular epidemiology (estimated at twice the average for the population as a whole). There are many factors that can be causative of cardiovascular disease. Some are listed below:

- Stress

- Genetics

- Diet

- Early upbringing (role of a manager, how to work with subordinates)

- Exercise regimen

- Work-life balance

- Family life

- Spiritual life

Executives, managers, and those who routinely deal with business and organizational issues seem to be particularly exposed to higher cardiovascular risk at an early age. Although each of the factors listed above should be managed to reduce the overall risk, one in particular seem to be elusive for many: Stress. In many managers of different racial makeup, where despite their near absence of obesity, suffer a higher incidence of cardiovascular affliction and early mortality.

An Antidote: To manage the overall risk and improve one's chances of a long and healthy lifestyle, a complete reinvention is required. The focus of this discussion is on stress management using counter-intuitive means. Other factors can then be integrated to bring an overall improvement in the risk factors, depending on how a reinvention can be fashioned.

One major area of stress for managers is their role. Managers (this includes everyone who has to shepherd resources) must understand their role to be effective. Few do!

A manager's role, as we have already presented, is to discharge the functions of a manager: *lead, plan, organize, and set up controls.* In addition, every manager is expected to do an *appropriate* amount of technical work. The trouble lies on how managers—starting with the first level and all the way up to a CEO—view this responsibility and how they discharge it. Since most managers—especially those who are immigrants—come from technical streams and rise in an organization from a hands-on position into management positions, they tend to view their basic technical background as their backbone skill. As a manager, this thinking can be detrimental to them and to their organization. How? Not letting go of the technical work and also discharging their duties as a manager can create a conflict within their own role that can rapidly escalate into a stress cycle that cannot be broken without an intervention.

Every manager must do work appropriate to the level. Studies have shown that, as previously presented in this chapter, most do technical work in *preference* to management work, because of their familiarity with it and the urgency with which it demands attention. How does this relate to managing stress?

The answers are simple: Technical work in an organization is endless. Undone management work, leaves those under a manager, rudderless and unproductive. When managers preempt their time, by doing technical work instead of the management work that *only* they can do, it creates a telescopic effect throughout the organization. For some immigrant managers, who rise from technical ranks—most do—this is further compounded by their communication style and this single factor alone can result in organizational dysfunction and distrust. Since the idea of a failure to most, and, especially to immigrant managers, is an anathema, they work even harder to bring control to their role.

As a class, some managers are not brought up in a culture of *straight talk*. This is particularly true of those from Asian (including those from the Indian subcontinent) backgrounds. Some even continue to reflect their upbringing by not treating their subordinates with equity. In addition, many are viewed as not open to a dialog and are seen as domineering, especially by Caucasian subordinates. To some an immigrant manager can be a mystery. Thus, a vicious cycle ensues. Stereotypical perceptions about lack of straight-talk, ease of access, and openness to learn, compound the problem many managers face. Such perceptions vitiate any attempts to bring a better working environment, where a manger is heading up an organization. Now, these managers personalize this plight and end up carrying that stress, without knowing how to release it or deal with it from early on. The result is that both the manager and the rest of the organization are stressed. So, what is the antidote?

An Antidote: A major breakthrough in stress reduction is to know the boundaries of management work and keeping the right balance between the management work and the technical work. Doing the management work that only a manager can do and knowing what it is are critical to this breakthrough. The second factor is to know how to open channels of communication. Breaking through that barrier, then practicing leadership behaviors that open channels of communication for straight talk can greatly reduce personal stress *and* improve organizational effectiveness.

Key Principles

Key Principles are a set of reminders, to managers and employees alike that guide their thinking, actions, and reflections when they are at crossroads.

Being aware of these principles helps in everyday existence in the corporate world and can save much of wasted effort, trial and error and surprises. Key principles are presented for each management function. On their face they may appear self-evident, even trivial. And, *that* is the point. Despite their simplicity and obviousness, their diligent application in everyday organizational encounters can mean the difference between success and failure. This aspect of managing is not different from what we see in our everyday life: often people think that although they understand these principles, somehow they are immune from it because of their simplicity. Some managers believe that they are smarter than these simple principles; hence they do not apply to what they do. For these people, experience is the best teacher.

General Principles

Leadership Force: The greater the diversion of views, the greater the leadership force required for unified action.

Need, Results, and Work: Needs are satisfied by results, which are the outcomes of purposeful work.

Value Creation: Value is created in a transaction, when parties agree that there is a mutual benefit as a result of that transaction

Manage Expectations: Managing expectations are important in a business transaction. This agreement is required on the part of all parties involved.

Alignment of Purpose: The greater the alignment of purpose in a given task, job, or career, the lesser the effort required to satisfy the needs of those who are engaged in it.

Work Separation: The most effective results are achieved by performing the management work separately from technical work. No amount of technical work can compensate for the lack of doing appropriate management work, at a time that it needs to be done.

Technical Preemption: When called upon to do management work and technical work, managers tend to prefer doing technical work.

Organizational Levels: The higher an individual rises in an organization, the more management they should perform. See Table-3 to understand how this happens.

Socratic Inquiry: It is much more effective for a manager to ask the right questions than to provide answers to those who come to them for advice. This style of leadership will eliminate the practice of having to go to the manager expecting the answers and foster the practice of self-reliance.

Organizational Entropy: The more complex and hierarchical an organization is, the more entropy (confusion) it builds that it must overcome to be effective. A manager's job is to intercept this entropy.

Ongoing Improvement: Organizations will tend to win, if they engage in relentless pursuit of improvement in every aspect of what they do.

Lead

Principles of Decision Making:

Decision Making: Motivation increases with the authority people are given to make decisions that affect their work and the results they produce from it.

Problem Definition: The more accurately a problem is defined, the more effective the decision leading to its solution.

Differing Perceptions: Facts may appear to differ, depending on the timing and point in time from which they are observed.

Sufficient Evidence: A decision can only be as sound as the assumptions and evidence on which it is based.

Practical Perfection: Waiting for a perfect decision is never as effective as making the best decision at the right time, evaluating its effect, and then making a correction.

Principles of Motivation

Reciprocity: The manner, in which an individual treats others, is the manner in which they will be treated, in return.

Human Reaction: People tend to react in terms of their own understanding and their emotional make up.

Mind Mapping: People will selectively hear what suits their agenda and ignore the rest until they are forced to confront it.

Participation: Motivation tends to increase as people are given opportunities to participate in decisions.

Communication: Motivation tends to increase as people are informed about matters affecting their own work.

Recognition: Motivation increases as people are given recognition for their contributions

Job Satisfaction: Contributions to organizational objectives increases to the extent people find in them satisfaction of their own personal objectives.

Change: Change tends to be more successful, by starting where people are and implementing only as fast as people can understand and participate in the change process. Change also happens faster if those involved in it clearly see the benefit, even though they themselves may not realize a part of that benefit.

Continuous Improvement: Change tends to be more successful by ongoing and small incremental steps.

Principles of Communication

Mind Mapping: Before communicating something that is likely to have an emotional impact, understanding a person's emotional state can help the communication.

Emotional Appeal: Feelings tend to overpower facts: Appeals to emotions tend to be communicated more readily than appeals to reason.

Usage Traction: The more often an idea is put to use, the better it tends to be understood and remembered.

Rapport: Understanding is made easier when there is a good relationship between those communicating.

Cognitive Dissonance: When two people do not get along together, their communication is likely to result in increased adversarial interpretation of what was exchanged.

Line Loss: The fewer people through whom a message passes, the better it will be understood.

Principles of Selection

Homogeneity: People tend to select new employees who are like them

Conformity: New people in an organization tend to conform to the habits of those already there.

Predictability: Past performance tends to be the best predictor of future performance

Plan

Principles of Planning

The Critical Few: In most situations, a small number of causes will have the greatest impact on the results. This is also knows as the Pareto Principle or the 80:20 rule (80 percent of the effect is produced by 20 percent of the factors).

Present Choices: Decisions made today will tend to limit the actions that can be taken in the future.

Horizon Flexibility: The further in time a horizon is projected, the more the flexibility in carrying it out.

Resistance to Change: The more a plan requires people to change, the more they will tend to resist it.

Organize

Principles of Organizing

Limits of Freedom: The greater the freedom of one group to encroach upon the freedom of the others, the less overall freedom.

Convergent Accountability: The more people to whom an individual reports, the more difficult it is to maintain accountability for results.

Minimizing Entropy: The more rigid an organizational structure is the more the entropy (chaos or confusion).

Principles of Delegating

Control Limits: Managers can safely delegate only what they can safely control.

Commensurate Authority: The less the authority given an individual, the more difficult the performance of responsibility for that individual.

Complete Accountability: The more accountability is fixed on individuals, the more effectively results can be monitored.

Setting up Controls

Principles of Control

Self-Regulation: The most effective form of regulation is self-regulation; regulate your own actions before regulating others.

Principle of Performance Appraisal

Self-Evaluation: The more effectively people can evaluate their own performance; the stronger their motivation to improve tends to be. This is why setting up the correct way to implement a 360 degree review, is critical to provide the feedback necessary to make self improvement.

Self-Improvement: The more honestly people seek feedback on their performance, the greater the chance of improvement in their performance.

Summary: Chapter-3: Management Basics

This chapter begins with the presentation of today's management challenge: Leadership.

It then goes on to outline the basic principles of managing. It starts with defining the four Functions of managing:

- Lead

- Plan

- Organize

- Set up Controls

Each function is expanded into its constituent Activities.

Central to managing any important activity, is an Accountability Agreement. It integrates all the functions and many activities described in the discussion, to create an unambiguous plan to manage an activity or project. To successfully execute any major undertaking or role, even for a non-manager, Accountability Contract is critical. A sample contact is presented.

A peculiar but very real problem of ubiquitous Management Work Gap is presented. Management work gap results from managers at each level doing inappropriate management work or work that others can do. The reverberations of this phenomenon pervade throughout an organization and create chronic problems associated with how work gets done and how critical management work takes a back seat. Understanding of this process is critical to improving managerial effectiveness in an organization. The pernicious effects of the Management Work Gap result in a stressed out workplace, inefficiencies, demoralized worker (and manager) and an unhappy customer.

The chapter ends with a listing of Key Principles that provide guidance to managers and employees on how to manage effectively.

CHAPTER 4

Managing Your Own Journey

"There is a loftier ambition than to merely stand high in the world. It is to stoop down and lift mankind a little higher."
—Henry van Dyke, poet (1852–1933)

Introduction

This chapter provides a foundation for many of life's transitions and challenges, including your quest to lift humanity a little higher. We reach a stage in life when we start to find its meaning. This is when we finally grow up. But, this, too, is a journey that we all embark on, and for which we need some rules as well as tools. Although much of the material provided here is applicable to job, career, and work-related issues, its applicability is quite broad. The material is more an arsenal of tools and rules one must learn during rites of passage, in our life's journey.

Day-to-day challenges in our jobs, including job and career transitions, are where we need guidance and some ready-made answers that fit our needs. They also demand a deep reservoir of energy and an awareness of our own capacity to deal with such junctures. These tools and rules are provided as a consistent framework around which we can build our ongoing defensive and offensive capabilities. These capabilities will allow us to succeed in an increasingly unpredictable and chaotic world of business in general and career and jobs in particular. During most of such junctures, our response underscores preparedness, more than finesse, in accomplishing what we set out to achieve.

This chapter has three main topics, to help improve your chances of success during life's journey, on almost anything from job or career transitions to dealing with our everyday challenges:

- Managing Challenges

- Getting Organized

- Understanding Yourself

This chapter also provides tools to cope with hurdles faced during challenging times; tools that provide some sense of control during the process.

Managing Challenges

When we are confronted with a challenge, we are assessing our capacity to deal with that challenge. In a way, during such assessments we are in a transition. Managing a personal transition comprises understanding the forces that drive it. How best to deal with these forces, common to all transitions can make these transitions meaningful and provide some degree of control to those facing them. It is this control that makes the transition a positive experience. The learning that comes from each experience validates our capacity to deal with them and gives us the confidence to confront even greater challenges. The following discussion presents the anatomy of a transition so that it is not a mystery.

Forces that are manageable drive personal transitions. Although no one can control the events that prompt a transition, understanding how to manage a career-or job-related transition or, for that matter, any transition, is critical for a positive outcome. The following discussion demystifies the various factors that manifest during a transition.

♠ What is a Transition?

A transition is a journey through which we travel to get to the destination, navigating through both time and emotional space. During critical transitions, our sense of time is warped and our emotions run deep. Many analogize such transitions as emotional roller-coaster rides.

During transitions, our life is changing; not ending!

Career transition can cause major trauma, especially if it involves finding new employment in a tanking economy. Navigating through such a transition can present a challenge that many are not prepared for and this includes getting settled at a new job in an unknown or even hostile environment. We can approach a transition one of two ways. One is to go and retreat, surrender to fate, and hope that things work out! The other is to take stock, find strength, and summon our innermost resources to discover what we are made of, develop new insights, and go on to conquer something to surprise even ourselves!

It is to this latter group this chapter—and this book—will be most helpful! This material is written for and is expected to be most helpful for those who deal with their challenges using the latter approach.

Regardless of the support we have around us, both emotionally and otherwise, we can control how we are affected by these challenges. The difference, in the way we deal with these challenges and how they affect us, is a matter of our preparedness, attitude, and our emotional constitution. We cannot control what happens to us in specific situations, but we can control how *we* deal with it! We can become victims or martyrs as easily as we can victors and masters based on choices only we can make. It is also a matter of what tools we have in our arsenal to deal with such situations that give us control over how we can do things differently and achieve the right outcomes. This chapter—and the book—provide many such tools.

Transitional Nirvana

Before we discuss Transitional Nirvana, let us first discuss Nirvana. After all, we are seeking this state in almost every endeavor we undertake.

Nirvana is a Sanskrit word that has to do with a state of bliss, and a state of existence where one is free from cycles of pain and suffering. In some Eastern philosophies, our existence consists of cycles of pain and pleasure. Unless we find ways of breaking this cycle we are stuck in it. Attaining Nirvana means breaking that cycle and finding bliss in our existence. Work Nirvana is a state of that bliss as it relates to our work life and it is achievable by practicing some of what is presented here, both in the chapter and in the book.

Adapting or even adopting what is presented here is a way to become free from career or job related cycles. This is *not* a religious practice; rather, it is a practice based on inner spiritual need and drive!

♠ Emotional Price

Emotional price is the non-physical energy expended in making a transition. Interestingly, the expenditure of the non-physical energy translates into physically depleting a body. Why? The physical, mental, and emotional resources are intertwined in our being, more than most realize.

When people are emotionally charged-up they are able to do amazing physical feats. When they are physically alert, their mental acuity is high, and when they are mentally sharp, their eyes twinkle. So, all these manifestations of existence are one and the same, except that what causes us to mobilize each is different. When one is challenged, as when going through a major transition, it is important to keep the three energy centers in harmony. The need for emotional energy is high when undergoing transitions, so it is important to keep a reservoir of the other two.

As is depicted in Figure-3, equilibrium between the physical, mental, and emotional energy centers is critical to overall health and harmony at any time, especially during a transition. This is why during a transition, maintaining a regimen that allows this balance is critical.

Another way to look at the emotional price paid during a personal transition, can be expressed by a simple relationship:

Emotional Price = Resistance to change + Resilience

Thus the emotional toll is high when our own resistance to change is high, ergo, fighting the change is bad. In a job situation, this change may involve something as simple as going back to a colleague, who has publicly disparaged you in a work situation, and seeking clarification of what was meant by it and vindicating your reputation. Additionally, taking this stance will forestall further such instances of disparagement and help you gain respect from your colleagues. The other option is to brood over what has happened, get angry, and hope that what has happened is in your mind, personalize it, and find some rationalization why you deserved it, and hope that it will not happen again!

Lowering our own resistance to change can go a long way in stretching out the emotional reservoir to deal with the transition. And, how does one do *that*? One way is to accept the inevitable and then positively look at how to quickly adapt to the changing circumstances. The concept of the Change Curve, Figure-4, describes how change happens and how to manage a transition through this change. Using some of the recommendations, it is easy to make this change speedily. Secondly, the emotional toll is inversely related to resilience. The higher the resilience—the ability to bounce back—the lower the emotional toll a transition is going to exact. Detailed discussion on resilience is deferred to the next section but it is important to know that there are exercises to become more resilient. They appear immediately following the discussion of the two additional factors that come into play during a successful transition presented below.

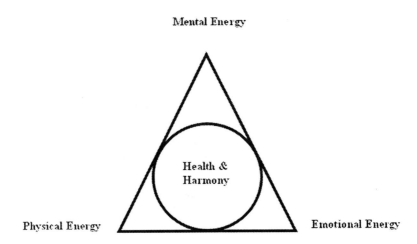

Figure-3: The Energy-Balance Trilogy

♠ How We Manifest to Others

There is a triad of factors integral to a successful transition. These factors influence how others perceive you:

- Managing your resilience

- Managing your chemicals

- Managing your fear or diffidence

Each of these is now discussed in the following sections, with specific tools to help provide a better outcome during a transition.

Managing Your Resilience

Resilience is a quality that allows you to bounce back from an unpleasant episode of a personal nature (trauma). Resilience lets you regroup and re-engage inner resources in a meaningful way to mobilize actions and move forward. One way to look at the power of being resilient is to look at its opposite: stiffness or rigidity! The classic metaphor of the mighty oak falling down in a gale-force wind and the supple but dainty willow plant bending in its path and yielding to its power, has much to convey in the way resilience can work. Those who are not able to yield to the powerful forces, temporary as they might be, can end up surrendering rather than finding themselves challenged by recognizing the power of these forces and then developing strategies to deal with them to rise to the challenge. Fighting these forces takes enormous inner resources, and then, when their power abates, there is no reserve left with which to move forward. Yielding to the forces on the other hand, gives the person a chance to regroup and then move ahead as their power wanes; it always does after a certain time!

To further understand resilience, knowing its components is a good start.

♠ Components of Personal Resilience

The following components are critical to assessing one's resilience in a transition:

- Knowing the situation and having a healthy perspective on it

- Having a deep understanding of yourself and confidence in your value

- Having a good support system: personal, professional, and social

- Ability to take action despite uncertainty and clarity

➢ **Knowing the situation and having a perspective on it:** Being open to different possibilities of how you can go through the transition can be a great resource in developing a healthy perspective. It is normal to not only take such setbacks personally, but also to *personalize* them. The difference between the two is, when you take something personally, you are holding yourself accountable for what happened to you and taking action to move ahead with it. This is healthy. However, when you personalize an adverse situation, you are trying to look at what you might have done differently to avoid it. The latter is a matter of mere speculation. For example, if you have just been sidelined in your job and you believe that if you had done something differently you could have prevented it, you are personalizing the outcome.

➢ **Having a deep understanding of yourself and confidence in your value:** This is the hard part. This is so because we identify our worth with how others value us. Our job—and the position we hold—is one measure of this value. When that is threatened it is easy to doubt our own value. Losing your spot of favored position is a temporary setback, a road bump. What Socrates said nearly 2500 years back is still relevant today:

"Remember that there is nothing stable in human affairs; therefore avoid undue elation in prosperity, or undue depression in adversity."

If this is the first time that you have run into a road bump and have to deal with it during a transition, consider it a wake-up call. If you have done this before, it is time to learn new ways to deal with what you knew from before. If you have never held a job—as a fresh graduate might—then it is time to find out how to cope with such situations and get ready for even greater setbacks in the future. Having a deep belief in your own value, worth, and ability to engage productively, are essential to developing confidence about yourself.

➢ **Having a good support system:** Having a good support system or network, is also key to successfully navigating through rough periods in one's life. Such a support system provides emotional, financial, mental, and physical resources. Most underestimate the size of their overall social and support network. The support system consists of personal, social, professional, and other connections. These connections are important in opening up additional resources. For example, if you know someone who has experience dealing with a situation similar to yours, they can be a resource. Having a career or life coach can also be a good resource. With such a resource, you are likely to get objective and expert input in dealing with your own situation.

➢ **Exercising the ability to take action despite, uncertainty and clarity:** In challenging times, it is easy to get paralyzed by overwhelming possibilities of actions and not knowing what actions are appropriate and when. Making a methodical plan and then discussing such a plan with someone within the support system can be a good way to move into action. They can also act as your checkpoint for progress. Once you start moving with a plan, you will feel less stressed and more in control, even though you are seeing little or no "action" initially. Remember, there is an inevitable delay between taking the right action and seeing its impact; much like a wall-mounted thermostat taking time to actually change the room temperature. Of course, in simpler situations, you can regroup using your own resources internally and learn how to cope to come out ahead.

Going With the Flow

Resilience can also be termed as "going with the flow!" The following story illustrates how this quality can help through life's ups and downs:

A very old Chinese Taoist story, describes a farmer in a poor country village. He was considered very well to do, because he owned a horse, which he used for plowing and for transportation.

One day his horse ran away. All his neighbors exclaimed how terrible this was, but the farmer merely said, "Maybe yes, maybe no." A few days later the horse returned and brought two wild horses with it. The neighbors all rejoiced at this good fortune, but the farmer just said, "Maybe yes, maybe no."

The next day the farmer's son tried to ride one of the wild horses; the horse threw him and broke his leg. The neighbors all offered their sympathy for his misfortune, the farmer again said, "Maybe yes, maybe no." The next week conscription officers came to the village to take young men for the army. They rejected the farmer's son because of his broken leg. When the neighbors told how lucky he was, the farmer replied, "Maybe yes, maybe no...."

The moral of the story, of course, is that the meaning of any event in our lives depends upon how we perceive it. Things do happen and we must learn to take them in stride.

Resilience Exercise

The following prescriptive exercise is designed to assess your resilience.

Tool-1: Managing Your Resilience: Exercise

To evaluate your own resilience, respond to the following items. Circle the number closest to your response and then add up the score at the end.

	Situational Perspective:	High 10-9-8-	Mid 7-6-5-4	Low 3-2-1
1	I have a sense of why I am feeling challenged			
2	I know why I am in transition now. With what was going on at work, the inevitability of this outcome was			
3	I know that there are less competent people in my own company getting ahead, and the extent to which I can disregard it is			
	Self-Understanding:			
4	I have a high confidence in my abilities to land the job that I deserve. The extent to which I can bank on it is			
5	I can reinvent myself to get what I want. My ability to reinvent, with some help is			
6	I can reposition within my own company. If that does not work, my ability to re-deploy myself is			
	Support System:			
7	The support I can derive from my own circle is			
8	My ability to grow the current network is			
	Taking Action:			
9	My confidence in planning and moving ahead is			
10	If the plan needs adjustment based on the outcomes, my ability to revise it is			
	Total Score			

If your score is 60 or higher, you can be considered resilient (be honest)! Practice behaviors that move you to a higher score.

* Managing Your Chemicals

This is the second factor that needs managing during transitions. It has to do with how others react to you. We, as chemical-generating organisms, are able to generate, among others, two hormones, and, in turn, *induce* the same in others. These two hormones dictate how others respond to us. Since job search is a social activity involving others, this is important.

The two chemicals contrast each other by their very nature, and how they affect physiologically and psychologically: one is epinephrine, more commonly known as adrenaline, responsible for helping us generate instinctive responses, and the other is beta-endorphin, considered many times more powerful than even morphine, a highly analgesic drug or a painkiller. Adrenaline helps generate fear, whereas beta-endorphin helps us become euphoric and joyful.

We are able to *induce* in those, with whom we interact, *their* adrenaline and beta-endorphin, creating an interesting dynamic. For example, if we are tense and self-absorbed with our own pain, we induce in those, who come near us, *their* adrenaline. Adrenaline release has one major affect on those who are experiencing its release: flight or fight! People are uncomfortable if you heap too much of your self-pity and pain in your interactions with them. Nature blessed us with this gift to react properly in the presence of fear. When one is confronted with a life-threatening situation, the release of their adrenaline causes them to instinctively fight or flight to save themselves from the imminent danger. So, if you cause others to release their adrenaline in your interaction with them, they simply walk away, rather than offering help! When people are suffering personal problems, as can happen from a job loss, their natural tendency is to indulge in self-pity, and tell everyone their woes. So, when meeting someone in a social setting, when in such a state, rather than launching into a tale of woes, try practicing an alternate behavior.

The preferred way is to start a pleasant conversation—talking about *them*. If you connect with the person, they will sense your body language and perhaps ask questions that may lead to a conversation where you bring up your needs. Even if the other person does not "get it," keep that interaction pleasant. If you, on the other hand, come on too strong with your woes, they may shun you from then on. You have caused them to release *their* adrenalin. In fact, in many interactions people will not generally remember what was said (facts), but how it was said (emotions) or the affect (how that made them feel).

On the other hand, when you come across to others as *genuinely* optimistic, positive and outwardly focused, joyful, and optimistic, their own reaction to your demeanor results in their body releasing the other hormone, beta-endorphin. This release causes others to experience joy and warmth around you. And, who does not want to be in that state? Putting others in this state can be a learned behavior!

Managing Your Chemicals: Exercise

The following exercise is designed to help you evaluate your response in different situations and how others may respond to you.

Tool-2: Managing Your Chemicals: Exercise

This exercise will explore your natural tendency to "induce" the good (endorphin) or the bad (adrenaline) chemical in your interaction with others. Respond with honesty to make this work for you. An adrenaline inducing interaction is likely to result in people walking away from you!

#	Behavior	(Endorphin Good	Adrenaline) Bad
1.	In my social interaction with others I am more apt to start with my woes.		X
2.	In my social interaction with others I begin first by asking about others and then sensing how I should hold my end of the conversation.	X	
3.	If others tell me how great things are for them when I know I am struggling, I feel uneasy.		X
4.	In a social group, when I know that I am in a bad space, I withdraw rather than using it to energize me.		X
5.	When I want someone to help me in my situation I do not waste time with pleasantries, I get right to it.		X
6.	When I face defeat, as a rejection or a setback, I withdraw from social activities and mope.		X
7.	When I face defeat, learn why and see others facing similar challenge, I keep my learning to myself		X
8.	Even when I know I am not doing well at work now, I have the ability to smile and keep my cool.	X	
9.	As I put increasingly greater effort to recover from my setbacks and fail, I feel down.		X
10.	I try to find faults with others.		X
11.	I generally believe that life sucks.		X
12.	When a series of things go bad during an early part of a work day, I assume that the rest of the day will follow suit.		X
13.	No matter how down I am I have the ability to make someone happy.	X	

If you have many X's circled on the right side of the column, clearly, you need to work on your attitude. Marking your own X on the "Good" side conveys that you have a healthy and positive attitude in the way you are approaching your job and its vicissitudes.

Managing Your Fear

The third and the final factor discussed here, that helps in transitional success, is the ability to operate without fear. How? When there is uncertainty, especially work related, there is angst, which can create fear. This emotion deeply affects those who let it run their lives. Fear creates its own adrenaline! This again creates others to see you as someone they want to avoid. Fear is something not kept inside ourselves as most think, it is something that is apparent to anyone who sees us; we wear it even without our knowing it. It is much like a strong perfume we wear that we can no longer smell! Fear impedes one's thinking and power to reason.

Fear, surrounding job uncertainty, can be managed since it is not instinctive fear. *Instinctive* fear is a gift that we are given to save our lives. It is an internally driven response induced when we know that our life—not our *existence*—is threatened as when someone confronts us with a gun or a wild beast we may encounter at camp unexpectedly. This instinctive fear puts our body in an automatic mode and impels us to react to it by flight or fight. Even under those life-threatening situations, the outcome is far more desirable when you are able to think rationally, and then act rather than react in panic. The only challenge is getting your mind into the thinking mode. Our response to *existential* fear can be managed to provide us the ability to create the best outcome.

During life's transitions, certain approaches we choose to adopt can help us. Recent studies have shown that those with an open mind, positive outlook, and without fear are more likely to come out ahead faster, than those who retreat, sulk, blame others for their woes, and move in fear. Fear and negativity around a situation can affect our mind by occluding it. An occluded mind is limited in its capacity to perform. Whereas someone who is fully engaged with emotional, mental, and physical resources can deliver so much more! This is why the first requirement, in a transition, is ridding of the fear factor! This is particularly true of job or career transitions.

Reminder: To successfully leverage one's internal resources and to mobilize untapped potential, becoming aware of the fear factor and overcoming the deepest fears are critical for a speedy transition to success.

Managing any transition *process* can be a rewarding experience, even though the episode prompting it itself can be emotionally traumatic.

Dealing with Sleeplessness

During intense transitions, it is normal to experience anxiety. Intense transitions can be those prompted by job situations, an impending termination or layoff, or anything that creates uncertainty, which leads to fear as we just discussed. Sometimes, this fear then drives certainty—the inevitable actually happens—which culminates in dread! During such episodes, it is normal to experience sleepless nights, or awaken in the middle of the night in sweat, and then lying awake with eyes wide open, wondering about what is next and finding meaning behind what is going on. In the quiet of the night, all negative thoughts multiply unchecked and create a paralyzing emotion from within. As situation deteriorates due to a declining economy, personal setbacks, and other factors, it creates further anxiety that impairs normal thinking. This is now a vicious cycle and it permeates our daily existence. Its effect is to slowly attack our own self-confidence and an ability to master our own destiny in an insidious and pernicious way. This fear that causes sleepless nights also vitiates our daily performance in all that we do to get out of the very situation that creates these nightmares. The best way to deal with this quandary is to recognize that such angst is common to most that have to face similar challenging transitions. Holding positive thoughts and painting pictures of blissful outcomes from these transitions can be good tools to combat these negative forces. Of course, thoughtful and visionary planning, diligent execution, and course correction, as learning is derived from ongoing efforts, must fortify such positive imagery.

Focusing on planned actions and holding the belief that the universe provides us our needs through our lessons, can be affirming. Such lessons make us strong and are proving grounds for our own inner strength of character. Accepting defeat in the face of adversity and retreating do not complete the intended lesson; they merely defer it. Additionally, one's self-confidence and esteem take a beating in this early admission of defeat. Maintaining a regimen, a plan, and diligent execution of the plan are important for success and early positive conclusion of such transitions. Remember *"Only the brave make the dangerous tenable."*—John Fitzgerald Kennedy.

Managing Your Fear: Exercise

This exercise is designed to assess your ability to control fear in situations that are not life threatening. Existence-threatening situations—loss of status, job, and money—do not warrant a response that is steeped in fear or one that is fear induced. In such situations it is normal to be in a state of quandary. But this is *different* from feeling fear!

This exercise measures your propensity to operate under fear in stressful situations at a job interview, social interactions with others, especially with those whom you consider to be in positions of power, and where the outcome of the situation can affect your future.

Tool-3: <u>Managing Your Fear: Exercise</u>

#	Factor/Score (write your response number for each item listed below):	Fear Factor High 10-9-8-	Middle 7-6-5-4	Low 3-2-1
1.	When I am called upon to prove my abilities, as in a meeting or a test, I become afraid			
2.	When I am in interactions with others where my abilities can be challenged, I become paralyzed with fear and my fear of failure or exposure is			
3.	For an important meeting or a presentation, no amount of preparation can rid the feeling that, if I fail, terrible things can happen to my future			
4.	No matter how hard I try, I cannot seem to shake the feeling that somehow, what I know and do not know will get exposed, and I will be humiliated			
5.	I am so anxious to make a good impression on those who matter to me, that I often leave feeling as though I have done poorly, because of my high degree of apprehension			
6.	No matter how well I do in an important interaction (as a presentation), I leave feeling that given another chance I would do even better			
7.	In important meetings, I feel as though the other person is in control and I am solicitous to them			
8.	For an important presentation, I keep reflecting on the past situations where I flubbed them, and keep thinking that it could happen again			
9.	In an important social or business interaction, my palms are sweaty before a handshake			
10.	I often fear losing my possessions if I lose my job for long. The degree to which this bothers me is			

Overall score:

Fear Rating:	70 and up	High degree of fear
	50-70	Somewhat fearful
	30-50	Healthy fear level
	30 and below	Almost fearless

Practice behaviors and thoughts that move you to the lower scores.

♠ A Transformational Strategy

During transition, to move ahead successfully at a personal level, being positive and optimistic greatly help. Here, success is not necessarily landing a job immediately, but rather, being able to manage the transition process with some adventure, fun, and personal control over it. Studies have shown that, over time, if you are positive and calm in taking on a challenge in the face of a series of defeats, you will end up on top. This is called the state of intelligent optimism, which entails, largely, being open to adventure, being positive, and holding the belief that you are in control, no matter how many setbacks you repeatedly encounter. The only possible caution might be that of avoiding *repeated* setbacks. Repeated setbacks must prompt an audit of the strategy and changing it so that you break that pattern. Behaviors that generate new avenues of hope must replace patterns of defeat. This is why identifying these patterns is critical before they take hold.

One of the worst feelings during the process of a job search is the frequent bouts of hopelessness and feeling out of control. This feeling is exacerbated when you are out of work and looking to get back in. This sense will be exacerbated in a tough economy. As disappointments mount, to what appear as seemingly perfect jobs, with each setback, rejection, or lack of response, your self-esteem plummets. As your confidence retreats, you start becoming a victim and lose your sense of control. You may even give up hope, if the same cycles repeat!

Studies have shown that those who maintain their perspective and optimism in such situations are better able to engage the full arsenal of their resources: wit, energy, intellect, memory recall, and composure. Why optimism? Because optimism activates your amygdala (aah-mig-da-la)—a very important part of your brain that increases your ability to positive answers to life's challenges.

In one study, when simple puzzles were given to a group of adults, researchers found that those who were comfortable within their own selves, fully relaxed, and ready to take on the challenge for fun, were consistently able to find clever ways to beat the odds and get the right answer. Those who were apprehensive, unsure, and afraid, invariably ended by giving up in frustration or taking too long by sequentially dealing with each element of the puzzle. Those who remained calm and were fully engaged with all their resources, were able to marshal their intuition and insights and were readily able to find some key or clue that gave them the edge to succeed more quickly. The research also found that those who approached their life positively overall, were far more likely to be able to deal with any adversity as a victor than as a victim! Similarly, in a job search, a positive outlook goes a long way in making you more desirable to others, and helping you reach your goal.

Staying positive and celebrating, even minor successes, and building on what works in a given situation can create a virtuous cycle. Success releases its own endorphins inside your body, which can help you far more than anything ingested externally in moving ahead to success!

Impediments to Transition

A job loss is often a cause for many changes in one's personal life. When everything is "normal" in a life, issues remain in the background and life sails "comfortably."

A sudden job loss can change that. In some cases its suddenness is immaterial. In a family situation, where two spouses share deeply ingrained but differing views around jobs steeped in their cultural upbringing, there is a potential for problems. These problems surface when even one spouse suffers a job loss. If the couple has not communicated individual views around jobs and what their job means to them personally, the changed circumstances can precipitate a surprise. Overcoming this difference and reconciling the two views after the job loss can take a surprisingly large effort and can affect their marriage or relationship. Marriages or unions that involve spouses or partners from different cultures are particularly prone to this surprise. One client's wife was from one of countries in the Pacific Rim. She held the belief—but never communicated to him—that his worth was tied to his job and his salary and that she was to manage the family finances. When his income stopped, she continued *her* lifestyle because she believed that his losing the job—even in a bad economy— was his fault and that she should not have to suffer for it. They could not agree to a scaled-down lifestyle after the job loss, and his top priority became saving his marriage.

A job loss can send shock waves in one's personal life. Understanding priorities, and then deciding how to move on in a job search, can take more time and effort than may be anticipated. Not addressing more important issues, before embarking on a job search can be a frustrating experience, because of the constant impediments they pose for an effective job-search campaign.

If the situation during your "normal life," does not warrant an audit of how each spouse feels about changed circumstances such as a job loss, it may be prudent to explore these views, and communicate them to each other, so that when setbacks do occur, there is little or no discord. This simple measure of prevention will allow one to freely move ahead during a transition with full focus.

A Philosophical Insight

During transitions, people find their lives becoming intense. Everything hits them hard and they start seeing things in a different light. A transition is a period of learning and growing. It too is a period of finding new meaning in the way our lives impact other lives. Some even see a major transition as a near-death experience, with an epiphany!

One rule worth reflecting on, during such transitions, is the rule of universal giving. The rule is: You must give in order to receive. In times of our own needs it is difficult to be giving to others. The following true story is probably an object lesson of this universal rule:

A Universal WGACA Story

WGACA stands for "What Goes Around, Comes Around." Often, in our lives, we encounter instances where we do not treat others in the spirit of the Golden Rule: treat others as you would want others to treat you! This is often perpetrated by our own selfishness, the values we adopt, and the choices we make in our own daily lives. During life's transitions you will encounter situations where lack of simple human courtesies may incense you. You may never hear from an interviewer, who gave you all the indications that you would be offered the job. You may never get a call-back, from repeated messages you left in response to something you had sent for a job opportunity. You may never hear from your "friends" because now you are in need.

The following story is a true tale, of how a simple act of doing the right thing, selflessly can result in something good at a later time. When times are tough and things do not seem to be going your way, it is easy to transfer that to others. Don't! As this story illustrates, you have the power to break that cycle and do the right thing!

His name was Fleming, and he was a poor Scottish farmer. One day, while trying to make a living for his family, he heard a cry for help coming from a nearby bog. He dropped his tools and ran to the bog. There, mired to his waist in black muck, was a terrified boy, screaming and struggling to free himself. Farmer Fleming saved the lad from what could have been a slow and terrifying death.

The next day, a fancy carriage pulled up to the Scotsman's sparse surroundings. An elegantly dressed nobleman stepped out and introduced himself as the father of the boy who had been saved. "I want to repay you," said the nobleman. "You saved my son's life."
"No," replied the farmer, waving off the offer. "I can't accept payment for what I did." At that moment, the farmer's own son came to the door of the family hovel.
"Is that your son?" the nobleman asked.
"Yes," the farmer replied proudly.
"I'll make you a deal. Let me take him and give him a good education. If the lad is anything like his father, he'll grow to become a man you can be proud of. And that he did. In time, Farmer Fleming's son graduated from St. Mary's Hospital Medical School in London, and went on to become known, worldwide, as the noted Sir Alexander Fleming, the discoverer of Penicillin.

Years afterward, the nobleman's son was stricken with pneumonia. What saved him? It was the very Penicillin that Fleming had invented. What was the name of the nobleman? It was none other than Lord Randolph Churchill, whose son, Sir Winston Churchill, went on to achieve greatness in his own right. Someone once said, What goes around comes around. Work like you don't need the money. Interview like you do not need the job; love like you've never been hurt; and dance like nobody's watching.

The moral here is to learn to give, even when you are lacking in some key resources. Give in your own way and accept nothing in return! If the boomerang effect does not follow immediately, it will in its own way, and *you* will know when it happens.

WGACA Exercise:

Looking at my own current situation, I have the following (can be more than one) to give to others who can benefit from it:

#1)
Describe it:

I plan to give it by:

#2)
Describe it:

I plan to give it by:

My own personal thought on WGACA is (this is optional):

♠ The Change Curve

The change curve is a nearly universal representation of any change that involves human affairs. A typical change curve is shown below:

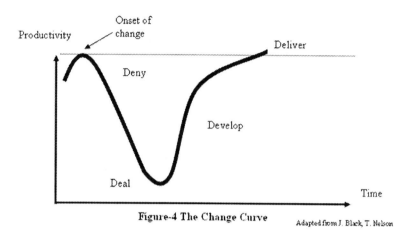

Figure-4 The Change Curve   Adapted from J. Black, T. Nelson

The curve shown in Figure-4 depicts the trajectory of our mindset and behavior when we are dealing with change. No matter what state we are in, change causes us to regress, before we are able to adjust to our new status. For example, when we lose our job, we are going through a transition. We go from being productive and feeling good about ourselves, *before* the onset of the loss, through becoming aware of it, and then going through a predictable process, following that change. This dynamic even applies when the change is positive. For example, when someone gets promoted or wins a jackpot, they need to adjust to their new state by going through a similar regressive transition.

Becoming aware of how change takes place, using the representation of the curve, helps those undergoing the change to manage it. The idea behind the change curve is to get past the stages that take away from being productive and, from a state of good mental and emotional balance, to another state of equal or better balance. This typically happens through a series of learning and coping experiences. The faster you transition through the curve and the shallower the curve, the easier it is dealing with change in a positive way and getting to the "other side."

There are specific interventions to accelerate the passage through the change curve to the next state in a four-state continuum. These four states are labeled in Figure-4 and described in Table-4, which also describes the interventions for a job transition. The idea is to quickly get to the next state on the curve and to come out reenergized and ready to take on the new challenge, by letting go of the past (the death of the past) and embrace the future (rebirth).

From State	Symptoms	To State	Intervention	Tools	Comments
Denial Inability to face reality and to pre-pare to act in a constructive way	Not accepting loss; denying reality. Anger; blame; regret	Deal	Support group; counseling, family members.	Discard past reminders; make plan. Use Tool-4 and Tool-5	Just talking about the loss can help!
Deal Accepting what happened and finding ways to move ahead.	Unproductive activities; frustration; feeling lost or even over-whelmed	Develop	Create structure, prepare a plan, engage in activities, and follow the plan.	Get organized. Daily schedule; measure progress and activities. Reward yourself.	Use help from others to create accountability for yourself! See Tool-6
Develop Defining specific actions to move forward and creating accountabilities	Feeling encouraged by progress; can see forward movement	Deliver	Coaching; support groups; increased emphasis on metrics Increased networks.	Expanding original plan to greater details based on what works.	Focus on your strengths that allow success in specific endeavors. Finalize résumé(s) and Marketing Plan
Deliver Delivering outcomes that are measurable, culminating in a goal previously envisaged	Feel good about the changed state and about accomplishments	Ready for next Perfor-mance Level	Doing postmortem, Learning from the transition and realizing what works for you.	Keep daily activity log; measure activity/progress. Reward yourself with something promised earlier.	Once you have mastered this concept, future transitions are easier.

Table-4: Understanding the Change Curve—Accelerating Change

Understanding the change process and how it can be managed, is key to staying positive and hopeful during any transition. Table-4 can help those in a job transition by following the prescription presented in the last three columns.

As one can glean from this table, a transition *can* last for an extended period of time, depending on circumstances. This is apparent from looking in the Tools column, in which the tools shown here are available throughout the book, starting with the next section. The best approach to accelerating change, is to go through the book and spot these tools (see Index) and come back to develop a better understanding of how to manage the change and create the most effective outcome.

✳ Tools to Accelerate Transition

The following tools can help you better deal and prepare for the transition. They are designed to help you emotionally accept the change and to take you through your change process:

> ➢ Change State (Tool-4)

> ➢ Transition Statement (Tool-5)

> ➢ My Truth! (Tool-6)

Each one is described below and can be used to accelerate the transition:

Change-State Tool

The change-State tool is a means of translating the concept of the Change Curve into an actionable exercise that allows rapid passage through each state of the change process. The Change Curve depicts how the change takes place and what some of the states are, during this process. However, to actually use this knowledge and to move through the curve, take a disciplined approach to behave in specific ways; so that, you merely breeze through each state than dwelling in it for any length of time. Each state is a necessity during change and passing through it is inevitable. Rapidly going through to the next stage, is what is needed to complete the transition productively.

A means to achieve this is Tool-4: Change State Tool, and is presented in this section, after the Transition Statement, because of space.

Transition Statement

A transition statement is an answer to the question that you yourself or others may ask. Why are you in transition? This transition could be a new job, getting into the grove of the new job, or something else. This statement is your honest response to help them help you, or to help yourself through acknowledgement of what you need. It also clarifies why you are seeking to complete the transition. An effective transition statement is brief, non-defensive, positive, and blameless. The following examples are illustrative:

"I recently changed careers and moved from high-tech to biotech. Although I was able to navigate through the process and get myself this job, I feel overwhelmed by all that is new to me. I must become familiar with the new culture, industry, and work, so that I can be successful here."

"Recent economic downturn forced my company to move its operations overseas, leaving only administrative and management jobs in the US. I am now looking for a design and drafting position nearby."

"After my marriage, I decided to take time to start a family and raise kids, until they were of school age. All three of my children are now in school and I decided to enter the workforce as an interior decorator. I am looking for opportunities nearby where I live."

"I recently immigrated to the U.S., on a green card. I was an architect in Europe for a number of years. I am now an intern at a second-tier architectural firm. Back home, I was a well-known professional, but here I feel as though I have just came out of college because, I must establish myself all over again. This is tough for me."

A transition statement should be both written and fit for oral delivery. The language and how it is presented are, of course, different. A written statement presented orally can sound stuffy.

Most transition statements may be presented when meeting someone. Often, they are your disclosure to yourself. The following samples can help someone who is struggling with the two versions:

Written

After HP merged with Compaq the two organizations were restructured to eliminate duplicate positions. Recent off-shoring trends have further affected the workforce at the new company and, as a result, I am no longer feeling secure at HP. I am now looking for opportunities in the IT support areas in a company, including those that are available internally.

Spoken

You probably already know about the big merger between HP and Compaq. This has resulted in ongoing reduction of the workforce. As this was going on, off-shoring further impacted those who were in the IT and software areas. I feel quite uncertain about my own job, even though I have worked there for over 20 years. I am now looking to leverage what I have learned into an opportunity within HP, or working at a company and am excited about the possibilities that are available!

Tool-4: Change State

Change-Transition Exercise
In my own case of transition, I am currently in state (From Fig. 4):

Reason why I am in this state:

Things I am going to practice to go to the next state:

I will know I am there because:

Things I am going to do beyond the next state:

Tool-5: Transition Statement

Now write your own transition statement in the space below:

Your Transition Statement

Written:

Spoken:

"My Truth!"

"My Truth!" is a private and personal statement. Sometimes you do not want to divulge all that surrounds your current situation. Sometimes you are not sure what you want, other than just a job. It is a good idea to be clear about the truth, so that you are honest with yourself. The better you are aligned with what you communicate and what your own truth is, the more authentic your campaign and more honest the outcome. Most have the innate ability to spot the misalignment between your words, and how you present them.

This statement is confidential and need not be discussed with *anyone*, if you choose not to.

During a transition, there will be moments of reflection, doubts, and apprehension, especially in a situation that drags out because of the circumstances. Having an honest "My Truth!" statement will act as a touchstone that one can come back to, to verify the authenticity of your intent. If your actions are misaligned with this statement, then there is a reason, and the reason can be found on *that* page.

Yet another reason, for this intimate disclosure stems, from the principle that if you deeply believe something, put it down, and own it; it has the power and ability to manifest. You can create your own future! Carrying the thought, will now become part of your being, and the universe has the obligation to owe you that gift. Just try it!

Some examples follow:

"I took this new position at my company, where I have worked for 12 years, hoping that I would get promoted and have better opportunities for growth. I think that I made a mistake in making this change, because there are no growth opportunities here and my boss is not pleased with what I have done during the past six months. Now I am worried about my survival."

Since my husband's layoff, things have become tough financially. He is too depressed to start looking and I do not know how long that is going to take. To support my family, I need to get back to what I did 15 years ago: doing office work and answering phones. Once he gets going again, I may not need the work.

I am going to have my first baby in about eight months. Once I have a child, I may not be able to work for a long time. I want to use this opportunity to keep my options open at this place, where I may want to come back. My manager does not know about my maternity leave, and I do not want to jeopardize my future. I do not know how to deal with this."

My current boss is giving me signals that I am not going to advance further in this organization. I need to find, for myself, if I can move up in an organization where I am appreciated and rewarded with positions of responsibilities. I must explore to see what is available inside as well as what is out there, before I decide to take an entirely different route, such as going into my own business.

Recent losses in the stock market have financially wiped me out. I need to find some startup that is promising, so that I can see it through its IPO, and then cash out on my options. Once I hit the one million dollar mark in cashable stock, I may just retire.

Tool-6: "My Truth!"

Write down your own statement now!

"My Truth!"

♠ Understanding Yourself

Transitions in our life are often marked by reflection and examination. Life's transitions are opportunities presented to us—gifts—that allow these indulgences. When undergoing such transitions, those who use these opportunities for engaging in self-discovery and in better understanding of their own purpose in life, find such episodes refreshingly rewarding—looking back! Although, in the moment, these episodes are stressful, looking back, most accept these opportunities to be a blessing.

This discussion on understanding yourself is presented here for two reasons: One is to help those who are in a transition understand themselves better, so that they become aware of how they handle their situations on a recurring basis. The second, more important, reason is to help them understand and manage some of their repetitive behavior patterns that can be puzzling and even frustrating to them. These patterns deal with their interactions with others. This is important to know in a job search, where your social and professional interactions with others determine what happens next. This section is presented, not so much to *change* who you are but, more importantly, to make you aware of how you may come across to others. Once that is known, you may choose to *manage* that behavior, to create outcomes that are more in line with your expectations.

Professional Evaluation

Professional evaluation is a service available from career counselors and other service providers that can provide insights into your career planning, especially if you are at a crossroads. Those choosing a particular academic path, also go through this as a part of their career planning process in high school and college. Career assessments are tools used by professionals and there are many available. Generally, do not expect to find anything new here from these assessments; just validation of what you already knew about yourself or that you suspected to be part of your experiences. Typically, such assessments provide a structure and a language for formally communicating these messages. One benefit is perhaps, understanding of your talents in a broader perspective of the overall job market, and how the currently available jobs can provide an outlet for such talents. New job categories are created continually and there are literally thousands of them. Having a ready list and some linkage of this list, with your own talent is a good resource for your own insights. Another tip, too: most of these assessments are available for free from a government Website that is updated frequently (see below).

Career Assessment

Many tools and assessment instruments are available for career targeting and planning. Strong Interest Inventory instruments can provide a solid, dependable, career-planning tool. The Strong Inventory measures participant's interests in a broad range of occupations, work activities, leisure activities, and school subjects. Its validity and reliability far exceed those of any other interest inventory. There is a family of Strong/career planning tools commercially available. These tools should be used to help those making a career decision, including:

- Those considering a career change

- Employees seeking more satisfying work within an organization

- Students exploring career options

- Organizations looking to retain star performers and key staff

- Midlife and older adults planning their retirement

A summary of various Strong-based tools is listed on http://www.cpp.com.

Another Website, managed by the U.S. government, is http://www.onetcenter.org, which provides free career assessments.

Personality Testing

There are many tools available for personality tests. One can get immersed in this pursuit and end up getting confused at the end. A simple and proven test instrument, however, is presented here. It is quick, inexpensive, widely available, well understood, and widely applied. So, if you ask someone within your circle what Type they were, more than likely you would get a response. This is the Myers-Briggs Type test.

Myers-Briggs Type Testing

The MBTI® is the most widely used personality-typing instrument presently in use. It is provided in several different languages and has been proven to be statistically valid and reliable. Many corporations, universities, governmental agencies, and the military use it to enhance team performance, communications, and organizational development. Individuals also use it to better understand their behavior and ability, to interface with members of their family or teams.

The MBTI® was developed at Stanford University, in the early '30s, by the mother and daughter combination of Isabel Myers and Katherine Briggs in an effort to operationalize the theories of the renowned psychiatrist Karl Jung (*Uyng*). It was used successfully during World War II in placing civilians in jobs required by the war effort. It has since been revised several times and is constantly being tested for validity and reliability. There is a whole industry based on this theory and how it is practiced. The instrument itself addresses an individual's preference for *four* personality traits.

The first acknowledges the individual's preference for Extraversion or Introversion. This dichotomy indicates how individuals view the world around them and whether they are energized by others and their surroundings or prefer to address the inner world of ideas and concepts. Being Introverted is different from being shy, which is a different quality; there can be shy Extraverts. Remember this is just a preference, not an either or. Everyone has a varying degree of both. In fact, this shading applies to all four traits.

The second dichotomy considers how individuals take in data or information. This can be either through the concrete method of Sensing (looking at data or using analytical means) or the more abstract method of Intuition. Differences between individuals in this area can create significant problems regarding how reality is viewed and, consequently, how individuals view each other.

The third dichotomy is the only one that is affected by the individual's *gender*. It indicates how the individual uses information in making decisions. The more logical and objective method is referred to as the Thinking function and is preferred by 60 percent of males. The more value related and subjective method is referred to as Feeling and is preferred by 60 percent of women. These differences can create significant communication difficulties at home and at work and, understanding this decision-making process can greatly enhance the functioning of an organization or family unit.

Finally, the Judging/Perceiving attitudes indicate how an individual organizes and operates in the outside world. This dichotomy is usually the easiest one to spot if you are Type watching. The Judging type will be systematic and decisive, while the Perceiving type will be noncommittal and open-ended. They like to decide at the absolute last minute! Differences in the way we conduct our lives can be quite annoying to those of the opposite attitude and need to be understood.

Each of the four attributes is independent of the others. These are determined by a self-administered test that has been validated over millions of samples and that has been refined and made more reliable over the past 50 plus years.

Why is the Type important in a job-search situation? For one, it dictates your approach to the job search. Job search is an activity that primarily involves dealing with the outside world and people in that world. Psychological Type plays a profound role in determining approaches that are likely to work for a job seeker. There are 16 MBTI® Types based on the four combinations of each type randomly grouped together. These types are shown in Table-2. While details of each type can be found in many sources, this discussion is limited to how each group of attributes influences your job-search approach.

Whether you are an Introvert or Extravert, you have "Extraverted functions," and these are very important during job interviews. For Introverts, these functions are auxiliary and less important aspect of their conscious personality. Reasons for this include:

- The reason for outward-focused activity in job search.

- The statistical prevalence of Extraverts in our society, resulting in what has come to be known as a "Western Extravert Bias."

- The need for communication and interaction as core job-search tools. While our introverted forms of communication can play some role, these tend to be relegated to second place in the job-search process.

In the table below the letters representing each dichotomy appear in groups of four, and what each letter means is summarized here for ready reference. Taking only one of the four letters, in groups of four, make up the 16 Types listed below:

I/E Introvert/Extravert Getting your energy (inwardly or outwardly)
N/S Intuitive/Sensing Getting your information (intuition or from sensing)
T/F Thinking/Feeling Making decisions (mind or heart)
J/P Judging/Perceiving Individual's world-view (black/white or shades of gray)

ISTJ	ISFJ	INFJ	INTJ
ISTP	ISFP	INFP	INTP
ESTP	ESFP	ENFP	ENTP
ESTJ	ESFJ	ENFJ	ENTJ

Table-5: The 16 MBTI Types

Career Transition Styles

How different Types handle their transition process is largely driven by their makeup. Since looking for a job is an Extraverted activity, extraverted styles dominate behaviors. Also, certain jobs require certain personality characteristics to be done well. A mismatch can result in much grief for both the employer and the employee. Therefore, your ability to understand this match, is critical in acing the interview and managing the selection process.

Job search involves Extraverted activities. Even though one may have a Introverted type personality dominant in their makeup, the Extraverted attributes become auxiliary to that person. For example "Perceiving" is an extraverted (outward-directed) category, because it has to do with how you interact with the outside world. One can perceive either by Sensing or by Intuiting. Same holds for Judging, which can be based on Thinking or Feeling. Thus there are four auxiliary characteristics that are present in any person, as shown here, along with their "themes":

SP   "Ready, Fire, Aim."
NP   "Look at all the jobs out there; I am overwhelmed."
TJ   "Here's what I can do for you; now, make a decision."
FJ   "We can be good together; I like you, so, what's with you?"

The following is a brief description of each of the four styles; see also Table-6 on the next page:

SP Style: This style is driven by perceptions, formed by data-driven activity. The focus is on taking in, looking at, and wanting data. S types look at raw data, form opinions, and perceive the outside world based on that intake. Since there are an infinitude of possibilities with the data flowing in, SPs often get overwhelmed and react by rationalizing that even if they hit a few of the targets with their "shot gun," they will land soon. So they engage in wanton activity: sending countless résumés, calling every possible lead, going to every job fair just to name a few possibilities. One antidote for SPs, then, is to plan, strategize, be selective, and take some risks.

NP Style: If SPs are mired in data, NPs are sure of their own insights! Intuitive types abhor structures and they take great pride in their ability to synthesize something from nothing—their own intuition. They see things that often simply may not exist. They will pursue opportunities and wonder why no one is responding to their "insights." This is further exacerbated if they are also language limited or poor communicators. N types are particularly poor at teaming and sharing a view with others; they have a hard time following the "pack." NPs tend to care less about their appearance and social norms, so they are at a disadvantage in social and corporate surroundings. Those pushing the far side of 50 can look older than they really are for this reason. So, if an older NP wants to go looking for a job and get ready for an interview, they should care about their appearance and social behaviors.

TJ Style: TJs are thinkers. They are at the core of the corporate world's executive cadre. The need for logical reasoning and closure is so dear to these Types that they find it difficult to deal with the FP types. Their focus makes TJ blind to people who factor in every thing they pursue. TJs are poor at small talk, or getting to know the person who is interviewing them; they want to get right to the point. They see people as a means to an end—their ends!

FJ: FJs are excellent relationship builders. Their networks are large and productive. Seeking harmony can be to the detriment of this Type, so they have to learn to manage that. You do not have to like everyone who comes across your path in the job-search campaign. Sometimes functional relationship can get you by. Some times F (harmony) can conflict with J (closure) in a relationship, so FJs have to learn to live with "enforced agreement." One strategy FJs can use to favorably impress their interviewers is to show solid logic and an ability to draw conclusions, without much rambling and digression. Since the J aspect drives for closure, being aware of the other person's Type can help.

Table-6: Transition Styles for Four Categories (Note your Type. Look for the two letters in it in the Category column below.)

Category	Transition Style	Behaviors	Antidote	Comments
SP ↓ (Sensing/Perceiving)	Bias to action. Just Do It.	Respond to raw data; look for more data; little planning; action without closures; ISTPs are more likely to search the Internet than network	Look for patterns; form strategy; form theories; think before acting; review results, learn. Form structure for closing open items; create self accountability	Before getting into action, prepare a plan on how you are going to get the most from each step; a planning step.
NP ↓ (Intuitive/Perceiving)	Anything goes with anything	Aversion to traditional structures; desultory habits; lack of follow through, forgetful. In tough job market "an absent-minded professor" is a liability.	Invoke your SJ style for structure and reality. Recognize that others do not share your "insights"; be patient with those who are more "S" than you	Solving problems that others do not see is a typical NP trait. If you must solve a problem, make sure it is recognized first.
TJ ↓ (Thinking/Judging)	Executive outlook	Plan and execute transition; goal driven; people-blindness; no subjective values; controlling. "Black or white" outlook; feelings have no place.	Know when to let go; seek out feeling and show sensitivity to people issues; relax; hiring is a people process.	TJs tend to connect well with higher-ups because of ethos. Remember, though, that your hiring manager is the one you have to report to.
FJ ↓ (Feeling/Judging)	Relationships driven	Easy networking; more tactical, less strategic; can take the feeling aspect too far and create discomfort with those who are ISTJs in the interview chain.	Think strategy, logic; manager assertiveness; temper your people connection with being detached in getting too close to others too early.	FJs do well in people jobs as customer relations, HR, training, front desk. Leverage these attributes if you are seeking such opportunities.

Type: Practice Exercises

Exercises based on Types:

You are an NP. What is your normal approach to your different steps of the job search and how would you increase the effectiveness of your campaign, if you knew this?

You are an SP. What is your normal approach to your different steps of the job search and how would you increase the effectiveness of your campaign, if you knew this?

You are a TJ. What is your normal approach to your different steps of the job search and how would you increase the effectiveness of your campaign, if you knew this?

You are an FJ. What is your normal approach to your different steps of the job search and how would you increase the effectiveness of your campaign, if you knew this?

Summary Chapter 4: Managing Your Own Journey

This long, but bedrock chapter covers many foundational topics critical to a career and job success. It also provides tips and tools for transitions that people encounter in their journey to attain career nirvana. In fact, internalizing what is presented here can be a life skill that can help in any transition, including a career transition! At its core, it prepares you to understand the most fundamental factors common to any transition. Internalizing what is presented here, can make the difference between floundering at a job or a career and mastering the career management process.

- Looking for a job is a transition and it must be approached with a process that can be managed to provide the outcome you desire. During a transition your life is changing and not ending!

- A transition is a life's journey that can be *planned* for, by reaching the right destination. This journey can be made adventuresome with some risk-taking and following proven methods.

- Recognize your own fear factor and work diligently to rid it. When you wear your fear others can see it, while you cannot. One way to overcome fear is to do something new that scares you every day and keep doing it.

- The emotional price you pay during your transition (any of life's transitions) is proportional to your own resistance to change and inversely to your resilience.

- Resilience is your ability to bounce back in an adverse situation and function at your full potential.

- In your interactions with others, you release two chemicals within your own body—endorphins (good) and adrenaline (bad). The same chemicals are induced in those you interact with and it is these chemicals that dictate how you come across to them. You can manage which ones you want to release, both in you and in others.

- If you feel defeated and sad, you carry that energy with you and spill that sadness around you. People try to avoid such energy instinctively. If you want people to help and support you, act positive even in the face of insurmountable defeat.

- Remember What Goes Around Comes Around: WGACA! People may mistreat you during critical periods in your life. They will get their just deserts, but you must manage yours on your own!

- The Change Curve shows how you can transition faster and with minimal pain and suffering. Practice the coping strategies. Five tools that will help you accelerate transition are presented in this chapter. The remaining tools appear later.

- Getting organized, physically and mentally are critical to launching and sustaining an effective campaign. Physical organization includes your workspace and arrangements, while mental organization includes your attitude and expectations. Develop a disciplined approach to your work.

- Career assessment and personality testing are some tools available for those who want to better understand their preferences. Myers Briggs® Typing tool is useful in understanding your own social style during your job search and how you use that knowledge to manage your own behavior. Working is a social sport unless you are a cyber junkie. Learn how to read people using this Typing technique and leverage that understanding to communicate more effectively and show a higher level of emotional intelligence (see Appendix-VIII: Emotional Intelligence)

This chapter has six exercises to help you to show you how to accelerate the change process and ease up the pain of transition. Three tools are provided to help you accelerate your transition. There are other tools when you are making a job or career transition and they are available in the author's *The 7 Keys to Dream Job: A Career Nirvana Playbook!*.

CHAPTER 5

Your New Job

"We are overpaying him, but he is worth it."
—Samuel Goldwyn, Hollywood Producer (1879–1974)

Starting a new job is always an exciting period in one's life. It spells the end of a transition—a difficult one if they are starting back from being out of work—and also spells a start of a new one. How long it takes to settle and develop a feeling of comfort, where one is more relaxed about their job, depends on the level at which they are entering a company. Regardless of the level of entry, there are a few common considerations one must be aware of to be able to not get into trouble settling down at a new place of employment.

With constantly changing employment models, how employers and employees view their mutual obligation is rapidly changing. With more and more employers now going the "contract" route, the expectations of what their agreement means beyond merely what is expected from a contract employee is difficult to state. But the fact remains, that professionals newly entering a workplace must follow certain rules to make their entry smooth and productive.

Different Strokes

As mentioned, each category of new employee faces a different challenge settling at a new work place. The following categories of employees are discussed in this paragraph:

1. Fresh graduates

2. Senior Professionals

3. Managers

4. Executives

5. New job late in life

6. Back after a major hiatus

7. Changing careers/industries

8. Immigrant worker

9. Baby boomer back in workforce

10. Rehired from retirement

The process of settling into an employer company varies depending on which of the 10 categories a new employee belongs.

Different Starting Points

We all enter our work life at different points in our life. This discussion is presented to show how starting a new job at different points in your life can result in different demands on you for your success.

New Graduates

New graduates—or even those starting out without a formal degree and who are pursuing a vocational path—land their first job with great anticipation. Even though they may have worked in their prior life, landing a "real job" after getting their freshly-minted degree has an allure all its own.

The following is presented as a comprehensive discussion that starts with the needs of a fresh employee, but goes beyond their immediate starting point. The reason this discussion is presented in this manner is because many young employees who start their new jobs do not have a clear perspective of how their first job can be the foundation for their remaining career and how it sets the tone for their success, immediate and future.

As this discussion is presented, its contents can help mid-career professionals by their reading the entire section, particularly the latter part. It is provided as a framework for those who want to leverage their first job into a solid career, rather than learn by trial and error as most do. For more on this see the author's *Pathways to Career Nirvana: An Ultimate Success Sourcebook!*

Your First Job

How you land your first job is driven by many variables. The most influential are your own vision of yourself, how you have managed your academic development, or otherwise prepared for what calls you, and the state of the economy. Here, academic development does not merely mean scholarship and grades; it includes how you rounded out your overall development and the perspective you hold of how the world really works. If you just graduated or set yourself for pursuing a new job, you are full of hopes and expectations.

Many graduate without knowing what they are going to pursue because they have little or no idea if a job provides what they are looking for. Many are happy just getting a paying job that allows them to apply what they have learned in their years of schooling. Many are so deep in debt, especially with the student loans and permissive credit card limits that they jump at the chance of making "real money." In such situations, and some others as well, many end up going after the highest-paying job available, regardless of the other factors, which become critical later in a career. Going into a job after being in a "spending mode" until then, warps the priorities with which one looks at how to go after the right opportunity. A higher starting salary can often seduce someone to make the decision that may bear out to be wrong in the long run, as it often does. Often, too, this means taking a job that pays well, but without knowing or fully understanding the long-term implications of the decision. Also, most do not realize that getting ready for the first job involves more than just pulling together a résumé and a wardrobe.

Deprogramming the Campus Mindset

For fresh graduates, their new job also turns out to be their first job. Many students do not look ahead during their college days to position themselves more strongly for their first job. Why? For one, they do not have a clear understanding of what the business world expects from them as a new entrant. Also, their main focus in college is on how to score top grades in their tests rather than how to make themselves more valuable to the business community. They simply do not know how to do things differently in college so that they are better positioned when they start their job search. And, when they do get to the point of getting ready for their search, the campus counselors immediately point them in the directions of how to write résumés and how to interview. This approach is an end run on how to get ready for the businesses world. This is the state of "unconscious incompetence." Most academic curricula and programs promote keeping students insulated from the realities of the business world because those who run these institutions take great pride in "academic purity!" The campus career-counseling center *sometimes* is not much help, either. Many, who staff it, are more involved in its administrative functioning and its political stature than almost anything else. Often, in a university setting, there is a very definite "caste system" and how a career center is run depends largely on who is running it. The purpose of this brief discussion is to move the student reader to "conscious incompetence." This is provided so that they can look for help or become aware of what they do not know.

Four years is a long time during the impressionable years to imprint a mind with beliefs that are counter to those that run the business world. This is why it is important to start changing your imprinting early, as you get closer to leaving your academic environment. On the campus the focus is typically on getting the degree quickly and making the grades. The academic focus is also on solitary achievements. In the outside world of the jobs, business, and economy all of this matters not as much as most think. Very few employers care to check how fast you graduated. Many do not pay as much attention to the grades (GPA) as those on the campus believe. So, what is important to the "real world?"

The following checklist may provide some insights on how to manage your student affairs more carefully so that you are better positioned to enter the business world:

➢ When engaging in part-time work as a student, summer internships, project work, final team project, or any other activity that defines your "brand," make a conscious effort to differentiate yourself. Rather than just doing what the job is, going out of the way to make something better for the employer on your own initiative has much more value. Create value beyond merely earning your paycheck. When you take on a class assignment, don't be a passive participant to hurry up the project, but provide creative suggestions to make the project unique. All of these differentiators can be on your first résumé and they matter more than your GPA. These factors show your independent thinking and your thought leadership.

➢ Many final-year projects are team efforts, especially for engineering and science graduates. Make sure that you participate fully in the team and understand how teams work. Most of the academic life is spent in solitary assignments and those graduating do not appreciate the value of teamwork, which is expected in business life. Make an effort to understand the team dynamic and how you made a difference to how your team performed. (Here, teamwork does not imply collaborating to earn a better grade than otherwise possible!)

➤ Take part in activities that are outside the academic sphere to develop your leadership qualities. Participating in the campus newspaper, student activities, taking a project to make the departmental laboratory or library a better place and so on. All of these accomplishments can be on your first résumé, and they will go a long way in differentiating yourself in your first job.

➤ Identify your own "development gaps" and make a conscious effort to overcome them. For example, if you are afraid to speak publicly, join Toastmasters or a similar group and develop your elocutionary skills. This will not only make you a better leader, but also give you some ammunition to strengthen your résumé beyond what most students do. This is now your differentiator. See Appendix-II: Conducting Effective Meetings about a reference to Toastmasters.

➤ In your senior year, take on someone who has just entered the college campus and help them in some way to make their life easier. Remember your own early days and see how it might have made it better for you. In doing this work you make yourself a better person and it is something you can write in your otherwise blank first résumé. In the business world this is called mentoring. Empower yourself to mentor others.

There are more examples of these activities in Chapter-8: Personal Capital, specifically in Elements of Personal Capital in the author's *Pathways to Career Nirvana: An Ultimate Success Sourcebook!*.

How these suggestions translate into a résumé for a fresh graduate is shown in a Before-After format (for a real but *disguised* graduate, Palmer Jones) in the same book. In that example, for the academic résumé the job seekers had kept his focus on the scholarly achievements. His original message did not capture the business world's attention because it does not speak the employers' language. The revised résumé, however, presents a good rounding out of Palmer's activities on the campus and shows how his using the business language to present his credentials, makes for a compelling résumé.

Other Considerations

The next consideration in pursuing your first job is how the economy is functioning or the state of the economy. However, regardless of the economy, there are more choices than most realize. Even if the choices are limited because of the economic, geographic, or political considerations, one must make an informed decision about their first job.

Why?

Sometimes, we operate in a state called the state of "unconscious incompetence." In this state you do not know what you do not know. Operating in this state in career matters is suicide. Why? It is difficult to change factors that become an integral part of your first job, once you have already started your career. Not being aware of them can create downstream difficulties in career matters. The first job is an imprint that is on a fresh page of an important chapter in your life that is hard to erase, once cast. This is why, regardless of whether you are starting a brand-new career after graduation or changing jobs, it is important to identify companies that not only provide the opportunities you are looking for, but also provide you with future possibilities and protect your career.

To a fresh graduate, a new job and the dawning of their career must not be a casual matter, although it ends up being treated as such by so many. There are various reasons why this is so. Perhaps the most important, and of which few are aware, is that going from being a student to being a full-time employee in the workforce is the single biggest transition one makes in their professional life. This is explained in more detail in the discussion of the Apprentice later in this chapter.

Before embarking on a plan to do a job search, fresh out of college, it is especially important for the newly minted graduate (for that matter, anyone looking for a job) to know the following rule of economic value creation:

For you to be gainfully employed you must easily be able to demonstrate that you create value at least three times your salary.

So, if you are shooting for a job that has a base salary of $80,000 annually, the potential employer should be able to benefit from you through your work to the tune of $240,000 (by a factor three times your salary). Sometimes this is difficult to assess, especially for a fresh graduate. Regardless, you must be able to deliver this level of value to qualify. And, where does this factor come from?

For one, you are not going to be productive from day one at the employer. They are going to train you to do what they want you to do. It may be nearly a year before the employer sees the rewards of your work (if you are still around). Then there is the benefits package—medical, dental, vacation, sick leave, and so on—that puts a burden of nearly 40 percent of your base salary at the entry level. There are overhead costs, contingency costs, and the profit, which you must provide. One key overhead element these days is the IT infrastructure costs. At HP for example, when the new CEO arrived in early 2005, his major focus was to reduce the cost of IT operations per employee from $18,000 to $6,000 annually! All of this adds up to about twice—or more —of your salary. This is why it is critical that during your campaign that you show a clear statement of value creation and the knowledge of where the value-creation opportunities are in the job that you are after. Merely showing knowledge in your field (academic, at that) is never enough. Also, merely parroting what is in the job description and stating in your cover letter that you can deliver what is required is *never* enough, especially in a tough market. You must anticipate what the needs are and know employer expectations and then exceed those expectations so that you can differentiate yourself form the rest, throughout your campaign.

The other thing, too, is that those entering the employment world anew often ignore their own sense of what is happening to them and the unmistakable signals that they get, as we all do, during their early days on their job. If something does not seem right, it probably isn't. Most ignore these signals and continue their jobs, only to run into trouble that is hard to deal with at a later time. If you feel that the fit in a job is not good and is causing you stress then you must seek help. Many around you may try to convince you that you are imagining these feelings because it is a new environment or a new chapter in your life. Seeking professional help, as from a career counselor or from a mentor is invaluable in the early stages. We, as humans, often have a tendency to inure ourselves to hardships, physical, mental, or psychological and martyr ourselves to a cause not worthy of this energy.

The Biggest Transition

Why is going from being a student to getting a full-time job is such a big deal? There are many reasons: the foremost is that being a student in your school, college, or university, you enjoyed a "rank" that few shared. You were the top dog in the highly ordered academic world during your graduation year. Many fraternities bestow unlimited powers on the graduating class, allowing them to "order around" any one else of "lower" rank, even those graduating barely a year behind them. You enjoyed certain freedoms of expressions that others respected and even promoted.

All of that comes to a sudden halt at the doorstep of your first job. In fact, your status completely reverses. In your first job, you are the new kid on the block. You don't know anything! Although no one says that to your face, the treatment and its implications become apparent in every interaction you suffer, even at the hands of those who are hierarchically "below" you. Your ability to adjust to this new treatment and how quickly you adjust to this shift determine how quickly you integrate in the new culture. Some bring their campus "nerdiness" to their jobs and expect the business world to respect it. They are the ones who find that their integration periods are the longest; some never do integrate and stay on the fringe, hoping that others my join in or that the future fresh crop of recruits will bring in more of their own type.

The Four stages

Once you are inside an organization, assigned to a job, you move through four distinct stages over your career arc that defines your career history, looking back. These stages are not restricted to your confinement to one employer; they cross employer boundaries, following wherever you go in your career; they are not employer specific, but are thematic in nature. The concept of stages came about nearly 20 years back when the then traditional hierarchies started disappearing and the deep command and control structure inside organizations started becoming flatter. Starting with the late '80s, many corporations came to realize that having highly siloed structures and deep hierarchies were getting in the way of doing business efficiently, primarily because they impeded the flow of vital information by creating a layered bureaucracy. This was also a juncture when information started becoming easily available throughout the organization.

The original command and control structure and the associated deep hierarchies inside an organization had migrated from the armed forces. Armed forces need a chain of command and rigid structure to protect the mission in which they are engaged. In a rigid hierarchy, information flows only one way—down. As information later became the brain of an effective management process and the currency of a well-managed enterprise, organizations became flat domains of titles and formal responsibilities. Formal authority vanished and was replaced by fluidity of information that governed the workings of an enterprise. Much of the organization functioned with informal authority and power vested in those who earned them. Organizations became more informal and egalitarian. Employees looked more for leadership than for someone to merely manage them as was prevalent in the past.

As a result, traditional ladder-climbing motivation was replaced by managing your career so that it evolved through a sequence of four stages as they are described here. Over the past two decades as organizations became more streamlined and effective, flattened hierarchies became the norm. These four stages are described below:

> ➢ Stage I: The "Apprentice"

> ➢ Stage-II; Individual Contributor

> ➢ Stage-III: Team Leader/Mentor

> ➢ Stage-IV: The Executive or Professional Manager

It is instructive to understand each stage so that how to effectively make a mark in each stage and make a transition from that stage to the next are clear.

The "Apprentice" (Stage-I)

An apprentice is the first stage in the evolution of a career. It is fraught with surprises, minefields, and rewards if you master the game. The "game" here is following the rules of the corporate world and the process that defines how things work in an organization, which are different from anything you have known in your past.

The job of an "apprentice" is such a major transition as we already described, that many fail their job within the first few months. Nearly all face difficult and painful adjustments. Even the best and the brightest suffer some of the surprising indignities of their early professional lives. From the perspectives of the hiring managers, only about 60 percent of the new graduates cut muster. About 10-20 percent meet or exceed expectations, the remaining are considered inadequate performers. These statistics are from the top ranking graduates of highly rated schools. What is the problem?

For one, coming out of the student mindset and the campus environment are one of the most difficult transitions for an apprentice to make. They look at their assignments as another term paper to be graded, full of scholarship and ivory-tower ideas.

To successfully transition into the apprentice stage, there are two phases: Initiation, followed by Maturation. During the initiation phase, psychological adjustments are the main focus. During the maturation phase development of competencies is the main focus.

Let us look at each phase more carefully.

Initiation

Initiation is the adjustment period of entering a new environment. The rules, expectations, and outcomes are a major source of learning to an apprentice during the Initiation phase of the first stage of their career. The biggest cultural shock is to going back to being a "rookie" again, as they did when they entered college. They all got the "second-rate citizen" treatment as they entered their first year. Slowly they earned their stripes and graduated to the top of their "caste system," allowing them special respect and consideration. This meant much to a graduating senior, or a doctoral student.

All of that "seniority" vanishes as these freshly-minted graduates enter the workforce. This is a huge adjustment and to many and a psychologically difficult one to make. Some never get past this shock. This may be one reason why the turnover rate of fresh graduates is nearly 20 percent in the first year and nearly 50 percent during the first five years. The cost of this turnover to the employers is high.

The other success factor in making a graceful transition into the Initiation phase of Stage-I is the ability to build relationships with those whose influence in the organization is unknown. Merely following what the boss wants is often not enough. You have to master diplomacy and tact as you navigate through the new landscape of the organizational world that is filled with mines, traps, and detours. This is, again, something that many schools do not teach. There the focus is freedom of speech and views. That view can be a deadly practice inside an organization.

The second factor that impedes a successful Initiation is managing your own expectations. Coming out of school with a freshly minted degree, every problem looks bounded, solvable, and tractable. The reality of the business world is that ostensibly simple problems morph into complexity due to a variety of factors, some of which are political. In this environment no one will bother to ask the opinion of a rookie. And this can be despairing to a hotshot graduate who has all the answers. Reconciling these two views is one of the greatest impediments to successfully completing the Initiation phase. Yet another behavior that can interfere with smooth integration during this phase is that once a decision is made, generally the debate ends and implementation begins. Those who come from the campus life fail to see the merit of this corporate dictum. They start challenging the decision or arguing its merit; a career thwarting move! To the academically minded upstarts, debate begins after a decision is made. In the corporate world the debate ends with a final decision and change begins.

One antidote for the challenge we just outlined, is finding yourself a mentor early in your days at the new job. A good mentor can be a sounding board for getting you to understand how the organizational world works.

The third challenge most new employees face, coming straight out of college, is that they think that they can solve all the problems on their own. Throughout their college days, individuality was at a premium. Collaboration was disparaged, even punished. In contrast, in the organizational reality, they are expected to collaborate and team-up to produce results. The sooner they reconcile to this reality, the sooner they can integrate themselves into the organization's culture and get past the Initiation phase and into the producing phase.

Yet another challenge a fresh graduate faces in the real world, is that their sense of speed with which events happen—events velocity—in the corporate world. In the campus environment they are used to solving bounded problems with speed, primarily because no one challenged their approach, nor did they have to have others buy into their solution or even the approach. In the reality of the corporate problem solving, collaboration, diplomacy, validation, and buy-ins are all challenges. Many young graduates get frustrated in the bureaucracy of decision-making and the time it takes to build a consensus.

This next challenge fresh graduates face, comes from the habit they developed during their college—going back all the way to early school—years. When given a deadline, they become master at deferring any real work until the deadline is just a few days away and then pulling all-nighters to get ready for the event—just as they did for their final exam or tests. After that they crash and become non functional again. This way of working is simply not compatible with the way businesses work. They constantly find themselves confronted with deadlines that never end!

The penultimate challenge most new graduates entering the workforce face is the task of reconciling their rigorous and ivory-tower approach to all the worlds' problems. For one, the academic world is disconnected with the realities of the economic world. This problem is further exacerbated by the recent trends that have accelerated in the way new job competencies are emerging. During the first five years of this Millennium, a sea change in job competencies has emerged as a result of drastic out sourcing, off shoring, virtual teaming and job consolidation. Work must be defined, done, and brought together in ways not known to the traditional worker. Academic institutions have not aligned their curricula to the new realities of the corporate world. As a result, a new graduate must think differently than what they were programmed for and for which they were awarded a degree. They must now change their mindsets, without compromising the basic principles they learned in school. This disconnect is not specific to what is happening in the turbulent times following the start of the new Millennium; it is now a fact of life.

And, ultimately, the new graduate must focus less on what they already know and more on how to learn what they do not. The mantra is *learning how to learn*. Learning how to ask the right questions to the right people is far more important than having all the wrong answers or even the right ones that no one is willing buy into. To a freshly graduated apprentice, this is one of the hardest challenges to overcome.

Maturation

As the Initiation phase is being conquered, concomitantly, technical maturation must be on the radar screen. During the period of adjustment and
Initiation, most are willing to overlook the deficiencies in the output of a new
graduate hire. This is understandable. But, once the honeymoon period is over,
marking the end of the Initiation period, the employee had better girded
themselves to understanding the standards of performance so that they are
quickly accepted as competent.

Competency is a term much bandied about in career parlance. Competency
in the context of this book is the ability to perform a task with skill that adds
value, with a defect-free outcome.

Competency entails the following elements:

➢ Knowledge

➢ Skill

➢ Aptitude (genius)

In the case of a new hire straight out of college, the Knowledge is what they
bring with them. The Skill is an embodiment of variety of complex factors that
are not obvious at first, but must be learned. It is the ability to effectively use
the knowledge to execute a task.

Aptitude is the special way of doing what you do. Incorporating a variety of
complex factors into a whole is what makes for this trait. In later discussion we
call this your genius. For now, we can break down this elusive attribute to some
concrete characteristics that bosses can relate to:

1. Accuracy: Ability to consistently deliver flawless work

2. Initiative: Ability to take action without being prompted and taking risk

3. Perspective: Integrate different views in synthesizing a solution

4. Intuition: Using uncanny insights to deliver solutions to ordinary
   problems and getting to the heart of an issue without sequentially
   and linearly going through an elaborate process of elimination and
   trial and error.

5. Collaboration: Knowing when to leverage collaborative solutions

6. Communication: Keeping others in the loop and communicating
   critical developments

7. Commitment: How consistently does the apprentice meet deadlines, despite obstacles, setbacks, and changed rules? How do they communicate possible delays and negotiate new deadlines?

8. Thoroughness: Being thorough is not taught in school. It comes from your inner drive to go beyond what is obvious.

9. Trust: Ability to consistently deliver, anticipate, and become predictable to others

10. Leverage: Ability to use available resources in a clever way and produce an outcome that looks like it took an effort much bigger than it actually did! This can also be called leadership.

11. Anticipation: Anticipating what the end customer or user would be delighted with is one of the most fundamental traits an employee can have. It is a skill difficult to teach but easy to spot.

12. Speed of response: Timely results and solutions to pressing business problem is a requirement. In this high-velocity environment speed of action is one of the leading differentiators.

This list may look intimidating to most. But, this is how an apprentice can make a mark during their "post-initiation" period. All these qualities listed above; together with skill and knowledge constitute competency. School curricula do not place much emphasis on all except perhaps the first one—accuracy.

Once an apprentice is able to demonstrate their competencies repeatedly in assignments, increasingly challenging, they earn their stripes as reliable contributors. This is a harsh regimen. It is easy to see why going through the Initiation and Maturation can be so demanding and why so few make it past the first year as we presented earlier.

♠ Conventional wisdom demands that a fresh graduate, newly employed, put their focus on dressing right, imitating the superficial, connecting with the power base, and socializing with the right crowd. Although none of these practices hurt, they are not enough. When political forces shift the power base and you are exposed to a different environment, all the veneer you so carefully cultivated can be quickly turned into trash. The fundamentals presented here will survive any organizational tsunami and will allow you to survive while others cannot.

Tools: Tool-4 and Tool-5

The following tools are presented to help those making this major transition from their college life to "real life" in an organizational setting. Two tools are presented:

✓ Initiation Transition Tool

✓ Maturation Transition Tool

These tools are designed to accelerate a transition from "college life" to corporate life. The first Stage of being an Apprentice comprises two phases. The first phase is the Initiation phase. The next phase is the Maturation phase. This tool is designed to accelerate a transition from the Initiation phase to the Maturation phase.

Tool-7: Initiation Transition Tool

#	Item	Rarely 10 9 8	Sometimes 7 6 5 4	Often 3 2 1
1	During conversations with colleagues at work, I brag about my campus escapades			
2	In a business meeting, I am quick to offer solutions and my opinions to a problem at hand			
3	When the support staff treats me as though I am a newbie and that don't know anything, while showing me the right way to do things, it bothers me			
4	At a meeting, if the general direction of a view is converging in one direction, I often jump in and show that there is yet another view worth considering			
5	When someone speaks disparagingly about my alma mater or its teams, I get angry and attack them			
6	If someone from another school that is ranked above the one I graduated from, makes a point, I go out of the way to show that I know more			
7	I bring to work my school memorabilia			
8	I bring to others' attention my high GPA			
9	I remind others that I am a fresh graduate and that my opinion should count			
10	I follow my own work schedule			

If you score less than 50 you have a long transition ahead of you; you may not even make it to the next stage.

Tool-8: Maturation Transition Tool

This tool is designed to accelerate your transition from the Maturation phase to the next Stage: Individual Contributor. **Note reversed scales from Tool-7.**

#	Item	Often 10 9 8	Sometimes 7 6 5 4	Rarely 3 2 1
1	On a tough problem, I come up with my own solution. Then I check with others to validate it			
2	In a business meeting, I listen to others' views and then form my own opinion			
3	I collaborate with a group of professionals to ensure that I get a rich perspective			
4	I think of the value I am creating and tie that contribution to how the company can benefit			
5	The pace of work (results) is too slow and this company should do something about it. This bothers me			
6	When I am given a tough deadline, I work long hours to meet my commitment			
7	Whenever I get a chance, I prefer to be working directly with the customer/client			
8	When I accomplish what is expected as a deliverable, I complete all the ancillary tasks			
9	When some task looks challenging or interesting I ask it to be assigned to me			
10	I am looking for someone to mentor me			

If you score less than 50 you have a long transition ahead of you.

The Apprentice and the Echo Generation: a Perspective

Typically, an apprentice is someone fresh out of college in their early 20s venturing into the business world. Although in an economy battered by job losses and job consolidations, it is not unusual to see someone "apprenticing" at a much later stage in their life. This discussion is addressed to those who are fresh out of college and into the workforce for the first time. It is also addressed for those who are going to be their supervisors, hiring managers, and otherwise wards of their career successes; someone in their late 30s, at the other end of the process looking after the apprentices.

The reason for the special write-up to address the needs of the echo generation, otherwise known as the Y Generation, is that this generation of graduates is unlike any other from the previous generation. One reason they are called the echo generation is because their demographic composition is much like the echo of their parents' generation. Typically, they represent someone born between 1981 and 1995. Y-Generation members in the U.S. are more than 80 million strong, about the same number as the baby-boomer generation to which many of their parents belong. The Y Generation is the largest consumer group in the history of the U.S. Other names for the "gen-y" include Echo Boomers and the Millennium Generation.

Members of the Y Generation have annual incomes totaling $211 billion, according to a study from Harris Interactive (2004). The study found that Y Generation spends $172 billion per year and *saves* $39 billion per year (a true anomaly!), and drives many adult-purchasing decisions. Consequently, the Y Generation represents the future market for most consumer brands. The study also found that pre-teens (ages 8-12) spend $19.1 billion annually, while teens (13-19) spend $94.7 billion annually and young adults (20-21) spend $61.2 billion. Nearly 87 percent of income for children under age 13 years is adult-supplied, compared to 37 percent of teens and seven percent of young adults, with teens and young adults relying mostly on jobs for their income. Why are these marketing demographics so relevant to our topic? For one, these adolescents coming into the job market have different expectations of money, what they earn, and what they do with it, including how they save and how all these relate to the jobs they have.

Marketing to Y-generation members requires using more involved techniques than the traditional ones used to attract their parents (a hint for their potential managers and supervisors). Member of Y Generation best respond to marketing methods that bring the message to places the Y Generation congregates, both offline and online (managers, watch out for the new "water cooler place."). Successful generation-Y brands are perceived as hip and popular, but without the air of heavy commercialism (managers, no BS!). TV spots that are 30-second sound bites do not work for this generation; they need peer persuasion (managers, be mindful of how you communicate with them). Also, Generation-Y demographics show that Gen-Y is more racially diverse, with one out of three members considering themselves non-Caucasian (managers, no stereotyping them). One out of every four members of generation Y lives in a single-parent environment and three in every four have working mothers between 1982 and 1995 (managers, remember missing a parent in the home life has a different psychological dynamic for these apprentices).

Their parents belong to the baby boomer generation (born between 1946 and 1964). They represent the values and norms of their parents, a rare throwback to the past generation raised on the culture of video games and instant messaging. This is an anomaly socially because most, who belong to the new generation, are known to rebel against their parent's generation.

However, with this social anomaly, which is now recognized as a given for this generation (Gen-Y), there are some behavioral norms that must be recognized, how they affect the corporate world in its expectations from this generation, and how must they be dealt with. The echo generation is found to have to following social characteristics that are worth making note of to be successful in the corporate culture:

- Respect for the elders

- Trust in the government (their parents rebelled against the government)

- Fiercely independent because of their confident buying power

- Prefer working in teams rather than working alone

- Participation is more important than achievement

- Highly networked and socially savvy

- Low attention spans (raised on video games)

- Must see immediate results

- Blunt in their communication (low patience)

- Low strategic skills; low planning skills

- Short on long-term vision

The reason this discussion is useful and relevant in the context of the Apprentice for this generation is because unless the "seniors" of the corporate world understand these characteristics that they (Gen-Y) bring into to their world, there is likely to be a disconnect or even friction as these new recruits from the echo generation make their way through the corporate world.

To keep things in perspective, it is appropriate to bring the Generation X in this discussion. The potential impact of the backgrounds of Generation Xers and Baby Boomers was reviewed to determine whether key factors and defining moments in their histories may explain the communication disconnect in our nation's workplace. Of special concern, the review sought to analyze the backgrounds of Generation Xers and Baby Boomers to find out how these perspectives influence workplace attitudes and perceptions. It is contemplated that, if these issues can be discussed openly, a more positive work relationship can be cultivated. Additionally, the techniques that could be used by Boomer supervisors to communicate effectively with Xers were reviewed. The results show that, despite a lot of name-calling and blaming, the American workforce and ethic remain strong, and Xers are, slowly but surely, altering the work environment in a manner that may ultimately benefit the family unit and reaffirm America's strong individualistic spirit. The purpose of this discussion is to flesh out how the unique backgrounds of Xers and Boomers influence a workplace and to develop a methodology for resolving workplace conflicts between the two generations.

As each new generation enters the workforce, conflicts are assumed and even expected, as each generation sets its tone and establishes boundaries, ground rules, and expectations. Perhaps no generation has entered the workforce with as much skepticism and diminished expectations regarding work-life as the generation referred to as "X." Prophetically, there have been substantive misunderstandings between Baby Boomers and Generation Xers. However, in order to remain productive, the great majority of Boomers who supervise the nation's 13th generation must understand the unique circumstances that have governed the upbringing of Xers and be willing to compromise their expectations regarding how they view work and its impact on them.

Individual Contributor (Stage-II)

As the Apprentice establishes their value and worth, they graduate to being an Individual Contributor. There may be no change in title, but when this happens, you *know* it. There is no timetable for this transition. However, typically it can be less than a year. Some, however, struggle with it as they suffer through an arduous transition process. Graduation to this stage is characterized by the following distinct attributes:

✓ Responsibility for a definable task, process, or client (s)

✓ Relative Independence within their task

✓ Self-managed timetables within the boundaries of the overall project

✓ Develop credibility for competent work

✓ Others seek their ideas for possible advancement of professional boundaries

It is interesting to understand that this transition is not time driven. Some stay in the Initiation phase for a long time, and, slowly, start getting the responsibilities of Individual Contributor. Although they no longer brag about their "college days," they do not exhibit the independent-minded professionalism that warrants their being called an Individual Contributor. Most are in the late 20s, but it is not uncommon to see a few in the 30s and 40s still struggling to make the mark in this stage. Some even retire barely having earned this rank. So, it is a combination of factors that drive professionals to achieve this stage.

Transitioning from Stage-I to Stage-II

There are five factors that accelerate the transition from Stage-I, Apprentice, to Stage-II, Individual Contributor. They are presented here as a list and discussed briefly:

✓ Independent decision-making

✓ Technical skills

✓ Confidence

✓ Initiative

✓ Synthesizing collaborative solutions

✓ Developing a reputation

Independent decision-making is one of the most difficult factors to overcome for young professionals. All their lives they have depended on others to tell them what to do. Although they are often good at following orders and delivering what was asked, doing something new on their own is scary to them. They lack confidence in their professional judgment.

Often, their boss thwarts this development to independent decision-making. Some bosses delight in making their subordinates dependent on their guiding them in every major professional decision. This relationship exacerbates the condition of dependence and is hard to break. The sooner you are able to recognize this need and accelerate your transition to independence, the better your chances of becoming an independent Individual Contributor.

Technical Skills is at the heart of the competency of an Individual Contributor. Understanding the intricacies of the job and being able to do the job hands-on is what makes one expert in their field. Technical skill does not mean technology skills, it merely means that whatever field in which you are engaged. So, for a lawyer, it is the knowledge of the law and the filing of the correct papers for the lawsuit; for the advertising accounts administrator, it is knowing how the client wants their message conveyed to the marketplace; and, for the accountant, it is knowing how to make double entry book-keeping in a business transaction. Without a solid foundation of knowing the ins and outs of a technical area, one cannot become a worthy Individual Contributor.

Confidence is your ability to take your competence to a level of inspiring others to trust you to do the right thing professionally. Confidence comes from having demonstrated competence and engendering in others that in a tough situation, you will not waver and deliver your best performance.

Initiative is when you are able to fulfill the task assigned to you with minimum intervention or supervision. This does not mean that you are not allowed to collaborate with others. It merely means knowing what you know and what you don't, and then seeking help, so that the task can be accomplished, all the while, learning in the process.

Synthesizing collaborative solutions comes from the ability work in a team setting. If you have confidence in your own technical abilities, you must be able to identify a piece of the puzzle that you can own in a grander scheme of things and ask others to contribute their pieces so that the entire puzzle can be constructed.

Developing a reputation comes from a focus that you develop in your own technical area. As you get good at what you do, others come to seek your advice. This gives you more opportunities to push the boundaries of your knowledge and learn more. This is now a virtuous cycle, catalyzing your reputation as an expert in the area of your endeavor. Publishing credible work in your area of expertise also accelerates reputation building in your field of endeavor.

Tool-9

Tool-9 is designed to provide insights into an accelerated transition form Stage-I (Apprentice) to Stage-II (Individual Contributor). Review the elements that help the transition and understand what behaviors you must practice to transition to Stage-II.

Tool-9: Transition Tool: Stage-I to Stage-II

This tool is designed to accelerate transition from Apprentice to Individual Contributor. Although there is no formal transition here, it is informally bestowed by virtue of how you are treated and how assignments are made in your work.

#	Item	Often 10 9 8	Sometimes 7 6 5 4	Rarely 3 2 1
1	Colleagues ask me about my views in certain areas of technical expertise			
2	When I speak in a technical or departmental meeting, my views are respected			
3	I am asked to collaborate on ideas, proposals, and business situations			
4	When I have some new idea and present it to a few, more of my colleagues come to know about it quickly through informal means			
5	When I am given a task, my boss respects the timeline for its completion			
6	My boss does not show anxiety around my progress on a task assigned to me			
7	My boss signs off on my reports, memos, and ideas with less and less intervention			
8	I get invited to meetings in other areas of technical expertise			
9	People stop by to collaborate with me on their ideas			
10	When I ask others to collaborate with me, they are willing			

If you score less than 50 you have a long transition ahead of you.

Stage-III: Team Leader/Mentor

In this stage there is a major shift in the job. Making a transition from Stage-II to Stage-III is not a matter of having "more" of what it took to get to Stage-II; it is "different." This is one of the hardest concepts for many professionals to grasp and deal with. Some of these "different" elements are nature and others, nurture. In the lexicon that is becoming dated, the person in this role was also called a manager. Please visit the discussion of the role of a manager in Chapter-3: Management Basics.

The best way Stage-III role can be defined is by imagining it as an interface between the highly technical work that makes the core of what an organization does and its business world. Thus, a person in this role straddles the two key areas of business boundaries: how it creates value by doing well what it does on the one hand, and then delivering what it does to its customers, clients, and the outside world in general to capture that value. The role of a player in Stage-III jobs is to be good at how to play in both these worlds.

The following characteristics are integral to those who play well in Stage-III roles:

✓ Deep technical expertise in one of many areas

✓ Good understanding of allied technical areas

✓ Strong personnel skills, including interpersonal and conflict resolution skills

✓ An ability to inspire, motivate, or impel others to produce good work

✓ A skill to develop others to make strong and competitive teams

✓ An understanding of gaps in the teams and identifying the means to eliminate those gaps

✓ A skill to translate customer needs into product requirements

✓ An ability to deliver product requirements through unique solutions

✓ A skill to mentor less experienced professional to reach their full potential

✓ A proven skill to lead teams with innovative ideas

In many contexts, the role of a Stage-III professional is seen as a manager. In today's world of virtual organizations, boundaryless enterprise, and global teaming, the word manager has come to mean more as someone who leads an effort of many, and not in its hierarchical sense, where the entire platoon is marching behind the manager. The concept has a simultaneous loose-tight connotation to the role. Although those in this role have had hands-on expertise in one of the many areas, which they supervise, they are removed from detailed work by one or more levels. See the Management Work Gap discussion is chapter-3.

The following characteristics help Stage-II professionals advance to Stage-III:

> Demonstrated expertise on one technical area

> Ability to deal with the outside world effectively

> Working effectively with ambiguity

> Collaborating with customers to translate their needs into deliverable products

> Understanding of how what they do in a team setting creates business value

> Generating new ideas and quickly mobilizing them into actions that generate revenues

> Mentoring other professionals.

> Networking with outsiders and positioning themselves as premier professionals

> Development of broad interests and competencies

> Developing others to take their place

> Taking responsibilities for their actions and for others; creating accountabilities

> Using conceptual skills to understand other technical areas

The transition from Stage-II to Stage-III is a discontinuous one. The reason for this discontinuity is that you cannot get to this stage by doing more of what you did so well in Stage-II. In fact, merely doing so, with no demonstrated aptitude for leading or managing, will vitiate any prospects of a successful transition into this Stage. This is one of the hardest concepts for Stage-III wanna-bes.

One reason is perhaps that the functions of those in this stage are so different from those who are in earlier stages. The managerial function can be described as one that involves *leading, planning, organizing,* and *controlling.*

These are merely the verbal (gerund) forms of the verbs used to define the four functions of managing in Chapter-3. In this context *controlling* is used to mean setting up of mechanisms in the management process so that events can be monitored for assessing their flow and effect on the workings of the organization and how changes in the way they happen can affect the right outcomes. This is why those who want to transition into this stage must be given special training and appreciation for these functional areas.

Tool-10

This tool is designed to help you understand what it takes to make a transition to Stage-III.

Tool-10: Transition Tool: Stage-II to Stage-III

This tool is designed to accelerate transition from Individual Contributor to Team Leader/Mentor/Manager. This is a formal transition and is not necessarily driven by how well you do in Stage-II.

#	Item	Often 10 9 8	Sometimes 7 6 5 4	Rarely 3 2 1
1	Colleagues ask me about my views in certain areas of technical expertise			
2	When I speak in a technical or departmental meeting, my views are respected			
3	I am asked to collaborate on ideas, proposals, and business situations			
4	When I have some new idea and present it to a few, more of my colleagues come to know about it quickly through informal means			
5	When I am given a task, my boss respects the timeline for its completion			
6	My boss does not show anxiety around my progress on a task assigned to me			
7	My boss signs off on my reports, memos, and ideas with less and less intervention			
8	I get invited to meetings in other areas of technical expertise			
9	People stop by to collaborate with me on their ideas			
10	When I ask others to collaborate with me, they are willing			

If you score less than 50 you have a long transition ahead of you.

Stage-IV: The Executive or Professional Manager

In this stage a professional has reached a level of seniority in an organization at a level at or above a functional director. These include director, vice president, COO, CEO, CIO, Chairman/Chairwoman, and sometimes, program manager.

At this level the world changes for those who are in it. Their focus of activities shifts from inward to outward. Their perspective drives their actions. Although someone in this position has risen from the technical ranks, and through Stage-III, the amount of time they spend in technical activities is less than 10 percent; the remainder of their time is being taken by the functions of management—leading, planning, organizing, and controlling. In exceptional cases its converse is true. For example someone who is a Chief Technical Officer or a Chief Scientist is expected to spend much of their time steeped in technical matters and then managing their implications as they influence the business in which they participate. Even in such cases, their role is to ask critical questions, and not spend time answering questions others ask. Even in their case, they spend little time on their own; they are in meetings most of the day or spending time with others.

The following attributes constitute what those in Stage-IV do to be successful:

➢ Providing organizational direction and vision

➢ Work at the interface with critical organizations

➢ Selecting, sponsoring, and developing key people

➢ Spend time away from technical activities and focus on leadership opportunities

➢ Ensure that leadership resources are used wisely and not frittered away fighting fires

Let us briefly discuss each to bring clarity to this topic.

Providing organizational direction is an act of leadership. To have a vision that is broad, yet specific that is well articulated and presented to others so that all understand it is one of the key functions of someone at this level. Although mostly CEOs or those at the helm have the grand vision, those at the levels below, including the level we are discussing here, are an integral part of that process. Even if they personally disagree with the vision that comes from the top, they have an obligation to permeate that vision across the organization. If such is not the case, they had better be looking for a change in their assignment.

Work at the interface with critical organizations is another key role executives play. They must identify which organizations are critical to success of their own and form bonds with them through their personal involvement. Their networks, influence, and personal connections at these organizations are what make them successful.

Selecting, sponsoring, and developing key people, is one of the major points of focus for people at this level. In fact, good executives spend nearly a third of their time cultivating leadership within their own organization and looking for talent that will enhance their own agenda.

Focus on leadership opportunities is critical for anyone at this level. Many come from technical ranks. It is easy for them to gravitate to their area of expertise and put their influence on matters that they are passionate about. This is counterproductive. Once you rise to this level of responsibility, you must learn to delegate all technical matters to those who are responsible for it. This does not mean that you cannot challenge a decision or a point of view stemming from a technical course of action. This merely implies that hands-on technical work is something you must stay away from, despite your temptation to get sucked into it.

Firefighting is the other area of waste that senior managers get sucked into. They act as a lightening rod of customer complaints and employee grievances. Although this is laudable, these activities take much of their time and create an environment of constant fire fighting and knee-jerk responses inside an organization. They should, instead, take their resources to develop robust processes for such problems and oversee their smooth functioning by monitoring these activities, perhaps by exception. Constant firefighting, especially at high levels inside an organization takes away much energy from creative and energizing pursuits. Such organizations wither and eventually die. See the Management Work Gap in chapter 3:-Management Basics.

The Executive and the Glass Ceiling:

One of the common barriers to advancement in an organization beyond the current level of management is called "the glass ceiling" to communicate the invisible nature of it. Although everyone feels its presence, it is particularly apparent to certain groups that feel discriminated against. They include women, minorities, immigrants, those with disabilities, and the "older" population of employees.

Often, there is a culture of promoting certain people from within that result in cliquey process that adds to this perception of the glass ceiling. Thus, to move from manager to a director, this glass ceiling may become apparent to some. Although this practice is discriminatory—hence illegal—it is very often difficult to prove discrimination. Besides, an organization's management has much discretion to manage it the way it chooses. Running an organization is *not* a democracy.

The best weapon against this barrier is to become aware of it beforehand. In other words, if you are a minority female entering a managerial position and your next promotion is director, it is best to start becoming aware of it and developing your strategies from the get go. To become a part of the "clique" you have to first reconcile to the idea. Then you have to work on it by seeking help, making an effort, and seeking coaching and mentoring. You also have to make your intention known to the "management" as early as you can. A good place and time for this is the annual performance review discussion. If the idea of belonging to a clique within your own company is abhorrent to you, then you may have to look for alternatives, such as moving to another company where the circumstances may be in your favor for advancement. For a savvy manager not to be aware of this situation within their own organization from the get go and then making an end run at the time when promotions are due is counterproductive or even suicidal (see Career Suicide below). At this level it is part of your job to know how to effectively deal with such challenges.

Career Implications

What we have presented so far is the panoramic view of how a career evolves. In this discussion there is an implied message of how you can chart your own growth within an organization and what needs to transpire before you can graduate to the next stage in your career growth. The narratives on the Stages and the tools provided are aimed at helping budding career professionals get a better stab at moving forward with their careers in a planned way. The discussion presented is in a highly condensed form, yet it provides a roadmap for those who are not familiar with the terrain. This is expected to be for those who just graduated from college and those who started out with their new jobs.

Developing Career History

For a career on the move, history counts. In fact, any upward career move requires a good résumé. This is a chronological fact sheet of your career and is the key instrument for making a successful move. Even inside an organization this can be a valuable tool to present your portrait to those who are interested in looking at you.

Often many professionals leave their fate in the hands of their managers. They expect that their managers have the best interest and insights about what is good for them and hence any actions their managers take should be in their best interest. Some even naively believe that their managers lay awake at nights wondering about the careers of their subordinates!

This is a view that can limit your career options. If you believe that your manager is staying awake at nights wondering about what next to give you as an opportunity or assignment to advance your career, you are mistaken.

To develop a history that you can leverage in your career requires, among other elements, a strong sense of career vision. Suffice it is to say that your career is in your hands and that you must learn to take charge of it early so that you can fill it with experiences that support your journey to the destination in your career vision.

Impediments to a Good Career History

In the matters of one's career, it is inevitable that one would encounter others who make it difficult for them to have a good track record in their pursuits. Why? For one, it is human nature that interferes with how it influences your pursuits, particularly if others see you moving ahead in competition with them. The following is a partial list of common factors that influence one's career path. Being aware of these factors can help in dealing with them.

- Professional Jealousy

- Organizational Politics

- Management culture

- The Glass Ceiling

- Incompetent bosses

- Organizational Culture

- Career Suicide

A brief discussion on each topic is presented here to provide a perspective on how these items, individually and collectively, influence the future of your career.

Professional Jealously is encountered when others see you as a threat to their success. In any field of endeavor, there is going to be competition. This is good for both—those competing as a group, as well as the one for whom they work. For example, competing athletes bring out the best in each other in what they do and thrill the audiences who witness them competing. It holds true in organizations. The only twist here is that people play vindictive, even pernicious games to bring others down with their schemes and, in the process, cause harm to themselves, those with whom they are competing, and the organization. Often these jealousies remain subterranean and sometimes result in healthy outcomes. But, unchecked and abetted by those who delight in their promotion, they can be quite destructive.

In their worst form, professional jealousies can cause those involved in them to mistrust each other. They promote an atmosphere of suspicion and paranoia. The worst manifestation of jealousies occurs when your own superiors undermine your professional credibility because they see you as a threat to their own cause. Very few feel secure and confident seeing their subordinates excel in what they do and making them look good to *their* leaders. But this perspective takes much self-confidence, integrity, and leadership, which few organizational managers are willing to display.

One way to deal with such encounters of jealousy is to see the pattern. If a colleague is known to have sabotaged your objectives in the past and interfered with your success, the best approach is to confront them and have a discussion. Without threatening them, develop an understanding of how you could collaborate and help each other. If this genteel and politic approach works for all involved, there is no need to escalate this matter to the chain of command. One rule of organizational survival is that for every action there is equal, opposite, and *escalated* reaction. The other rule here, too, is that those who bring the complaint first, get the third degree!

If however, the jealousies escalate, then you must involve your superiors and resolve the issue to everyone's satisfaction. When an issue raises itself to this level of attention, there is a cause of concern and you must take all the necessary precautions to protect your professional future and your welfare at the place of work. The following checklist is provided as a guideline in such situations:

- Identify the pattern of behavior; don't go into denial by thinking that you are imagining it. If you sense it, it is happening.

- Approach the person who is behaving in a counterproductive way and see if talking to them in a non-confrontational way can help. Having a coffee or lunch is a good forum for such discussions.

- If the behavior persists, meet the person again in a less friendly and more business-like approach and caution them that if the pattern continues, you may escalate the issue to your boss. You may have a different boss than the person who is persecuting you!

- If the behavior continues, see your boss in an informal setting and put them on notice. Ask for advice. Do not present the matter as a complaint.

- Continuing jealousy should result in a three-way meeting (four-way if there are two bosses, one for each of you) with a formal memo about the meeting to your boss and what agreement was reached.

- If this continues, you have two choices: ask for a transfer or quit; escalate your complaints by increasing their tenor or import.

Organizational Politics can be defined as a code of conduct you must adhere to in order to protect your prospects of continued employment at your place of work. Those in power inside an organization set the tone of the conduct by virtue of their ability to advance their own agenda. Those who oppose it create their own band of followers and the factions continue to battle their agendas. All of this happens below the surface so that there is no track record of memos, meetings, or any other formal process by which these individual agendas become points of contention to be resolved in arbitration inside the organization.

Often, senior executives subliminally promote this to happen to see who wins out and then they make their 'formal" decision to ensure that the favored one wins out. These are treacherous areas of organizational landscape and should be avoided by those who have solid professional skills to back their work. Often those who do not have a solid footing inside an organization or those who are trying to undermine the current organizational order start these petty games and they create an undercurrent of support by employing skullduggery and subterfuge.

Getting involved in organizational politics can be tantamount to career suicide, especially if you are new to an organization and do not know the full scope of the games being played and who all are involved.

Management Culture is the environment created by the style of senior leadership that forces the rest of the organization to align itself to it. Once again, there are the written rules ("content") of this culture and the unwritten ("context") ones. Part of the management culture is the norms that are established of management behavior that are expected of others. Some of these norms are formal and others a loose set of guidelines and practices. This is the glue that drives the management process and makes the organization move forward (or backward). Knowing this culture can be critical to a career success.

The Glass Ceiling is a metaphor for a perceived or real barrier that prevents employees from penetrating the ranks beyond where they feel stuck. In an earlier discussion we presented the concept of the glass ceiling as it applies to executives. But here, this is at all levels of employment. Women, minorities, those with disabilities, "aged" employees, immigrants, and other groups of employees feel especially discriminated against in a workplace because of their special status. There are many resources available, including books, Internet resources, and coaching to deal with the issue surrounding this barrier to advancement. (see Index).

Incompetent Bosses is yet another minefield one must deal with in an organization. Partially such an outcome is the manifestation of organizational politics we just discussed. If a senior manager has an agenda that they want to advance and they foresee resistance in their path, they usually appoint, in strategic places, those who buy into their ideas. In extreme cases, this can involve sexual favors and blackmail or fraud. Sometimes those who fill such slots are called "yes managers" in acknowledgment of their willingness to go along with whatever their boss, who appoints them, decides to advance as a cause.

If you see this happening inside your organization, more as a pervasive practice than an anomaly, you may want to seriously consider finding yourself another company to work for.

Organizational Culture can be yet another factor that can cause career reverberation. It can be defined as a set of norms and values an organization adopts or embraces to advance its own agenda or vision. It is a combination of both good and underhanded practices that can affect your career. A culture of fraternization can lead to an environment that can be toxic to many who have to live with it. If top management connives to ignore such transgressions, you may want to ask yourself if this is something you can live with and then decide what strategy you are going to adopt to deal with it so that your career is not compromised.

Professional Suicide is deliberate behavior of those who sabotage their own careers by acting in ways that guarantee a negative outcome and result in their career getting trashed. Often it is a cumulative effect of pent-up stress, frustration, and a sense of hopelessness caused by how an organization treats them. Professional suicide is a culmination of a spiraling cycle of increasingly damaging behavior that one embraces and then pursues it until their goal of killing their own career is reached. When on such a path, it is best to recognize it and get immediate professional help so that the inevitable outcome can be derailed and the career brought back on track.

Some of the more typical suicidal behaviors are described below:

- They suddenly quit their jobs for others far beneath their capabilities, even when they have to fight to stoop to such low-level jobs.

- Some become disruptive and do things for which they must know they will be fired

- Some suddenly "retire" on the job and work with minimal effort.

- Others get caught up in daily fires and refuse to keep up with technical advancements, becoming obsolete.

- Others develop psychosomatic complaints of backaches, headaches, and ulcers.

- Some, told to slow down by their doctors, are not able to and seem headed for physical suicide.

All of these behaviors result in their careers going in the negative direction. When these behaviors start to show, immediate action must be taken to change the course of action and protect a well-nurtured career.

Résumé Thrillers, Fillers, and Killers

As one navigates through their career, there will be occasions to grab assignments of your choice, get assigned to what comes your way, or just while away your time awaiting a juicy project. Each of these assignments have a place in your résumé and how it creates a message of impact to the reader about your career, in matters not just of how you package that assignment, but rather, how that assignment itself helps your value proposition.

If you have a crystallized career vision, it is clear how you want to develop your career "history" so that your future value will be dictated by the power of your contribution and how you managed those critical assignments. This is why having a vision helps you look ahead and seek out assignments ("thrillers") that provide rounding out your career in ways that help your future path. Constantly being vigilant and having connections internally can help ferret out assignments before they become publicly available. Putting your boss on notice for specific future assignments is also a good idea. The best time to do this is during the annual review.

Résumé killers are those projects where the assignment did not advance your career and the outcome set you back in the way it worked out, such as a major product that failed, a campaign that got a black eye, and so on. It is best to anticipate such projects before they land on your résumé and manage how they are reported and perceived, both internally and externally.

Résumé fillers are tasks that clearly take up chronology but do not have any substantive outcomes worth reporting. What they suggest is that you were considered "idling" or were sidelined in the organization when you report such assignments in your chronology; not a good thing for career advancement.

Being aware of these three categories of résumé entries is a good guide for watching out for what you get assigned during the course of your career.

Looking Ahead

During a career track, it is always a good idea to keep holding a forward-looking vision. Looking back can help somewhat to see how what you have done is going to look on your résumé. Looking ahead has to do with what we presented in the previous paragraph: each future assignment must put you in a light that allows you to show how you have developed and grown in your career. Your manager is not going to worry about that; you must.

The best approach to managing your résumé message is to visit it every six months and look at it objectively. This is the time to take stock and meet with those who are in a position to provide the view that allows you to evaluate how what is emerging is going to help you in your future. This can be managed proactively as mentioned here.

Protecting Your Prospects

Once again, this strategy of protecting your prospects must be done proactively. If you trust the organization to give you assignments that are in your best interest you might be surprised to see that, as time goes by, all you have is a portfolio of assignments—a smorgasbord—that may not serve you in the best and leveraged way in managing your career. This is where having a mentor in addition to having a good relationship with the boss and those around you greatly aid your cause. Never underestimate the power of those who have your interest in getting you what you are looking for. Never underestimate the power of advice coming from someone who has experienced first-hand lessons from the school of hard knocks.

Venturing Out

If your persistent efforts to keep your résumé sharp and marketable get frustrated and you are not able to recover from a few bad assignments, it is time to contemplate moving. Do not expect for things to change suddenly. If your manager has failed in two promises in getting you the kind of assignment you need to keep your résumé sharp, it is time to start shopping your résumé for an outside job. In such cases, do not make idle threats. The best approach is to line up another opportunity and then walk into the boss's office and quietly announce that you have made a decision to move on, without giving out details as to why.

Established Employee

Much of what is presented in the previous section applies to someone making a transition into a company as their career evolves. Some may enter a company as a natural progression of their career, when they decide that there is an opportunity to expand their career somewhere else. Sometimes, in larger companies, this move can be from one organization to another within the same company, either initiated by management, or by the person.

This discussion is presented to address each category of the following transitions:

- Transition within a company
  - o Self-initiated transition
  - o Management-initiated transition
- Transition outside a company
  - o Transition is good times
  - o Transition in adverse times

Transition within the company

Self-Initiated Transition

Self-initiated transition within a company is usually prompted by personal considerations. They are listed below:

- Stagnation in the position
- Organizational relationship(s)
- Lack of opportunities, including the risk of job loss
- Expanding your career horizons

Each is briefly discussed below to provide a perspective on how to best manage the transition to the new position.

All self-initiated transitions have an unwritten rule: you must prove yourself to the new organization without any benefit of the leadership giving you a preferential treatment. This treatment is usually accorded only when the transfer is initiated by the management for its own benefit. In such cases both the management and the individual benefit.

Stagnation in the previous position could have resulted from any number of factors. In most cases, however, it is the environment within that organization that is the cause of such a condition. If it is not, anyone making such a transition must evaluate how much of that stagnation was caused by the perception by others of self-induced work habits. In all likelihood, if such were the case, self-initiated transfer is likely to be a more challenging undertaking as most organizations will find ways to block it. But, if such a transition were to materialize, anyone making this change must first make a self-assessment of the reason for the change and take responsibility for self-generated causes that prompted this transfer. Usually such episodes are not one sided. Without such self assessment, the same cycle is likely to repeat even faster, and then yet another transfer within the same company may be difficult.

One approach for a fresh start at the new position in the same company—different organization—is to find a coach or a mentor who can help in the change. The change must be of patterns that cause self-induced stagnation. Often, such a condition is a combination of internal and environmental factors. The fact is that the environment can be changed to a large extent by changing your own behavior and attitude. This is why making an honest assessment of the causes, and then creating accountability for change, can be a good first step. Having an open dialog with a coach or mentor can be a good start.

If the reason for the stagnation is more perception than the reality, then changing perception in the new workplace must be a top priority. One approach to changing perception is to organize a campaign to honestly communicate your activities to those whose perceptions matter in the future. One way to start such a process is to send regular memos, white papers, and meeting notices where what you do is disseminated. Collaborating with other thought-leaders in the new organization is also a good move.

Relationship in the previous organization can be a major factor in deteriorating job prospects for someone in a company. Relationship is a two-way street. Once again, an introspective and honest assessment must be made to identify patterns of behaviors that result in adverse or non-productive relationships. If this pattern is not understood and broken, and replaced with its productive and healthy counterpart, the same cycle can easily repeat. Once again, having a mentor or a coach can be a good start to self-correction of behavior patterns.

Lack of opportunities including risk of job loss is a common factor for many to seek a transfer within a company to a different organization. If a transfer is made to another organization, it is a good idea to understand how you can leverage the learning from the one that you transferred to, help in improving its prospects. This is not only possible, but highly desirable to create new value in the organization. Often, an organization's leadership is responsible of capturing new opportunities and translating those into growth plans and for the organization and its members, who can grow with it. So, the strategy here should be collaborating with the leadership to identify new opportunities and then defining a role that you can play in advancing the organization so that all can benefit and grow with it.

Expanding career horizons is often a major factor for those in large companies to make a move on their own. If the target organization has opportunities not easily available from the source organization, then clearly claiming those opportunities as you start your stint in the target organization is important. If the target organization is rapidly growing, carefully vetting the right opportunities is critical before taking on new responsibilities. Going in with a plan and then discussing it with the leadership of the new organization is a good way to start the new stint.

Management-Initiated Transition

Management-Initiated transition is generally a good sign. This usually means that someone has done well and is being moved around to get exposure to other challenges within the company for ongoing career advancement. Of course, the converse can also be true, where a valuable person is not delivering their worth in an organization and the management is assessing whether the person needs another chance to prove their mettle inside the company. In most cases the person involved knows the circumstances for the transfer and must make use of that awareness to situate for a proper transition.

Transition outside a company

A transition outside the company is prompted by any number of factors. Typical among them: glass ceiling, stagnation, layoff, disagreement with management and so on. Most of these factors are negative in their connotation. In such cases, it is natural for the exiting employee to be down on the company and express that in some way during the transition, either to the exiting company or to the prospect company.

This is not a good idea. Keeping a positive outlook, no matter what the circumstances of departure, is desirable. Even though companies may not care, it is the people who hear that view or share it, that can create barriers in the future, without your awareness.

Also, during the transition process—interviews, meetings, etc.—it is to your advantage not to discuss proprietary information about your current employer with the new one. This can have negative repercussions from two views: one they may not trust you to keep their information confidential if they were to hire you; they may get what they need and then not hire you.

When starting at the new company having a good plan of engagement and managing the expectations for both sides—your own, and the chain of command—is critical to success.

The other dimension to success at a new company is relationships. Anyone beyond the individual contributor is going to have to work with others in a social environment. As your seniority goes up, relationships become growingly important. Understanding who the key players are and then managing each relationship well from the get-go are important as you navigate your new life in the organization.

Transition in good times

When a transition occurs at a point in your career where you are doing well, landing a new job is exciting, even when you are already established in your profession and you have a certain "style" that may be hard to change. Coming in with this advantage gives you certain momentum that can carry you through the initial transition and into your new job where you are well ensconced. The following points many be worth remembering to avoid any backlash, especially for senior professionals, that may result from their lack of sensitivity to the existing company culture:

- Do not disparage traditions that may be well entrenched in a culture by making open comments, or avoiding certain events where you presence as a senior member of the team—or even an executive—is expected.

- If you want to dismantle traditions—if you have the power to do so—do so in a gradual way and assess the reaction of the work group. Suddenly changing long-standing traditions without due concern to those who respect them may create an unhealthy backlash.

- If you want to start new traditions, also try on a smaller scale and see how the group takes to them

- If you offend someone or a group by imposing something that you consider must be changed, do so in a way that is healthy and respected.

Transition in adversity

Transition in adverse times entail your having gone to another company when you suffered a setback—a layoff, demotion, or a firing. In such cases, assume that those who work at the new place already know why you joined them, but at the same time you can be positive about your outlook on it. Do not pretend that you transitioned under great circumstances, but you do not need to dwell on that beyond some casual reference.

Managers

Managers and those who have people reporting to them in the new organization have a particularly challenging role during their inter-company transitions. Knowing the style of management and the culture of the new organization are critical to a successful transition. If a manager (anyone with that title and, up to, and, including, Senior Director) moves to a new organization, they had better learn to accommodate the existing culture with their own style rather than its converse. If they come on too strong and muscle their way in to the new organization, they may succeed until their newness wears off. Then, after the organization gets used to their style, they may have the entire organization rebelling against them in a covert way to subvert their agenda. If this happens, the future of such a manager is very limited.

In such positions it is much more effective to create allies and build relationships before moving on with your own agenda, no matter how urgently you think that you must do this to make your mark.

Newbie managers, who are promoted from their largely hands-on technical role into the position of management, find this transition, even without the burden of having to switch companies, one of the most difficult. They keep going back to their comfort zone to validate who they are, and, in the process, forget their most important aspect of their new role: relationships. So, when a newly-minted manager undergoes yet another transition to a strange company, they must be vigilant that they do not revert to their old calling: doing technical work to compensate for their lack of getting traction in the relationships department.

One reason why this strategy does not work well, is that the two approaches to getting one situated in a new environment are, once again, orthogonal. This is the same argument we presented in the discussion of the Management Work Gap, in Chapter-3. Just as no amount of doing technical work can compensate the demands of doing the right management work, no amount of doing technical work can result in building relationships at the new place of work. Only express efforts that result in building planned relationships can do that. So, for managers, building relationships must take priority over the temptation of doing technical work, just to show your new colleagues how good you are in your own field of endeavor.

This transition is even more challenging for the mid-career professionals and the baby boomers. Why? Because of their seniority, they are expected to be masters of their technical domain. So, if they have shied away from building relationships and socializing at their previous employers, they had better change their attitude and priorities at their new employer, otherwise they may face a similar fate there, too, particularly, if they transitioned out of their old company in adversity!

Executives

Anyone with the title of a vice president and above, including the CEO falls into this category. In such a transition, it is best to first take time to understand the people who report to you and see their perspectives, even though you may not agree with them, before pushing forward with yours.

One of the immediate undertakings such leaders embark on is major organizational change: layoffs, shutdowns, reorganizations, cutbacks, and so on. Such seismic changes must be led by the initiating executive in both spirit and actions. For example, if a CEO initiates a cost-cutting initiative and installs policies in place to monitor costs down to the supply of pencils and clips, they had better discipline their own actions and hold off on buying their own corporate jet for travels. Such moves are blatantly insulting to the employees and result in long-term resentment that is hard to overcome. Often, those in the baby boomer age group convince themselves that they have earned their keep and can do whatever that they want, while expecting the rest of the organization to follow their initiatives. In this context a quote by Eleanor Roosevelt is apropos: *"Great leaders do not ask their followers to do things that they would not do themselves."*

New Job Late in Life

New job late in life can be exciting, especially if you find your dream job as you enter your "mature years." This period will vary from being 40 to 60 and beyond. Recent studies have shown that an average worker retires with $58,500 to their name. With the ongoing assault on their retirement accounts and pension plans, many American workers dread entering their twilight years with long life spans ahead of them, a threat of higher inflation, reduced benefits, and a fixed and paltry sum to their name. Many are looking for reentering the workforce soon after their retirement.

One of the major challenges faced by the baby boomers returning back to work at a new job, is that their boss is likely to be a GenX or GenY newbie. GenX are those born between 1965 and 1980 and GenY are those born between 1981 and 1995. As we will later discuss in Chapter-8: Taking Care of the Customer, those in GenX, GenY categories have a blind spot in the relationship dimension. This is now a double-edged sword. In terms of how they will treat you, you may find the whole interaction patently lacking in the relationship dimension. They may even treat you with condescension. But, if you take it in stride and show that you can be an asset in an organization lacking in the relationship dimension, you could soon make a place for yourself.

Yet another category of a worker in this group is one who has never worked until late in life and who is now in the need of a job. Having your first job late in life (or after many years of hiatus) can be a daunting prospect. The best approach is putting aside your pride, treating the many workers, even your manager, who may be half your age, with due respect and ignoring the condescending attitude towards you, that may be initially apparent, as you start working or as you even navigate during the interview process.

It is a proven fact that older employees are nearly twice as productive as their younger counterparts in how they work (little wasted time, very little learning curve, and strong work ethic). This is somewhat counterintuitive to many, who see the younger workers as having more energy and staying power than their older counterparts. The older worker is likely to go after their assignment in a more deliberate and planned way, taking into account the years of experience that they have under their belt. So, a younger manager bringing on board a baby boomer to their department is setting a new standard of work in their department.

The best way to leverage this advantage is to mentor those who are open to learning. Collaborate with those who are able to create a "win-win" outcome and then sharing with them your "secrets," that can only come from learning first hand. Here, even though you may not have had "work" experience, if this is your first job, late in life, your life experiences are equally as valuable to the younger set as your work experience.

Back after a major gap

Many baby boomers are returning to work after a major hiatus in their work life. This is especially true of the woman workers, many of whom decided to take time off to raise their families in their thirties and then relied on their husbands to provide for the family. After about 20 years of this, many have come to realize that after the kids have left the nest and after learning that their husbands' retirements may be in jeopardy, that they had better find some avenues to generate incomes for themselves.

Coming back to work after many years of not working can be a daunting experience. The best strategy is to be clear about the job you are going after and then update your skills and bring them to be competitive in today's job market. The other hurdle to face then is the age barrier. Using some of the strategies mentioned in the previous paragraph it is not difficult to reenter the work force and get integrated with dignity to start productive work life again.

The greatest challenge for such baby boomers is the culture shock of working again. If you do not have the political savvy to navigate successfully—most don't—then it is a good idea to take this learning in stride and integrate that into your routines. A wayward behavior in this department can cost dearly in terms of future prospects, and this late in life it is something very difficult to recover from.

Changing Careers/Industries

Changing careers or industries late in life is difficult but not impossible. Some transitions are easier than the others. For example, going from high-tech to biotech is a natural transition if you choose the right functional area to pursue. It is tempting to go through intensive training to learn about the industry before making a transfer. With such a strategy it is normal to land at entry-level positions because of the industry change. This can be avoided by choosing a different strategy. When going from one industry to another, it is best to choose the target industry to have some landing advantage coming from the industry you are leaving. For example, going from high-tech to biotech the advantage is a disciplined product development process, cutting-edge IT infra-structure, fast cycle times for most processes, and so on. Leveraging these advantages into a new job cross industry is a much better strategy that allows you to land at a comparable or higher position than is possible with the "train and gain" approach.

For more on this see the Author's *The 7 Keys to a Dream Job: A Career Nirvana Playbook!* Key-3: Presenting Yourself: Playing Golf with Tiger Woods on how this is done with examples.

Immigrant worker

In the context of this discussion, an immigrant worker is someone, who has been in the U.S. for a number of years, but is not fully integrated into the work pool, socially, psychologically, and emotionally. It is said that it can take up to 10 years for someone to integrate to a point where their work habits and cultural norms become seamless with the working population. Some companies have a predominantly immigrant culture. There are some start-ups in the Silicon Valley where the predominance of Indian and Chinese cultures is noticeable. For someone of the dominant national culture to integrate into such a company, which also has predominant culture of the same nationality, the integration will be much easier. But, when this happens, the company comes to be labeled as an "Indian" or "Chinese" company, making it difficult for it to grow beyond its initial stages.

In any case, for an immigrant worker to reengage in the context of this book and who has been in the U.S. for less than 10 years, it may take a special effort to make the transition that entails finding the right job and then coming on board where they feel productive. Although such workers make excellent employees because they focus on their assignments and commitments and rarely stray, how they are able to integrate with the rest of the workforce is something their manager has to worry about.

Baby boomer back in workforce

Many baby boomers who have found themselves out of work in their mid careers or who have come to the retirement point, must consider alternative avenues of getting reemployed. Those who have lost employment in their mid careers—those in their 40s—must find how to make the existing momentum their ally. There are various ways to get back into the workforce and many of them are presented in detail in the author's previous books, including *The 7 Keys to Dream Job: A Career Nirvana Playbook!*, and *Rehired, Not Retired: Proven Strategies for the Baby Boomers!*

Rehired from Retirement

Rehired from retirement can result from either being called by your previous employer or by pursuing your own dream to jump-start your career. In any case, getting back into the workforce entails integrating back into the workforce. Many of the guidelines and recommendations presented in the previous paragraphs apply to this situation and it is recommended that those who fall into this category carefully review this material.

Transitional Tribulations

Career and job transitions are never easy. Getting into a new job can be a sigh of relief, especially if you are or have been out of work, even for a short while. However, this complacency may be short lived. Yes, it is great to be landing in a new place of employment, but it is foolhardy to underestimate the transitional challenges many face in today's growingly uncertain corporate world.

Recent job market upheaval has made everyone inside organizations edgy. Everyone is looking over their shoulders to see if they are at risk in some way that may compromise their job. A new element—you—inserted in the mix of things in an environment that is already clouded with apprehension and suspicion can exacerbate the situation. This is particularly true of older workers— baby boomers[1]—who are often finding themselves landing in organizations where their peers are much younger and even their bosses not much older than the peers. Apart from the age gap, these workers are also experiencing a "cultural gap" and are finding it increasingly difficult to align their values to those of their peers. This is not a casual matter and those who see themselves facing this challenge must recognize it and take special actions to make sure that they are not rejected as "antibodies" when they try to get integrated in a culture that appears suddenly foreign to them. This is not an indictment of their inability to integrate, but a commentary on today's reality.

Disappointments and Regrouping

What has been presented so far may sound idealistic to many in today's uncertain economy and the turbulent corporate climate. With mergers, acquisitions, consolidation, and restructuring on the rise, nothing is certain. So, to stick rigidly to what is presented here for career advancement may be foolhardy. What is presented is a process that outlines how certain things can be managed in a career to protect your options and preempt certain situations. There are no guarantees in life so, when things change, one must learn to regroup, take stock, and re-chart the roadmap by learning what the changes are. Learning does not come from planned successes, it comes from failures that teach us how to regroup and move ahead. Plans are based on ideal assumptions we make about what we know. There is so much that we do not know, that most

---

1. See author's *Rehired, Not Retired: Proven Strategies for the Baby Boomers!* to understand this better.

plans, especially in precarious times, as we are increasingly facing, have to be tentative with your ability to regroup and redefine you journey. It is this ability that is going to drive your career success and not the firmness of your original plans. Most confuse achievement with success. The latter is a matter of chance, the former, a matter of your own efforts.

Some Survival Tips

As a new employee, you have an advantage. The advantage comes from your perspective from being a fresh pair of eyes looking closely at your evolving and emerging work environment. This perspective is often invaluable in catching things that otherwise go unnoticed. Once you become part of the scene you no longer are able to see things with this perspective and, more importantly, your input will be treated no differently than those of all others who have been there a while.

As a new employee you may be given assignments and responsibilities far beyond what you expected or discharged in your last job. Unless you find this to be overwhelming, the best strategy is to try to rise to the challenge. Once you take on the challenge and plunge into it, you may be surprised by your own ability to handle it and how much help that is available from those around you. If, on the other hand, you protest the assignment as too onerous, you may lose your edgy newness and quickly loose your sheen. The new assignment and challenge may also empower you to venture taking new risks and boldly address what lies in front of you and conquer it. You may surprise yourself.

The second piece of advice is to be aware of gathering impediments to your success and obviate any setbacks that may result from it. For example, if you are managing a project—a new responsibility for you—and you see an impending obstacle to completing one of the milestones due to non perform-ance by one of the team members, you must immediately take action by first confronting the team member and then escalating it to the appropriate chain of command to remedy the situation. The best strategy, again, is, rather than whining and complaining, predicting what you see as happening and how it would affect the customer and using that predictive power to create an appro-priate corrective action. An effective strategy, too, is to go to the higher ups, not just with the problem, but with two or three alternative solutions that can immediately remedy the situation. Even presenting a recovery schedule and contingency plan may be appropriate after alerting the affected people in a non-judgmental way.

A new perspective always lends itself to an unbiased observation about events that may not be as obvious to your colleagues and even your boss who may have been working there for a while. Use this advantage to further your cause in project execution or whatever assignment that you have been given.

Confidence, poise, equanimity, and trusting your instincts can go a long way in forging your own path to success at your new job. Those who wait to get used to the new place rapidly become part of the background and fade into oblivion before they even recognize it themselves.

Summary Chapter-5: Your New Job

This chapter is aimed at providing new employees a roadmap of how to position themselves for success from their first day on the new job. The following 10 categories of professionals are discussed in this chapter:

1. Fresh graduates

2. Senior Professionals

3. Managers

4. Executives

5. New job late in life

6. Back after a major gap

7. Changing careers/industries

8. Immigrant worker

9. Baby boomer back in workforce

10. Rehired from retirement

Considerable discussion is focused on the fresh graduate, since getting out of college and into the job market is the biggest transition in many ways. In this discussion, how to make a smooth transition from the "campus" mindset to a "business" mindset is presented in detail. Additionally, the four stages of professional development: Apprentice, Individual Contributor, Team Leader/Mentor/Manager, and an Executive are presented to help understand how to navigate through each stage to the next and what factors drive that journey. Understanding this process is critical for anyone to navigate through their career. A tabular tool for each stage is provided to show what factors propel you to the next level from your current career rung.

Some discussion is also presented on common barriers to executive advancement as the "Glass Ceiling" to make readers aware of how to deal with them. Common impediments to career advancement are presented. A good understanding of these is central to managing your career and the rate at which you move ahead. In today's uncertain climate, this process offers a roadmap and not a guarantee of success. What is important is the ability to manage the process, being flexible, and using your own resources (see chapter-2: Managing Your Journey) to regroup when things suddenly and unexpectedly change. The destination is not the main focus of this process.

Understanding the difference between achievement and success is critical to this attitude.

A discussion on how to move within a company is also presented to make readers aware of the factors that go into such moves and what they can do to manage this process.

Each of the 10 categories of "new" employee faces a unique challenge in integrating in their new job, company, and community. In this period of growing uncertainty, the environment inside organizations has become increasingly inimical to new employees. There is less trust and camaraderie with a growing apprehension around any change that happens inside an organization, and that includes a new employee. Transitioning into the new job is more challenging for new employees because of these factors. They must be vigilant in their initial adjustment and even seek help or coaching to make this a smooth transition, regardless of how seasoned they are in their experience.

CHAPTER 6

Charting Your Career

"Always aim for achievement, and forget about success."
—Helen Hayes, actress (1900–1993)

This chapter deals with your ongoing efforts to attain your vision at your new place of work and beyond. It does not matter if you started your job right out of college—or that it is just your first "career job"—or that this is a job after you have been displaced from your previous one, or that you just wanted a change to refresh your career. Getting settled at a new place, and then having a vision to move forward in a planned way, are important to create a career path that is not just a random happenstance. Many believe that a career "happens" to them and not the other way around. Nothing could be further from the truth.

Anyone can make a plan and then execute that plan to ensure that their career is a success. For a more complete discussion on how an established and proven framework can make this possible, please see the Author's *Pathways to Career Nirvana: An Ultimate Success Sourcebook!*. This book posits a 10-element career-management framework that allows anyone to understand the factors that drive a career and how they can be managed to navigate that career in the right direction.

The focus of this chapter is to present some commonsense insights into how to manage your everyday affairs at a place that you believe provides opportunities for your advancements. This is a place where you honestly believe that if you "follow the rules," that you will be accorded commensurate rewards.

Deciding on a Path

Some of this discussion has already been presented in Chapter-5: Your New Job, under the section, New Graduates. There, the discussion was not just limited to fresh graduates, but was expanded to show how their progression in their subsequent positions can be planned and how that can be brought about. In that section, there were tools presented to accelerate these transitions. Here, in this chapter, we are going to present specific actions that you must take to ensure your success.

Central to any achievement is a vision one creates around it. Once the vision is in place, meaningful action can make that vision a reality.

Career Management Framework

Few know how to manager their career. Most let their career "happen" to them. One reason why this is so, is, perhaps, because many do not know of a systematic approach to career management. In the absence of such an approach, they resort to a trial and error approach. This can be both frustrating and expensive. It can lead to an unfulfilled life and missed opportunities.

A systemic career management framework evolved out of working with thousands of clients who came looking for career advice. This framework is the topic of an entire book previously published. See the author's *Pathways to Career Nirvana: An Ultimate Success Sourcebook!*, for more details. Although *Pathways,* posits the rationale for this comprehensive framework and then describes each element in individual chapters, this discussion here is limited to the summary of that topic.

Development of the Framework

Most approach their careers as a series of episodes resulting from stringing together their job experiences. Few understand and know how to plan, manage, and manifest a rewarding career in a planned way. One reason for this course of action is that there is no unified framework that shows and guides those who want to approach their own career as a grand plan. Secondly, most treat their career experiences as a series of discrete episodes. Studies have shown that when a situation is presented as a disconnected series of events, people can manage it if the number of elements is seven plus or minus two. Thus, once the number exceeds five to nine discrete elements, depending on the individual, most are unable to recognize the thematic connection or unity in a meaningful way. However, if there is an overarching framework that connects seemingly disjointed elements, it is much easier to deal with any situation that the framework addresses, regardless of how many elements the situation presents.

Yet another way to look at the framework providing a useful career roadmap is to look at it as a tool that allows you to "connect the dots." Connecting the dots has to do with finding patterns in an otherwise random course of events. So, if a career encompasses many episodes of jobs, assignments, and accomplishments, using this framework can help develop a theme, which can be leveraged into a message much more compelling than merely presenting the episodes as discrete events.

While researching thousands of career professionals who were pursuing a change in their careers and helping them through their transitions, it became apparent that they needed a consistent framework and a model with which they could work and rely on for getting some guidance in the way they make career decisions. Career Management Framework is the result of working with many such professionals, at all levels and stages of their careers. It embodies a consistent and universally applicable foundation on which any career decision can be made. It is an intuitive and systemic model of 10 most commonly encountered elements in a career that can be identified even before a career gets started. In addition to this framework, a process is needed to make this framework come to life to allow charting of a career. This is discussed further in each chapter that expounds on each of the 10 elements of the framework described in *Pathways* (see Figure-5 on the next page).

The framework is systemic because the entire model forms an articulate and interconnected whole in a way that is unique. Systemic also means that any one element can affect all other elements, one at a time, and together. How much impact one element has on the others is a matter of various factors. But the way the model is presented, it simply means that each element influenced *all* others, not just the ones close in proximity to it, as it may appear in the graphic rendition of the model. The implications of this model are discussed below, element-by-element in a summary form, as an overview. Detailed discussion can be found in the book, *Pathways to Career Nirvana: An Ultimate Success Sourcebook!*.

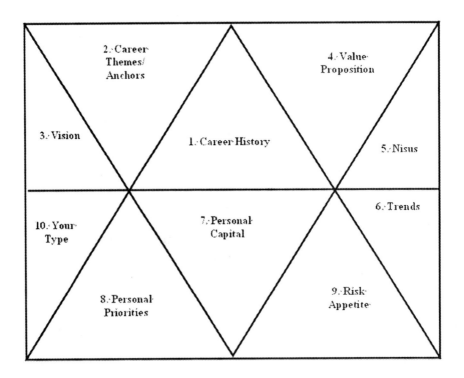

Figure: 5: Career Management Framework

At any time in a career, your forward-looking professional success depends on your:

1. Career History

2. Career Themes/Anchors

3. Vision

4. Value Proposition

5. Nisus: your perfective-urge or endeavor

6. External Trends that define what is going to happen

7. Personal Capital

8. Personal Priorities

9. Appetite for Risk

10. Personality Type

1. Career History

More than any other element, career history has the most bearing on your present and the future. It establishes the arc that defines your career trajectory. How high that trajectory reaches and how much it spans, is dependent on the "slope" of the arc and momentum of a career, much like pitching a baseball. A more detailed discussion on these topics is in chapter 2: Career History in the author's *Pathways to Career Nirvana: An Ultimate Success Sourcebook!*, but it is sufficient to mention now that it is important to manage your career history so that you can always leverage it for your next move or to consolidate the one in which you are currently engaged.

There are various ways of managing this important element. One way to manage it well is to look at your current position, responsibilities, and momentum. If you can easily leverage that into a position that takes you to the next level of responsibility then you have managed your career well. This concept of career momentum and spring boarding applies to all stages of career development, even at the start.

Career "history" can also be mapped out looking ahead by carefully considering possible opportunities and assignments in a position and then going after those in a deliberate and systematic way so that you are given a chance to prove yourself. This entails taking some risks and putting yourself out in front and center and facing exposure to challenges that come with it. However, when done in earnest, and politic way, it can advance your career faster that almost any other avenue. This is primarily because you are now driving to your own destination to achieve what you want.

2. Career Anchors/Themes

These are your beacons that shine throughout your career and dot your path with noteworthy achievements. They typically have a theme. For example, if you are a great troubleshooter, then every time a project or a situation got into trouble, you jumped in and rescued the project and, maybe, even the company, through your skill. These themes define your career history. They light your career path, looking back, with metaphorical signposts and provide the illumination to your course ahead.

3. Career Vision

This is the vision you hold for yourself. If you are clearly able to see what you want to be doing and able to articulate that vision in a written message that moves those who read it then you have a compelling vision statement that is worthy of a pursuit.

One way to develop a realistic vision is to take a piece of blank paper and draw a line in the middle. On the top half write your vision or dream.

On the bottom half write your reality.

The more clearly you are able to write your vision or dream the more clearly you can implement a plan to realize your dream.

4. Value Proposition

This statement is your value proposition. This is how you create value for the target employer or an organization for which you are responsible. One element of this value proposition is your genius. Your genius is a gift you have that allows you to do things in ways different—and better—than anyone else can do them.

5. Nisus

This is your physical and mental drive that allows you to accomplish your set goals. It provides you the power to propel forward despite adversity, obstacles, setbacks, and other impediments. This is your spiritual will that allows you to conquer your set goals. This is your driving force that takes you to attain perfection in what you yearn to achieve.

6. Trends

This is the only external element that factors into the overall framework that is out of your control. However, how you discern it, interpret it, and leverage that into your career campaign is entirely within your realm. We already presented some of this is chapter-1: Today's Workplace.

7. Personal Capital

This is the sum total of your goodwill that you have bankrolled in your career. This accumulated goodwill can be leveraged in your career as if it were capital or a bank account.

8. Personal Priorities

Throughout our career we experience different personal priorities, primarily because different stages of our life present different career choices and opportunities. How we manifest at these different points is driven by these priorities.

9. Risk Appetite

Any venture involves risk. It is generally true that the greater the risk, the greater the reward. Making a choice in career involves taking calculated risks.

10. Your Type

This is the Myers Briggs personality Type that drives your social interaction with others as well as how you manifest to them. Any career pursuit is a social activity with a business focus. Almost all jobs require a certain personality flavor to fully engage and to create a productive outcome. Extensive research is available that links a particular Type to a job category. This knowledge can help those who are making career choices to narrow their options and explore paths that are more promising, based on their own Type. This is a suggestive element and not a definitive one in a career decision. One reason for its existence in the framework is because, although your Type is fixed, how you become aware of it and how you manage your behaviors can change the way you present yourself to others.

Implications

The implications of this career management framework in practicable terms are many. For one, it provides professionals with a comprehensive roadmap on which they can plan their career journey. It is as useful to the freshly minted college graduate as it is to someone going through a mid-career crisis. This framework is not presented as a panacea for all career related challenges and yet, it is provided as a potent tool to make important decisions in that realm.

Rationale

The impetus for developing this framework came from working with nearly 2,000 professionals who were facing some career challenges during the job-market quake that jolted them, and many others, in the early months of 2001. Here, in the Silicon Valley, where most of these professionals resided, the near-seismic shift was triggered by the dotcom meltdown that began in late 2000. Their plight was further whipsawed by the rapid and accelerating off-shoring trend that precipitously eroded employment in high-tech; even its fallout to other industries was brutal. Ongoing mergers, job consolidations, and acquisitions further caused many jobs to disappear.

Grim as this picture appears, not all had to face this fate. Many simply gave up because they believed that jobs, once gone, were not coming back. Not having the tools to refashion themselves in a productive way, many took the easy way out by accepting whatever was available to re-engage. Many executives ended up as greeters at major retail chains and superstores, wearing aprons with "How may I help you" printed on their backs. Of the nearly one million, who were high-tech refugees in California alone, that flooded out from the relentless layoffs during the two years following the meltdown, more than half simply gave up and migrated out of the industry. Many took jobs that paid them the minimum wage. The survivors who were lucky enough to be missing out on all the layoff excitement, did better, but were under the constant threat of looming lay offs.

One reason for this unfortunate outcome is that no one knew how to leverage their past, repackage themselves and find opportunities that were not apparent in a market turned upside down. There were plenty of opportunities that lay dormant. They went unclaimed because neither the job seekers nor the companies knew how to bring them to life to leverage the uncertainty to their advantage.

The same scenario applied to those who kept their jobs and were wondering about how to deal with the ongoing threat of uncertainty. Without an actionable framework, tools, and some guidance, they continued to do their jobs, hoping that some fortuitous event will extricate them from their predicament and put them on a path to bliss.

The challenge of how to capitalize on the career momentum and to leverage that into the next major opportunity was daunting to many. Working closely with those who came to seek guidance, there were nearly 2,000 unique data points to find a pattern, and then from that, construct a generalized framework that would provide an answer to all those who came seeking it—a key to the way out of their predicament and to their future. This framework would also provide them specific enough knowledge to make it work for them and not merely provide a generalized set of possibilities. Using hypotheses, testing them, experimenting, and putting them to trial to validate raw concepts, the framework slowly emerged as a possible answer that would serve those seeking to move forward in these uncertain times. As more tools began shaping up for each element of the framework and as more and more clients began seeing success in the approach, they embraced in refashioning themselves, the 10-element framework emerged and then crystallized, as it is presented here.

The next step was to validate this framework with clients by working with them to help their reinvention. As more and more embraced this framework, the ideas that made it practical and the tools that provided the answers to the "what next" questions in a new endeavor, the universality of what is presented here became more and more apparent. Once clients owned the idea of this framework, they got excited about taking it apart—remember, many were engineers!—and using their own test case as a proving ground for its validity. Some even challenged many aspects of it, hoping to prove it limiting or even wrong, only to come back even more convinced that they bought into the right idea and that they were on the right track with its use.

The battle testing of this framework was not merely limited to high-tech refugees, economic orphans, or even those unaffected—the survivors—during this upheaval; it was proven by many other professionals who came from a variety of industries as banking, insurance, law, services, consulting, even physicians, health-care professionals and pilots from bankrupt airlines during the same period. Additionally, the concept was field tested with those in other geographies within the U.S. and abroad. With each test came some additional insights, which brought new perspectives to making this framework practicable for all, without making it too general. What emerged was a robust, battle-tested, universal career management framework that has survived the test of one of the most challenging job markets in remembered history.

How to use this framework

The application of this framework depends on where you are in your career and transition. If you are in college to get a degree, or a fresh graduate, some of the elements of the framework may puzzle you: Career History, Career Themes/Anchors being the most apparent. If you are out of work and looking, then your top priority is finding yourself employment again. In this circumstance, your priorities are different from someone who is doing well and is looking to leverage that momentum into a better position. And yet, to each facing a transition, there is something that you will find worthwhile that opens up your perspective.

This is a *systemic* model. This means that all the elements are interconnected to each other that produce the outcome you desire. Each element influences the others. This is what systemic means. There are relationships between every element and every other element, in turn.

The "Vision Thing"

In the Career Management Framework just presented, Vision is an important element. In managing your career, vision is central to its success. Why? Vision gives you hope and purpose. It can provide energy to your everyday pursuits in ways not otherwise possible. It nourishes your soul with inspiration that flows from the very core of your being. No major career has ever attained its goal without a vision, early in its life. In many cases, these visions are not some public proclamations or documents that are open for scrutiny. No, these are private, well guarded matters of import to those who seriously pursued them to achieve what they set out to do.

What is the difference between a vision and a goal? The former is a grand, inspiring, and overarching statement of purpose. It is energizing by virtue of its audacious yet achievable —plausible—nature. It is crafted in a language that shows thought, insight, inspiration, and energy. A goal, on the other hand is a subset carved out from the vision that defines a bounded achievement that would lead to the vision. In terms of its language, it could be more mundane and matter of fact. For example, "Putting a man on the moon before the end of this decade" is a vision, whereas building the first booster rocket within two years, is a goal that makes the vision possible. There is yet another pesky element in this lexicon: an objective. An objective is a measured goal. For example, in this illustration, building a booster rocket with a certain thrust and within a certain dollar budget would be a consistent objective.

What is the difference between a vision and a dream? A vision is a realizable dream.

A career vision does not start with the first job; in many cases it starts early in life. But, to some, having a vision early is not easy. They explore different options and delay committing themselves to a vision until later in life, when they have more clarity. It is often ironic that one does not always know what they should be doing until they get a taste of it. This is not much different from having an appetizer to increase your appetite! So, formulating a vision at the doorstep of a first job is an appropriate juncture. For some, even doing this later is also not too late!

Vision is not vaporing about some grandiose goals, but it is about achieving something that *appears* unattainable! And, yet, when one focuses on it and pursues it per plan, they can achieve it *with* effort. Mere effort, though, is not enough. It requires timing, luck, and a strategy. Tools often help in accelerating this process because they provide the means to achieve an end. So, in this section some tools and exercises are presented to make visioning a working concept for those who have trouble with it. At the end of *this* process, you are expected to have a vision, if you want to achieve what you desire. Although having an early vision is to your advantage, a vision at any time in a career is better than having no vision at all!

The Vision Dichotomy

There are two ways to approach the vision process. And, yes, visioning is a process and not a task, as we just presented. Developing an exciting vision that energizes and creates an all-consuming pursuit is critical to successful attainment of whatever you set out to do. However, there are two approaches to a vision:

One approach is based on a secular objective and anther at a deeper level. This does not mean that one excludes that other; each could complement the other. Let us take an example.

A secular approach to career planning is based on your specific financial needs that you draw up with timelines. Some of these considerations are: when to get married, when to have children, their education, buying a home, and finally, retirement. You define your cash flow needs and the nest egg size to secure the retirement you envision. Once these pecuniary objectives are identified, you define what career tracks offer these rewards in their manifestations and pursue how you are going to follow them. Of course, there is some thought of a plausible profession in this mix, but that is secondary. Typically, this reflection is perhaps going to take place after you have your degree or at a point in your life where you have already made some commitment to what you aspire to be in the way you completed your coursework.

This is an opportunistic approach to career planning. There are many who follow this path. How many times have you heard high school students say *I want to be a malpractice attorney and make a killing!*

Money can be a great motivator to many and they pursue whatever profession and career lets them achieve that objective. The downside of this approach is that, since it is based primarily on material objectives and not much more than a superficial desire to be financially independent, when the objective starts falling short of its goals, there is no emotional reserve to compensate for that loss; there is no inherent reward for having pursued your passion! The other aspect of pursuing such a path is that wherever there is easy money, there is much action. Those who are in it for the money alone cannot compete with those who are in it for their love of it. Even in a promising field of endeavor, it is very difficult to compete with someone who is in it for their love and passion, when all you are after is the money! If such a pursuit becomes difficult as more and more competitors crowd the field or things suddenly change, due to shifted fortunes, it is difficult to recharge yourself, because whatever you are pursuing is not from your heart.

Yet another manifestation of this approach, is when things are not going your way, fear drives many decisions. Because there is no deep conviction that drives your actions, it is difficult to keep the fire from within stoked that often gives that energy or courage, hope, and inspiration to those who work from deeper beliefs as is possible with this approach.

The approach to visioning based on what stirs your passions allows—nay forces—you to tap into your genius and makes you come alive. Career visions based on such foundational values tend to have a bedrock quality to them that is difficult to shake.

Starting Early

Many, who have successful careers, get on their career paths by the time they are 20. There are many Nobel Prize winners, especially in physics, who received their prize for their work they did in their early 20s! Not all have this insight or resources to be able to achieve this feat. How many times you have heard adults in their 40s saying, One day I will figure out what I want to do when I grow up!

In order to pursue a vision that is attainable, it is to your advantage to start early in your life to form this vision. A vision formed in vacuum is likely to be vacuous as well. To form a concrete vision, it is necessary to have some ownership to the process and a realistic plan to achieve the vision. Otherwise it becomes just a dream. Sometimes, starting your first job can be a shot in the dark for many. But, regardless, starting such a job gives some insights into how the professional life works than any other experience you may have to get a first-hand view of a career. Another point, too, is that a vision does not have to be a stone tablet. It can change based on circumstances, insights, and changed priorities. It is this dynamic that makes the *process* of creating a vision so exciting!

Once you have started in your first job, it is easy to ascertain whether you are in your element. A good job and the environment, in which it is carried out, speak much about what type of life you would be leading. If this work sustains you in your everyday life, then you have become part of something that is worth looking into deeper to see if this is a way of life that you find satisfying. This includes money, recognition, rewards, advancement, job satisfaction, growth, and everything else that sustains you.

If, however, you landed your first job with some planning, expectation and effort, then, more than likely, there is less uncertainty about your station as a starting point of a professional career. However, this is not a guarantee. Often, what you envision from a naïve perspective is not how it pans out, once you experience it first hand. If the initial experience after planning, pursuing, and landing your first job confirms the expectation, then you are probably on the right track.

If the first job, on the other hand, presents a disappointing picture of work life, then you must explore to see if the particular job you are in or the employer is the cause of that disappointment. The next layer is the industry. If any one of these explorations provides a clue to your lack of a positive feeling about the situation, then you must quickly explore further to validate your hypothesis. You cannot go on hoping that things would improve if you give it more time. When you surrender to this possibility, more than likely, you will inure to the circumstances and reconcile with lowered expectations as time goes by.

It is interesting to recognize that fewer than 30 percent of the professionals give any thought to this dimension of joy in what they do. The remainder, nearly two thirds of the professional pool, engages in what they do merely out of their economic need. To those who belong in this vast majority of willy-nilly professionals, there is a great opportunity to change the status quo by looking deeper.

In any case, let us examine this dichotomy in detail to explore how to proceed to the next stage of vision formulation.

A Good Fit

A good fit in your first job is an encouraging signal. It speaks for your ability to fit in with the "establishment" and create value that others appreciate. You derive a degree of satisfaction perhaps unknown to you in your past existence. If you just stepped out of a college campus, you will realize that creating value in an economic context has its own sense of accomplishment. It is different from getting great grades in school.

A good fit in your job is also characterized by an inner sense of security, confidence, excitement, anticipation, and a sense of timelessness. Time flies by when you are engaged in your endeavor. Although money, recognition, and reward are important they become subordinate to what drives your everyday actions. If this feeling is present, despite everyday challenges of the job, politics, and occasional setbacks, then you can assume that what you are engaged in is your calling. You must look deeper in yourself to go through this vision process and work towards actualizing yourself.

This concept of actualizing yourself comes from the Hierarchy of Needs that Abraham Maslow proposed nearly a century back. This is known as the Maslow's hierarchy of needs and is shown in Figure-6, as a part of the following discussion.

Maslow's Hierarchy

Abraham Maslow is known for establishing the theory of a hierarchy of needs, positing that human beings are motivated by unsatisfied needs, and that certain lower needs must be satisfied before higher needs. Maslow studied exemplary people such as Albert Einstein, Jane Addams, Eleanor Roosevelt, and Frederick Douglas, rather than mentally ill or neurotic people. This was a radical departure from two of the chief schools of psychology of his day: Sigmund Freud or William Skinner. Freud saw little difference between the motivations of humans and animals. We are supposedly rational beings; however, we do not act that way. Such pessimism, Maslow believed, was the result of Freud's study of mentally ill people. He blasted those schools by asserting that the study of the crippled, stunted, immature, and unhealthy can yield only an abnormal psychology and a crippled philosophy. Skinner, on the other hand, studied how pigeons and white rats learn. His motivational models were based on simple rewards such as food and water, sex, and avoidance of pain.

Maslow thought that psychologists should, instead, study the playfulness, affection, and positive traits of living beings. He also believed that Skinner discounted things that made humans different from each other. Instead, Skinner relied on statistical descriptions of people through modeling. Yet, despite their limitations, both pioneered a breakthrough in mental processes and explained some of the basic behavioral patterns, albeit focused on the abnormal.

Maslow's hierarchy of needs was an alternative to the depressing determinism of Freud and Skinner. He felt that people were basically trustworthy, self-protecting, and self-governing. Humans tend toward growth and love. Although there is a continuous cycle of human pathology, he believed that violence is not what human nature is meant to like. Violence and other evils occur when human needs are thwarted. In other words, people who are deprived of lower needs such as safety may defend themselves by violent means. He did not believe that humans are violent because they enjoy violence. Or that they lie, cheat, and steal because they enjoy doing it.

According to Maslow, there are general types of needs (physiological, safety, love, and esteem) that must be satisfied before a person can act unselfishly. He called these needs "deficit needs." As long as we are motivated to satisfy these cravings, we are moving towards growth, toward self-actualization. Satisfying needs is healthy; blocking gratification makes us sick or evil. In other words, we are all "needs junkies" with cravings that must be satisfied and should be satisfied. Else, we become sick.

Needs are prepotent. A prepotent need is one that has the greatest influence over our actions. Everyone has a prepotent need, but that need will vary among individuals. A teenager may have a need to feel that a group accepts them. A crack addict will need to satisfy their cravings to function "normally" in society, and will not worry about acceptance by other people. According to Maslow, when the deficiency needs are met, at once, other—and higher—needs emerge, and these, rather than physiological hungers, dominate the organism. And, when, these in turn, are satisfied, again new—and still higher—needs emerge, and so on. As one desire is satisfied, another pops up to take its place.

Physiological Needs

Physiological needs are the very basic needs such as air, water, food, sleep, and sex. When these are not satisfied we may feel sickness, irritation, pain, discomfort, etc. These feelings motivate us to alleviate them as soon as possible to establish homeostasis or equilibrium. Once they are alleviated, we may think about other things.

Safety Needs

Safety needs have to do with establishing stability and consistency in a chaotic world. These needs are mostly psychological in nature. We need the security of a home and family. However, if a family is dysfunctional, i.e., an abusive husband, the wife cannot move to the next level because she is constantly concerned for her safety. Love and belongingness have to wait until she is no longer cringing in fear. Many in our society cry out for law and order because they do not feel safe enough to go for a walk in their neighborhood. Many people, particularly those in the inner cities, unfortunately, are stuck at this level. In addition, safety needs sometimes motivate people to be religious. Religions comfort us with the promise of a safe secure place after we die and leave the insecurity of this world.

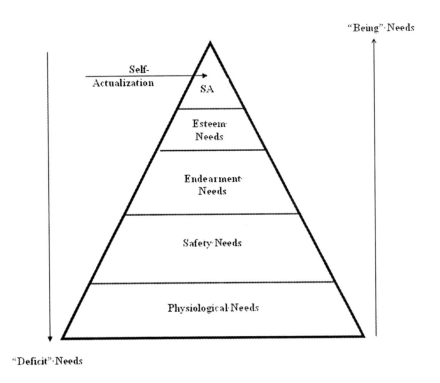

Figure-6: The Hierarchy of Needs

Endearment Needs

Endearment and belongingness are next on the ladder. Humans have a desire to belong to groups: clubs, work groups, religious groups, family, gangs, etc. We need to feel endeared (non-sexual) by others, to be accepted by others. Performers appreciate applause. We need to be needed. Beer commercials, in addition to playing on sex, also often show how beer makes us convivial. When was the last time you saw a beer commercial with someone drinking beer alone?

Esteem Needs

There are two types of esteem needs. First is self-esteem, which results from competence or mastery of a task. Second, there's the attention and recognition that comes from others. This is similar to the belongingness level; however, wanting admiration has to do with the need for power. People, who have all of their lower needs satisfied; are seen often driving expensive cars. This is perhaps because doing so raises their level of esteem. "Hey, look what I can afford, you nobody!" Esteem needs are endless. Rich want to be wealthy; the wealthy want to be the wealthiest; the wealthiest want to beat their second-ranked counterpart by an increasingly greater margin, and so on. This is human nature. This is what keeps us striving for greater goals.

Self-Actualization

The need for self-actualization is the desire to become more and more what one is; to become everything that one is capable of becoming. When people function at this level, their motivation transcends secular needs. They are operating at their Essence or spiritual being. People who have everything can maximize their potential. They can seek knowledge, peace, esthetic experiences, self-fulfillment, and oneness with their surroundings. It is usually middle-class to upper-class students who take up environmental causes, join the Peace Corps, or go off to a monastery for these reasons because their lower level needs are met and they are looking for deeper meaning to their existence.

It is this quest for the deep that drives us to see self-actualization.

The Discontinuous Realm

The depiction of the hierarchy of needs in the manner of Figure-7 and the narrative that follows is a reductionist view of how our purpose plays out in our lives. In its simplest interpretation, the graphic conveys the impression that to actualize, one must sequentially and painfully go through the preceding four stages to achieve this nirvana. And, if that were the case the majority will never experience the epiphanous moments that we all encounter, albeit occasionally. The Universe grants us sporadic glimpses of such existence to make us aware that such states are not for only the blessed, but for all to share, pursue, and achieve.

Attainment of the *nirvanic* state does not imply the end of struggles. As one journeys through their career and life, obstacles, enemies, jealous colleagues, and adversities continue. As one rises up the hierarchy, though, their influence in our life and how we react to them become more and more irrelevant. When you are at the bottom of the hierarchy trying to survive, the view you hold of those who appear to have attained the state that you are yearning for, is an idealized view of the reality as you see them enjoying. However, the reality of those actually in the state is quite different. Those, whom you look up to, face a different level of challenges in their own ways. The force that sustains them, though, is their own belief in their cause and how they are able to rise above the mundane obstacles. This is a constant human struggle and condition.

None of this discussion is intended to disparage the attainment of the higher ideals. It is merely presented to put into perspective the reality that no matter how high you travel in the hierarchy, there is always something that you lack. The only question is, how it manifests in your daily existence and how it drives your future actions. For example, even though you have made enough money to be called wealthy and achieved some degree of self-actualization, many feel the need to amass even greater wealth as they continue to enjoy their state of self-actualization. Such is the nature of the lower-level needs and the basic human nature.

The only approach to attaining true self-actualization or nirvana in a career—or life—is to shift the focus from getting and having to being and becoming. What is the difference? The main difference in the two attitudes is that in the former, there is always something that is lacking and there is never enough: what is portrayed as "Deficient Needs" in Figure-6. Material needs as fortune, fame, and possessions are never enough for this mindset. In the latter approach, it is your attitude of prosperity that recognizes that pursuing attainment of further material needs is futile and the focus must shift to the inner quest: peace of mind, a sense of contributing, a sense of fulfillment and so on: this is depicted as the "Being Needs" in Figure-6.

Another Perspective (Herzberg)

Although Maslow's model does a good job of showing how employees—or anyone else—find motivation to get ahead in their job, a more recent model by Frederick Herzberg has drawn much attention. This is called the Hygiene-Motivation Model.

Researching nearly 200 engineers in Pittsburg in the 1950s, Herzberg found that the factors that made these engineers, individually and as a group, feel exceptionally good about their work and their environment were not opposite of those that made them feel negatively. Herzberg used this research to posit a two-factor theory. In this theory he proposed that human beings have two sets of needs:

- Lower-level needs to avoid pain and depravation;
- Higher-level needs as a human being to grow psychologically

These needs must be satisfied at work as much as any other sphere of human activity. He concluded that some factors in the workplace meet the first set of needs but not the second, and vice versa. The former group of factors are called "hygiene factors" and the latter, "motivators."

"Hygiene factors" have to do with the context of environment in which a person works. They include"

- Company policy and administration
- Supervision
- Working relationships
- Working conditions
- Status
- Security
- Pay

These factors are important, but they do not promote job satisfaction; they prevent job dissatisfaction, in the same way that good hygiene does not promote good health. Once introduced, they increasingly come to be regarded as rights to be expected rather than incentives to greater satisfaction and achievement.

"Motivators" (also referred to as "growth factors") relates to what a person does at work, rather then the context is which it is done. They include:

- Achievement
- Recognition
- The work itself
- Responsibility
- Growth
- Advancement

Herzberg maintains that both set of factors are needed because they are not opposites of each other.

One interesting aspect of Herzberg's theory is that pay is a dissatisfier. This is because in the short term, increasing pay or inducing someone to work for higher pay can work, but soon it becomes an expected parameter.

Vision and Action

One approach to creating a vision, is to become aware of success paradigms within the realm of your own surroundings. A paradigm is a pattern or set of rules that produce what is intended. Vision is not an abstraction. It is, rather, a goal based on what you perceive to be *your* ideal. In formulating a career vision, it is expected that there is some ideal that you have in mind. Typically, this can be a person who has achieved what you desire, or a position that is your goal as an ultimate reward for your life's work. Often, this vision evolves and changes with time. But, unless you have a clear idea of this end state, it is difficult to achieve it.

The vision one holds of an ultimate point of their career, does not have to be a position or title, or something even described as known. It could be a concept, an idea, or even an ideal. But, one requirement for it to be a realizable vision is that it is S.M.A.R.T. This acronym stands for Specific, Measurable, Actionable, Realistic, and Time-bound.

SMART Vision

Developing SMART vision requires hard work. It also does not happen overnight. It is a process that requires commitment, constant attention, and nurturing. It evolves with time. Some realize such vision early in their lives, some late. Realizing does not mean attaining the vision, it simply means that you have reached a point where you can own your vision and then start pursuing its attainment. Some have a clear vision of their "being" and the needs associated with it—the being needs—early in their lives. Some get to this point late in life—in their retirement years—and some never even brush with it.

A Tool

One tool that can help catalyze a practicable vision is called a "Horizontal Line" tool. It is simply a horizontal line drawn in the middle across a page, dividing it into two parts; top and bottom. In the top part of the page, you write your current state in vivid detail; in the bottom half, the desired state, also in vivid detail.

The best approach to starting this process is to start with the end in mind. A ten-year horizon is realistic. Some may want to go beyond that time span and create even a grander vision. The only caveat in such an undertaking is that if something gets derailed in the early part of the process, it can cause some discouragement because now the final goal or vision is so lofty. In such cases, some simply give up and let their life guide them reactively, a bad mistake!

Once the ten-year span is covered, the next step is to start looking at shorter spans and start filling in the intervening years in a graduated way so that the vision is sequentially mapped out to the end point of ten years.

Tool-11: Vision Mapping Tool

10-YEAR VISION

HAVE:

Position: Junior Engineer
Salary: $68,000
Reporting to: Group Lead
Responsibilities: Delivering designs on time and to requirements

WANT (4)

Position: Vice President Engineering
Salary: $245,000 (today's dollars)
Reporting to: President, COO
Responsibilities: Entire engineering department of 450 (today's reality)
Achievements: At least three patents to my name, great professional reputation as a creative engineering executive,
Time Span: 10 years

Note: There is some danger in setting out a vision this far out in an increasingly uncertain world. This tool is valid for any case of a vision, but this specific illustration is offered as a case in point.

Tool-11: Vision Mapping Tool (Continued)

FIVE-YEAR VISION

HAVE:

Position: Engineering Manager
Salary: $100,000
Reporting to: Director, Design Engineering
Responsibilities: Entire hardware engineering design department of 65
Achievements: At least two patents to my name, great professional reputation as a c creative hands-on engineering manager
Time Span: 3 years

WANT (3)

Position: Director Engineering Design
Salary: $125,000 (today's dollars)
Reporting to: Vice President, Engineering
Responsibilities: Entire engineering design department of 125
Achievements: At least two patents to my name, great professional reputation as a c creative hands-on engineering lead
Time Span: Five years

Tool-11: Vision Mapping Tool (Continued)

FOUR-YEAR VISION

HAVE:

Position: Engineering Group Leader
Salary: $100,000
Reporting to: Manager, Design Engineering
Responsibilities: Entire hardware engineering design department of 65
Achievements: At least two patents to my name, great professional reputation
as a c creative hands-on engineering manager

WANT (2)

Position: Engineering Group Leader
Salary: $100,000 (today's dollars)
Reporting to: Manager, Design Engineering
Responsibilities: Entire hardware engineering design department of 65
Achievements: At least two patents to my name, great professional reputation
as a c creative hands-on engineering manager
Time Span: four years

Tool-11: Vision Mapping Tool (Continued)

THREE-YEAR VISION

HAVE:

Position: Junior Engineer
Salary: $68,000
Reporting to: Group Lead
Responsibilities: Delivering designs on time and to requirements

WANT (1)

Position: Engineering Group Leader
Salary: $100,000 (today's dollars)
Reporting to: Manager, Design Engineering
Responsibilities: Entire hardware engineering design department of 65
Achievements: At least two patents to my name, great professional reputation
as a c creative hands-on engineering manager
Time Span: 3 years

After mapping the "have" and "want" scenarios for your career are completed, you have the gap of what needs to be accomplished to go from the present state, to the "wanted" state. Once that journey is mapped out, it is easy to take each element of the "gap" and then describe what it would take to close that gap. Now, you have a roadmap for achieving your SMART vision. This plan now includes your goals, timetables, measurements, and progress hooks. Progress hooks are markers or signposts in your journey to the vision destination that continually tell you how far you have come, and how much more you have to go, to achieve what you set out to do.

The Vision Mapping Tool starts with a grand vision that may be five or 10 years out. Once you have clarity on that vision, with a realistic (yet aggressive) time frame (the "T" in SMART), then it is easy to break it down into manageable time spans, so that the goals of each time horizon do not appear too daunting.

Once this vision mapping is done, the companion action plan must be prepared to make the vision actionable. Once that action plan is prepared it needs to be validated by those who have the power to make it happen. Typically, these are your immediate supervisors and the chain of command.

A few words of caution: Holding out a specific vision for more than a few years can be dangerous. In an uncertain world, few things remain steadfast for that long. However, the concept of visioning that spans any length of time is valid, as long as the process is clearly understood. The other factor in this context to remember is that accommodation and flexibility are important in an uncertain world.

The other caution, too, is that this specific illustrative example is indicative of a deeply hierarchical organization and that it assumes that for the period of the vision—10 years—the business and organization are going to stay "stationary." In this economy, both these assumptions are precarious. However, this illustrative example is presented to show how a vision can be drafted and how a tool can be used to operationalize this vision.

Action Plan

Once the vision is mapped, the more important step is to prepare a detailed action plan. Each action plan carefully shows how you are going to move from your current position to the next and what you have to do to achieve that goal in each step. Action planning has to be done at each vision level and then rolled up to the final vision, so that the plan is seamless in accomplishing the final objective.

A sample action plan is shown for one objective (of the three that are shown as illustrative examples).

Making it Real

To execute the plan you have prepared in detail, you must get the concurrence of those who can help you achieve it. Discussing it with your immediate supervisor at the appropriate level of the plan is a good start. You must present it so that it does not threaten your supervisor. You must present it so that they look at it as an opportunity for them to move up and let you take their place. Otherwise it might not work.

Discussion of plans that go beyond your supervisor's level is also not appropriate, as some may perceive it as too ambitious, or even inappropriate. You must get the concurrence on specific goals and objectives that are outlined in the plan. It is these actions that will enable you to move up, primarily because your immediate supervisor has implicitly "blessed" it!

Higher-level plans must be handled with discretion. You may want to discuss it with your mentor or career coach.

Notes:

Tool-12: Action Plan

Action plan for (Your name):

Moving from Junior Engineer to Group Leader

Actions:

1. Demonstrate competence in leading projects with increasing scope and complexity

2. Lead successfully the development of next two generations of product revisions

3. Mentor junior engineers

4. Complete recommended training for team leaders

5. File at least one patent application

6. Author three technical papers and publish in major journals.

7. Achieve outstanding performance reviews during the next three cycles

Making the Plan Real

The purpose behind making an action plan is to start a process of discipline and commitment to your cause. Once there is ownership and support, purposeful action can make the difference between achieving your goals and missing them. You must be vigilant to new opportunities and obstacles to your plan.

If something new crops up, and it can help you in your pursuit of your goal, volunteering to take on this challenge can be a positive demonstration of your commitment to advance. Similarly, if there is a problem, as might happen due to a lost proposal, cancelled budget, or any other setback, you must put the welfare of the department and your boss's interest above your own, in order to protect your long-term prospects.

Vision and Metaphors

Why is vision so important to success?

A vision is a crystallized view of what is to come and what motivates our action. Without a clear vision it is difficult to marshal enough inner resources to pursue anything meaningfully. Developing a compelling vision is one of the most difficult challenges in life. Perhaps it is this reason why many go through life without a clear sense of vision. A vision is different from a goal. A goal is a destination, which one may or may not achieve. But, a vision is an inspiring force that drives people to pursue a purpose with uncommon commitment. Goals can follow from a vision but the converse is not true. It is the force that makes us become who we want to be. The process of achieving the vision we set out to conquer, forges us into becoming something that we cannot otherwise do. A goal is attained; a vision may never be attained! A vision charts a journey, a goal ends it!

After having a vision, a plan is required to make that vision a reality. A plan lays out the details of actions necessary to achieve the vision and what must happen for the vision to become reality. A vision without action is a dream; action without a vision is a nightmare!

There is yet another driver in our lives that makes us get up every morning and put our heart and soul in what we do. That driver is the metaphors for which we live. Metaphors crystallize our commitment to a cause and makes what is otherwise abstract, concrete in our minds. Joseph Campbell, the author, philosopher, and storyteller, insists that we live and die for metaphors; they are that powerful in how they drive our existence.

In one of the episodes, oft cited in this context, is the story of Spartacus, the slave who mobilized the fellow Roman vassals in an uprising to free themselves from an oppressive existence under their ruler. As they were all fleeing Rome, on the outskirts, the Roman soldiers caught them. After surrounding the band of slaves with his army, the general, who knew that Spartacus had led the rebellion, but did not know what he looked like, demanded that Spartacus step forward. There was no doubt in anyone's mind what was going to be next¾imminent death! But despite that dreadful certainty, every slave stepped forward and proclaimed that each one was Spartacus! Why? The metaphor for being free was so compelling to each of those who had followed Spartacus; they did not care if they died believing in that vision.

Such is the power of having a vision and holding metaphors that are dear to one's heart!

Laying a Foundation

To achieve the vision you set out to conquer, a solid foundation is required so that you can build your career advancement campaign on that foundation. Depending on your level and career momentum at the time of your entry at a company, how you go about this process is critical. The following elements of this foundation are presented so that those who have a plan and a vision as we presented in the previous section, can start laying this foundation:

> ➢ Having an internal compass
>
> ➢ Relationship with your boss
>
> ➢ Relationship with you chain of command
>
> ➢ Your social capital

Having an internal compass

The internal compass here refers to the person or position that you aspire to achieve in your organization. Normally, there is someone at a level high enough that inspires you. This person could be even three levels above you and not directly in your chain of command. But, all the same, this person can serve as your beacon and it is good to recognize this person's power in your career advancement.

One approach to leverage this resource and benefit from its power, is to acknowledge it and then seek to connect with it in ways that serve you, and the company. In many companies there are formal mentor/protégé programs that encourage such arrangements and relationships. But, before getting into, or even committing to, such a program, it is best to meet with your would-be mentor and have a personal discussion, without mentioning that that is what you wish your relationship to be. Once you get acquainted then you can explore further to see if such a person is compatible with your make-up and will provide the mentorship critical to your advancement.

Working within Your Group

Although having a loadstar within your own organization is a good first step, the activity that solidifies your journey in the direction of your vision, is your own group in which you are expected to perform. If you are planning for a senior management position as you advance, a solid foundation of technical skills is critical. A solid technical skill in your area of expertise is paramount in any successful career. This does not mean that one needs to have *technology* in their skill set. Here, technical merely refers to any specialized area that defines your expertise in which you function.

Mastering the skill in which you wish to engage is critical to the ongoing success in a career, even though you may never need that skill in the later stages of your career. This sounds contradictory. This is so, perhaps, because it is not that the mastery of this skill gets you to the vision you are aspiring, but that it gets you *going* in the right direction. It is not the content or the knowledge that you have mastered that is your ticket to the aspired vision that you hold, but, rather, it is how this prepares you to make that vision yours! It is not the skill that is the real asset you acquire, but it is the *learning* of how to acquire that skill that is your asset. Once this learning of how to learn is internalized, expanding that process to other endeavors comes naturally. And, it is this mastery of learning that prepares you to conquer new vistas to advance towards your vision.

Working well within your group allows accelerating this process of learning. This is why developing good relationships within the group catalyzes the ongoing journey towards the vision. As one grows professionally, advancements into management entail building good relationships with those who can help you in your role. So, the sooner this relationship skill is mastered, the faster is your ascendance towards your vision.

Managing Upwards

Managing upwards entails making sure that your chain of command is fully confident of your ability to deliver what they expect, and then some. Most find this a difficult task. Most do not realize that merely doing good work, or even great work is not enough in most organizations. Because of an organization's highly political nature, what is done with good intentions is not what is seen by those who are in positions to assess its merit. Intermediaries can influence their thinking based on how they want to present you to those who matter. Often, you are on your own. Often, too, the "baggage" that accompanies a person can get in the way of creating the right perception at the right levels. This baggage can include your personal peculiarities, past history that may be adverse, or just not having the "right image" inside the right circles. And, to many, this is difficult to know, let alone manage, all these factors that can militate against their organizational and corporate well being.

One reason for this difficulty is that most believe that their managers and their chain of command should have a clear idea of what they expect from those who report to them. Of course, this is generally true, but communication is not always perfect. Besides, most managers have hidden agendas that are not always apparent to those under them. The most obvious being that the manager coveting their boss's job. Some of the subtler hidden agendas can be undermining a colleague's initiative, getting more visibility to something that they have done, getting recognition for their group, etc.

Successful upward management entails knowing these hidden agendas up the chain. Not all agendas up a chain are in synch, which create additional challenges for those who are intent at managing well upwards. One obvious way to move yourself up the chain of command is to move your immediate boss up, freeing up that slot for you!

It is often difficult to know these hidden agendas. Sometimes, it is difficult even to know the overt agendas. Managers work hard at communicating overt agendas through regular, and staff, meetings, but if one wants to get ahead, going out of the way to flesh these out and then finding out how you can support these agendas can be at the heart of long-term success in an organization. Anticipating what your manager might be expected from their chain of command and then apprising, or even helping the direct manager with, the need can go a long way in ensconcing—even ingratiating—yourself for a favorable view. One word of caution: before fully supporting your manager's agenda—overt or hidden—you must make sure that they are "in" with their higher ups. If they are not, then if they were to suddenly disappear, you might be next in line with the same fate!

Knowing that the immediate boss is on the "outs" with the higher chain of command creates awkwardness in the relationship with them. Knowing this, and managing the relationship with caution, can only help you when your boss is finally out and that slot needs filling with someone from the inside that upper management now trusts. Having a cozy relationship with the ousted boss can only compromise this trust. Undue loyalty to your ostracized boss can only hurt your long-term prospects. This does not mean that you can disregard your boss and compound their problem. Remember, that person is still your boss and has the power to write you up in their assessment of you, in ways that can thwart your efforts in the future, no matter how much your higher chain of command takes to you!

Appendix-I: Managing Upwards has more details about how to do this process right.

Managing Downwards

Managing downwards is somewhat a complement of what we just presented—managing upwards. There are some differences, though. The main difference is that managing downwards also entails managing sideways. This includes all your peers and others who see you as a team player at their level within the organization. Managing these relationships entail being straight, open, and respectful of others. One of the challenges many—especially managers—face is their ability for "straight talk." This involves being direct, forthright, and not evading an issue, no matter how unpleasant a situation. When these situations relate to individuals, some mangers, especially immigrant managers, take devious routes to their handling. For example, in an unpleasant personal situation that involves someone below them, they may say something to a third party, who will, then, convey the information to the affected employee. This is an inappropriate way to handle a personal situation, but it is not uncommon to see this, even at the CEO and Board of Director levels.

About Annual Reviews

In many companies, annual reviews are treated episodically! This means that the annual review is an event that piles up because a reviewing manager simply does not get a chance to do the review in a systematic way and as a process that culminates in delivering a meaningful review at a meeting once a year. For someone who has worked hard and has looked forward to an honest appraisal of their work in a timely manner, this can be disappointing. Such treatment of a review and the affected employee has far greater impact on the morale of the employee and the organization in general than most realize.

In Chapter-3: Management Basics, we presented the concept of the management work gap. Part of the reason this gap exists, and part of the reason why managers do not do the work that only they can do, is that they are too busy doing technical work or inappropriate management work. Performance reviews is one of the most sacred task of a manager because it entails developing people. In the function of *leading*, we identified this as one of the pillars of that function in that chapter. Deferring, short changing, or paying a lip service to the performance review process can conduce in a manager's loss of credibility, both up and down.

Everyone who is slated for a review must take charge of that process well before it is due. Many companies now do a 360-degree review. In this method all those who work with you—up, down, and sideways are invited to give an input on your performance. This is done blindly, so that the person who is being reviewed knows to whom the review forms are sent, but does not know who wrote a particular review (as opposed to a double-blind process, where neither side knows the identity of the other). Those who are going to provide an input to the process must be identified early and their inputs must be gathered in a timely way (the "system" does this automatically, but still needs an oversight). Another tip is letting your manger know that you are up for a review, and then set up a time, well in advance, on their calendar to avoid any surprises.

The 360-Degree Process

Many organizations now routinely use the 360-degree process to conduct an ongoing review and progress assessment of their employees. In most cases the focus is more on measurement and less on development. As a result, the true spirit of the process is lost to the basic human condition—beating out the other guy!

The true spirit of a 360-degree review is development. Our own development comes from our knowledge of ourselves and how others see us in our own working environment. This is where a 360 can be invaluable if used properly. Many who undergo this process, are driven more by looking good than becoming better at what they do and how they do it. As a leader, each level of leadership has certain competencies that define your success factors. If you display and conquer these competencies, you are deemed effective at what you do and are ready to move on to the next level of leadership challenge. The word leader applies to everyone in this context, not just those in managerial or executive positions. An individual contributor can—and must—be a leader in what they do. So, taking a 360 in its true spirit is important. What is the true spirit of a 360? Giving the access to those from whom you can learn rather than those who admire you or from those with whom you have reciprocal agreements, so that you both rate each other accordingly.

The true spirit of a 360 that is properly designed is to identify for yourself the direction in which you want to grow, then finding those who can give you inputs in the context of your development needs. There are typically 15-20 key leadership competencies identified for a successful leader. If you pick five of these that are important to your moving forward and development as a leader, that is a good start. Finding the right people to provide the input on your 360, then taking their inputs in a positive and constructive way, are critical to this process. Once you get the inputs, meeting regularly with those who provided these inputs and checking your progress and seeking ongoing feedback are the essence of the development process. Learning is painful and that is the point. Every act of your learning something about yourself is traumatic to the ego. Once you learn to overcome that trauma, you are on your way to growth and development in ways that is almost joyous.

A 360 performance review process, at its core, involves measurement of human performance. As such, it is subject to the fallacies of the human condition. In its true spirit, a well executed 360-degree performance review is an opportunity to learn about what is going well, and what can be improved on, in furthering your own development, as well as the organization. Done poorly, it ends up being a great communication tool that blocks learning!

How?

Most like to make sure that they get a favorable review from those whom they chose as their reviewers in the 360-degree process, so they chose them accordingly. This strategy can prevent new learning, although you have found a great way to receive communication formally. In a small sample of reviewers, it is not difficult to surmise who might have written a certain assessment about you, because the context is clearly known. In view of this, and the relationship the reviewer already has with you, carrying out such a review merely reinforces what you already know. It does not add any new insight to the review process, nor does it create an actionable outcome. There have been instances when a manager, after seeing their 360 degree review results, called those whom they suspected as having provided the negative inputs to intimidate them by stating that they plan to retaliate in kind. Such tactics vitiate the 360-degree review process.

Yet another area that gets attention often is the trend of the data. When 360 reviews are done over time—longitudinal data—it shows a trend. The person being reviewed is tempted to look at the trend data and surmise that they are improving or declining in their performance, depending on the data for that time period. This can be misleading. This is because from year to year, many things change: assignments, managers, reviewers, and everyone's perspective. As a result, there is "noise" inherent in this measurement. Paying attention to the "noise" factor can lead to unnecessarily wasting time dissecting precise data that is not that accurate anyway. This is why those who provide feedback on the 360 reviews must be well trained in how they interpret the results and then communicate effectively.

The best approach to doing an effective 360-degree review is to solicit inputs from a diverse group of participants around you and use this as a learning and development tool, rather than as a "feel-good" tool.

Please see Appendix-VI: The Annual Review and Raise for further discussion.

About Salary Increases

In many companies, the annual performance review coincides with the salary increases. In some companies, these events are decoupled merely to keep the focus on the performance review and development, separately from the salary increase. Often, when they are combined, the salary increase dominates the overall discussion and the performance and development part gets the short shrift.

Often, salary increases are based on a budget and then an "average" that is fairly tight around a mean. If you want to negotiate a different—and higher—salary, the best approach is to prepare a case why you should get a higher raise, then present it during the salary discussion. Relative value creation and absolute performance are some of the factors that can be considered during this process.

Getting What You Want

Although this discussion can take place at any time during the course of a year, the best time to do this is at the performance or salary review. Once again, this is a process of communication and give-and-take. Normally, making a list of what you want then presenting that in terms of how the immediate organization, your manager, and your company can benefit from it more than you personally, can work well.

Although the concept of "straight talk," we discussed earlier, may appear to contradict it, it is not inconsistent with it! How?

In getting what you want from someone else, there has to be a consideration. No one gives away anything, even if it is free to them. Even a gift has strings attached to it! So, the best approach is to acknowledge this fact of the human condition, and approach your needs or wants from that perspective. In approaching your boss to present your needs, an assignment that is a résumé builder such as a trip that exposes you to new insights, a meeting that increases your visibility or a pay raise, are all examples of such needs.

The best way to frame your request is to first assess how your boss, or the organization, will benefit from their giving you what you want. That is the WIIFM factor (What is in it for me?). For example, if you want that résumé-building assignment, one approach that might work, is to first research the assignment and figure out some angle that positions you favorably to address some special need that project has that you can readily address. Writing a memo or an email, after briefly presenting your interest in person, to your manager can stake a claim that is going to be hard to ignore. Being persuasive and persistent are two factors that can conduce to your success in getting that assignment.

Similarly, asking for a raise that goes above and beyond the set budget, can entail doing research on what the department, and your manager, are going after to increase their standing in the organization. Then, having a meeting with your manager on how you can contribute in measurable terms to that cause can be a good starting point. Once you meet the goal then going back to the manager and claiming your credit can take you a step closer to getting what is now your right to claim. Another factor to consider is to do some comparative salary benchmarking. Salary surveys are available in the industry, and using that data to show why you belong on a different salary curve, in addition to doing the assignment we already presented, can make your case for a raise ironclad. Many believe that they deserve a higher salary because they have greater obligations—higher mortgage, more kids, a sick parent, etc.—which require them to have a greater take-home pay. Such arguments are specious and cannot result in getting what you are after.

This approach to getting what you want in an organization is pretty universal. Even if you desire something from a colleague who constantly competes with you, presenting your argument with the properly framed WIIFM can conduce to your success. In this case it is a win-win!

Some resort to other, less effective, strategies to getting what they want. Such strategies include subterfuge, backstabbing, rumor mongering, threatening to escalate the cause, etc. Such tactics usually backfire in the long run. For example, see in Chapter-4: Managing Your Own Journey, A Philosophical Insight: A WGACA story.

Summary Chapter-6: Charting Your Career

At any time in a career your forward-looking professional success depends on your:

1. Career History

2. Career Themes/Anchors

3. Vision

4. Value Proposition

5. Nisus: your perfective-urge or endeavor

6. External Trends that define what is going to happen

7. Personal Capital

8. Personal Priorities

9. Appetite for Risk

10. Personality Type

This list represents the 10 elements of a unique career-management framework that is universal. Each of the 10 elements is described in the narrative following the presentation of the framework. Much discussion is presented on the vision part, with the concept of vision in one's career and identifies the role vision plays in career success. The two somewhat dichotomous paths for forming a career vision are identified without showing a preference to one or the other. How a typical career is launched and how it progresses in a typical course are identified.

The motivation for career advancement as presented in the Maslow's hierarchy of needs identifies the basic reason people strive to achieve greater goals in their lives. In this hierarchy, unless the lower needs are met first, higher needs cannot be and are not pursued. In the ascending order these needs are:

1. Survival

➤ Safety

➤ Validation and endearment

➤ Security

➤ Nirvana or Self-actualization

Examples of what it means to be in each state of needs are presented in this discussion.

Another perspective of what motivates people in their work is presented in Herzberg's model of Hygiene/Motivation factors. A list of factors in each category is presented.

An Action Plan Tool is also presented to make the plan real for those who find it useful to take the vision concept to its practicable level for everyday use.

How to manage upwards, downwards, and your annual review is briefly presented in this chapter. There are appendices that cover these topics in more detail.

CHAPTER 7

When Things Go Wrong

"Our life is not about getting and having, but it is about being and becoming"

—Lord Krishna, in *Bahgawat Geeta*

Life is a cycle of two things: enjoyment and challenges. Here, we could have chosen the "good-bad" pair to be rather obvious about how life is—work life or otherwise! But, good and bad are relative terms, and how you perceive one in contrast with the other is a matter of context. For example, your getting laid-off, at once, is not a good thing, but often, it can be a blessing. The reason it can be a blessing is because it forces you to explore other opportunities and perhaps reinvent yourself, which can lead to richer possibilities. In today's society, we often judge what is happening to us in the context of its immediacy and how those around us perceive it. The life's vicissitudes are a constant of the human condition in all its manifestations.

Many expect their life to be a liner progression of good things. Such a view of the flow of events in our life is unrealistic. Why? This is simply because our life is about experiences and our ability to learn from these experiences. Life is about being and becoming and not about getting and having, as the quote so clearly admonishes at the head of this chapter. Learning is often not without its own pain. We often eschew learning because we do not want to go through the pain if we can avoid it. In our everyday life, we do this by failing to tell someone who has mishandled a situation by giving them appropriate and timely feedback. When we ourselves handle something poorly or even marginally, we avoid asking for feedback because we know that if the truth came out, we would be mortified. We often take great comfort from those who agree with us and, despite the fact that we can learn from those who do not by seeking insights from them, we often shun the opportunity to do so. Often, too, is that when we are asking for feedback, we are really seeking only the positive, because the whole truth can often be painful.

A Chinese Parable

The following Taoist parable illustrates how taking things in stride can be a healthy avenue to dealing with life's ups and downs.

The moral of the story, of course, is that the meaning of any event in our lives depends upon how we perceive it. Things do happen and we must learn to take them in stride.

The purpose of this chapter is not to philosophize events that change our existence or impact us in a way that is at once painful. Rather, it is to provide some avenues to avoid ongoing pain and possibly thwart, or even obviate, more serious consequences if events took their own course.

A very old Chinese Taoist story describes a farmer in a poor country village. He was considered very well-to-do, because he owned a horse, which he used for plowing and for transportation.

One day his horse ran away. All his neighbors exclaimed how terrible this was, but the farmer merely said, "Maybe yes, maybe no." A few days later the horse returned and brought two wild horses with it. The neighbors all rejoiced at this good fortune, but the farmer just said, "Maybe yes, maybe no.

The next day the farmer's son tried to ride one of the wild horses; the horse threw him and broke his leg. The neighbors all offered their sympathy for his misfortune, the farmer again said, "Maybe yes, maybe no." The next week conscription officers came to the village to take young men for the army. They rejected the farmer's son because of his broken leg. When the neighbors told how lucky he was, the farmer replied, "Maybe yes, maybe no...."

Why Things Go Wrong?

In any endeavor where humans are involved, things often go wrong. One reason is that we do not live in a perfect world. Another factor is human beings bring with them their own "baggage" to their place of work: fears, insecurities, prejudices, indifference, and ambitions. The result is this mindset conduces towards behaviors that are often counterproductive in a workplace. When such behaviors come from the higher-ups in a chain of command, employees are left to fend for themselves, often at a loss at what to make of these aberrations.

In today's organizations, where employees are stretched doing diverse tasks and doing multiple roles, just to keep their jobs, conditions rapidly deteriorate because few take the time to set things straight before they are communicated to those who are chartered with their execution. And, as they get off track, it is difficult to bring them back on track and mend the relationships that drive how individuals work together. The following list is suggestive of how and why things go off track for someone:

1. **Cognitive Dissonance:** Two people sometimes just cannot stand each other. Sometimes this condition is instantly apparent, sometime it grows with time. When this happens between a superior and their direct reports, trouble brews and it is difficult to set this straight. The best course of action is to surrender and start looking outside the group or company.

2. **Miscommunication:** Some people are not good communicators. When miscommunication becomes chronic, it damages the relationships between the two individuals. Acknowledging this early and then taking remedial steps by both parties can be a good start.

3. **Favoritism:** Although this is immoral and unethical, it is not illegal because it is hard to prove. When two people in an office go beyond their professional relationship, this factor can vitiate the good-faith efforts of those who work in their environment and are trying to do an honest job. It is estimated that nearly 25 percent of office workers engage in a personal relationship that goes beyond just being a good office buddy. In reality, this vitiates a good working relationship between the two, and worse, creates a morale problem for the rest, as well as a toxic office environment.

4. **Incompetent boss:** When the boss is incompetent, it is difficult to do your work competently and expect to be appreciated. Others, who are

also like the boss, often can subvert your best efforts and ingratiate themselves with the boss to further vitiate your efforts.

5. **Misunderstandings:** Misunderstandings occur as a result of misperceptions, wrong assumptions, miscommunications, and false expectations. These misunderstandings often lead to frayed relationships because those involved do not take the time or the trouble to repair any damage caused by such misunderstandings. Often, their egos are involved and both parties find it beyond their realm to get to the bottom of a deteriorating relationship to make it better.

6. **Having your own agenda:** This is often at the root of many dismissals, demotions, and career reversals. It is not uncommon to have an agenda that you find exciting—for you! Typical examples of such agendas are: chasing your favorite project, going after some capital purchase that will make things "better," interfering with someone's project to advance your own project, etc. How you marshal such agendas can be at the heart of your perceived impression within your own organization.

    It is not unusual to have an agenda that goes counter to what is already in place organizationally. However, harboring such an agenda and then overtly socializing it can often create difficulties for the person promoting such an agenda. If you find yourself in such a situation, the best approach is to pause and decide if promoting such an agenda through subterfuge can be tantamount, at worst, to a career suicide or, at best, to compromise your job or prospects at the current employer. The best antidote for the "agenda fever" is to check with others for signals and then decide if you should continue in the same organization or move on to other groups within the same company or move on to other employers.

7. **Goofing off:** This is one of the more common situations for many, who do not like their job and who are looking for more "challenging" roles for themselves. Occasional goofing-off is not uncommon, but when it becomes chronic it is a warning for more grave things to come in the future. In more bureaucratic organizations, where the chain of command has its own inertia, finding challenging assignments can itself be a challenge! So, in resignation, many just start doing as little as they can get away with or even goofing off as a part of their work routine. Such behaviors include arriving late to work habitually, leaving early, taking long lunches, disappearing from the office for hours, not to be found on the premises, whiling away time surfing the Internet, making personal calls, and engaging in sending personal messages via the company email system.

Such behaviors do not go unnoticed. Colleagues, or even the boss, act naïve but they are never dumb. Otherwise they would not be working where you do! So, it is only a matter of time before you get hauled into the boss's office to have an unpleasant discussion about your performance. This can quickly lead to a written warning, followed by a Notice of Concern. Once the initial meeting takes place, it is very difficult to bring things in check. After that meeting the train of events is almost inevitable.

The best strategy to avoid a showdown when you feel stultified in your job is to recognize it and decide to move on. One last thing you may want to try, to buy some time, is to preemptively approach the boss and suggest some challenging assignments that you can undertake to improve things in the organization. If any of the suggestions get approved, at least you can buy some time implementing these suggestions and get energized for the duration of that effort. If the effort is successful, it can be a résumé builder. While this is underway, you must actively start looking for a change either inside the same company or outside.

Early Warning Signs

When things go wrong they do not happen as a single episode. Often, issues escalate and the one who is in denial over the train of events that have taken an adverse course, is surprised when something precipitately occurs to change their status vis-à-vis the other person. If this other person happens to be the boss then it is something from which it is difficult recover. So, what are some of the early warning signs of your getting into trouble? The following is a partial list of such signs:

1. You do not get invited to important departmental meetings

2. You suddenly get dropped from the distribution list of emails and memos that you routinely received

3. When you enter a room, people suddenly stop talking or start whispering

4. You do not get invited to group lunches

5. Your close associates do not look you in the eye while engaging with you

6. You start getting no-win assignments with unreasonable schedules

7. When you attend a meeting, many attendees ignore your comments, especially your boss

8. You do not get a birthday party; everyone else does

9. When you go on a vacation no one misses you

10. Your colleagues do not keep their commitments

11. Your boss may make snide public remarks alluding to something that you did

This is only a partial list of how things happen in a social setting of an organization where you are no longer a star player. Not all of the listed behaviors are exhibited nor do they start manifesting at the same time. This is gradual, and that is part of the problem. The reason that this is a problem is that it is easy to go into denial over such events if they happened slowly and sporadically. However, the incidence of such behaviors is unmistakable, and the best approach to dealing with it is to make a decision to move on!

Regrouping

Regrouping entails catching early, when things start going off track. For the person involved, this is one of the most difficult things to recognize. Most deal with setbacks episodically and do not look at the patterns that form a train of events that takes its own course in an unstoppable way. Some who are paranoid by nature take on an apposite view of every little setback and episode and magnify it to either overreact to it or to get sympathy from anyone who takes the time to offer it to them. For those in the latter group, one approach, perhaps get some coaching (not therapy!).

One approach to dealing with things when they take a perverse turn is to be aware of them and deal with them, one at a time. This is difficult for most. Why? This is mainly because of the basic human condition that deals with not wanting to confront anything that pains us. The following list summarizes some regrouping strategies that allow for changing a course of action that may be otherwise inevitable:

1. Understanding what is happening and then recognizing it

2. Getting to the root cause of why this may be happening

3. Identifying those who are involved in the process and then finding out who the main player is

4. Admitting to yourself objectively what you may have done that triggered the change that is now redounding to your detriment.

5. Meeting with those who are affected by your "actions" and then having a "straight talk" about your role in it and what you may have done differently.

6. Meeting with your boss and getting their view on the situation

7. Making changes in the way you behave so that those with whom you have had a conversation can see that you are making earnest efforts to make things right

8. Seeking outside help as a counselor, a coach, or a mentor

9. Going out of the way to set things right, especially for those who may have been affected by your actions (or inactions).

10. Taking an initiative to be positive about others and the organization.

One of the greatest challenges for those who are suddenly exposed to setbacks, organizational ridicule, or an exile is keeping their perspective and riding out the storm by acknowledging early, their own errors. Personal heeling takes time; organizational heeling takes even longer. So, if it takes a long time for such a person to re-ingratiate themselves with others in their group, it is something that they have to work on riding it out.

Some Recovery Strategies

In a career, or even a job, it is common to have ups and downs. No one goes monotonically and steadily up in their every endeavor, because if they did, then it is perhaps because they wanted to be safe and take no risks. And, because there is no failure in such a trajectory, there is also no learning! Failure is learning's handmaiden,

If any setback or failure is taken in stride and context, its occurrence becomes less troubling. It also provides for some recovery strategies that are otherwise not possible. When those who are involved in such episodes during their careers do not look at these events as times to grow and find out for themselves their true self-worth by dealing with them in a constructive way, they are missing out on major opportunities to discover themselves. Reacting to such episodes emotionally and not taking action to overcome them in a constructive way are a suboptimal way to deal with life's challenges. What is even more potent in such situations, is taking preemptive action before a train of events gets out of hand, making it difficult to stop when you want to.

One reason why many, who suffer poor treatment at their job, do not fight back, or even make an attempt to redress the wrong, is because of their belief that they must have done something wrong to deserve it and that they are unable to marshal a fight with their employer. They also fear retribution in the form of poor references, increased harassment prior to their physical departure from the organization, and organized indifference by their colleagues during their remaining tenure at their job. Although some or all of these apprehensions may be valid, harboring these beliefs and then cowering in fear and resorting to inaction are your worst strategies.

Any reasonable employer is going to salvage what has already been invested in an employee and do everything possible to prevent further damage to either side. In fact, in most cases, employers are more apprehensive about retribution from the affected employee than is apparent to most. There is always the chance of litigation that can create problems for the employer if the employee decided to pursue a claim because of perceived unfair treatment. In this litigious society, employers are not willing to risk tying their resources in protracted litigation or even arbitration if they can avoid it.

In view of this dynamic, if any employee feels mistreated or even suspects such treatment, it is well advised to pull all facts together and meet with their boss and the HR representative. While this is underway, they must also actively start looking for a job outside, without regard to how their current employer will reference them.

Having a job outside your current company can put you at a great advantage at a time when you are being adversarial with your current employer. Once you have a job in hand, you can ask for a severance package under the veiled threat of a legal action if the situation warrants. Actually going through the legal process can, however, be to your detriment. This is because your entire future employment prospects now hinge on this fact. Future employers are reluctant to consider favorably, employees who are prone to legal recourses.

Throwing in the Towel

Once you have gone this far in the process, it is time to take decisive action. Often, the best course of action, particularly if you already have a job lined up, is to ask for a severance package. Many progressive employers willingly give four-to-six months' salary in consideration for not pursuing a legal course of action. Even if you do not have a legal basis for suggesting such a course of action, many HR representatives do not want to tread on this basis. How such a suggestion is made when you are negotiating your exit is not always easy, but not that difficult, either. It is a matter of circumstances and having the courage and conviction to do what is right.

Once you take this course of action and chose to follow it, it is best to take it to conclusion and walk away from the company with a substantial check in your pocket, without paying a penny of it to a lawyer.

Summary Chapter-7: When Things Go Wrong

Things often go wrong during a career. It is rare when everything goes right and there is no cause for concern. There are the following seven factors that typically result in things going off track:

1. Cognitive Dissonance

2. Miscommunication:

3. Favoritism:

4. Incompetent boss

5. Misunderstandings

6. Having your own agenda:

7. Goofing off

The following ten factors can help you regroup when missteps occur:

1. Understanding what is happening and then recognizing it

2. Getting to the root cause of why this may be happening

3. Identifying those who are involved in the process and then finding out who the main player is

4. Admitting to yourself objectively, what you may have done that triggered the change that is now redounding to your detriment.

5. Your close associates do not look you in the eye while engaging with you

6. Meeting with those who are affected by your "actions" and then having a "straight talk" about your role in it and what you may have done differently.

7. Meeting with your boss and getting their view on the situation

8. Making changes in the way you behave, so that those with whom you have had a conversation can see that you are making earnest efforts to make things right

9. Seeking outside help as a counselor, a coach, or a mentor

10. Going out of the way to set things right, especially for those who may have been affected by your actions (or inactions).

11. Taking an initiative to be positive about others and the organization.

Despite your early and diligent efforts, if it is not possible to recover from being off track, it is best to consider a move and leave your employment for better opportunities. Whenever possible, avoid using the services of a lawyer. Try working with the HR and others yourself.

CHAPTER 8

Taking Care of the Customer

"The customer is not buying what you think you are selling to him."
—Peter Drucker, management guru (1912–)

In any organization, customers must come first. As we laid out in Chapter-3: Organizational Basics, an organization is the soul of the business it serves. Yet another analogy would be that the business is the "content" and the organization is the "context" in which the content is delivered. Without the customer, the business would not exist. Here, we differentiate between the customer and the end user. A customer is the one who pays the bills and the end user is someone who benefits from the value created by the organization. In today's complex business ecosystem, there are many players, and differentiating them and attaching the right labels to them can be difficult. But, the fact remains that regardless of the actual label someone bears, and regardless of the role they play in the value chain, if they are at the receiving end of the value chain, to the "right" of where you participate in it, they are your customer. Those participating to the "left" of you, then, using the same metaphor, would be suppliers. Here, the adjectives "right" and "left" are used to denote the side of the consumer/provider in relation to the producer business, and not as its political leaning.

Customer Focus

Taking care of the customer is one of the most basic needs in a business. Yet, the skill required to do this correctly is not appreciated in a way that results in organizations having the right approach to improve a customer experience, as a disciplined process. Often, organizational factors override customer needs and, as a result, customer experience is relegated to whatever processes allow employees to be expedient. For example, if an issue or customer complaint is parceled out to a functional department, its own mission will always take precedence; customer will come second. . The result is a dissatisfied customer at best, a customer defection and a slowly dwindling business at worst. Most fail to realize that a complaining customer does not see the "silos" that those within an organization are so married to. The rub lies in the differing perspectives of those inside an organization and those who deal with it as customers. Those inside an organization see it as "siloed," whereas those on the outside, including the customers, see it as monolithic.

Why is this chapter part of this book and not other issues an organization deals with on a daily basis? The reason is simple: not making the customer central to your role in *any* organization can be deadly, regardless of the role you play in it. The closer you are to the customer, the more critical this role becomes. On the other hand, other issues an organization faces are less critical and their influence more parochial.

This chapter is aimed at providing some guidelines on how to understand a customer and how to deal with the customer issues in ways that is not obvious. Using what is presented here can create a customer-centric culture that will change the way your business operates. There are hundreds of books written about how best to deal with customers and how to increase customer satisfaction. The material presented here is designed to provoke fresh thinking and provide some food for thought on how to manager customers *differently*.

Customer Management Hierarchy

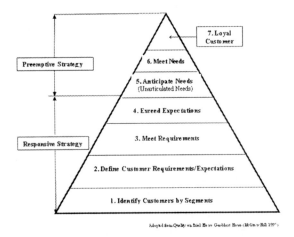

Figure-7: Customer Management Hierarchy

Generally, customers can be classified as belonging to a hierarchy as shown in Figure-7. A brief discussion of each element follows:

1. **Identify Customers by Segments:** Although a customer is a customer, a company must have a strategy to treat each category of customers differently. Although this smacks of discrimination, this is how a business can derive the most benefit from each type of customer it garners, nurtures, and deals with. As a class, all customers must be accorded some basic treatment that is equitable, fair, and that which gets more customers to want to do business with you. But, at the same time, there must be deliberate inequities that are designed to treat customers that are more valuable to a company, in ways that enhances how they are differentiated from the rest. Segmenting customers by their value, immediate potential, and future possibilities, must be a core skill a customer management process must possess.

2. **Define Customer Requirements and Expectations:** Meeting customer requirements is the most basic function of any business. Requirements are essential value elements that deliver what the customer is paying for. They represent what is functionally exchanged in a transaction that satisfies the two parties engaged in that transaction. So, if a customer went looking for a car, they expect that car to deliver the basic requirements of transportation, safety, quality, reliability, reasonable appearance, and a fair price. When these requirements are met, the customer may consider parting with their money, in exchange for that automobile. If the requirements are compromised, then there is no reason for the customer to enter into the transaction.

   Customer expectations are another matter. If requirements are the threshold for a transaction to occur, expectations catalyze that transaction. Requirements are the customers' perceptions of how the required product or service should be delivered.

   Requirements and expectations have a different place in a transaction: exceeding requirements does not create greater value in the minds of the customer, because this approach does not deliver greater value to the customer. For example, a typical automobile has a life of 12 years before it is retired. So, for the upholstery supplier to make seats that last some 30 years would add no value to the OEM in its purchase. Making such a seat would add cost without adding value. If the same seat remained comfortable and durable throughout the life of an average car, that expectation would be worth some additional value to the customer. Exceeding expectation can create loyalty, exceeding requirements does not!

3. **Meet Requirements:** Once the requirements are known, meeting them is at the basis of any transaction where the buyer is willing to consider parting with their money as a fair trade for what they are getting in exchange. This is why merely meeting the customer requirements is a "Responsive Strategy." Without such responsiveness, there is no customer!

4. **Exceed Expectations:** As you go past the requirements and capture what will make the customer want to come back—understanding their perceptions and making efforts to satisfy those perceptions—you will get increasing business as a result. Take for instance, the automobile example: if you were to take it to the service station for its routine maintenance, you expect the car to be maintained according to some checklist. If the center also delivers the car on time, treats you with courtesy, and goes beyond what you had come to reasonably expect then the center has exceeded your expectations and you are likely to come back the next time.

5. **Anticipate Needs:** Once the expectations are exceeded, or at least met, the next level of attention, centers around *anticipating* customer needs. Anything from this step forward is considered a Preemptive Strategy. This typically means thinking ahead of the customer. So, in the case of the automobile that is being serviced, as we just presented, if you were to come pick up your automobile with your four year old son, who gets off school at 3:30, then having some toy and a snack for him as you pay for the service and check your car, would be anticipating your needs and meeting them. Such needs, when met, have far greater power in their ability to generate loyalty.

6. **Meet Customer Needs:** This is a constant cycle of anticipating needs and then meeting them ahead of the competition. As you increasingly get better at anticipating customer needs and meeting them, your competitors are going to do the same. Those who stay ahead of the curve are going to be the leaders in the loyalty movement and are going to keep more customers coming back to them.

7. **Gain Loyalty:** This is the final step in the ladder of customer experience. Getting to this sweet spot is hard work but worth more than can be described in words.

The Kano Diagram

The goal of any business is to capture customers and drive them to becoming loyal followers of the company's products and services. As is obvious, loyalty comes from not just delivering what each segment of customers requires, but going well beyond that on an ongoing basis, in order to constantly wow them. The challenge to keep customers interested in the company's products is ongoing, because no matter what innovations you introduce to get customers' attention, competition is going to catch up to, and even preempt, your next move. To appeal to the customers' buying tastes, the producer must provide full panoply of features that fall into three categories: Required, Expected, and Exceptional.

The required features are standard features that reflect the current state-of-the-art for the product offered. In chapter-2, Organizational Basics, we introduced the concept of the Hygiene Factors in providing employees a reason to join your company. Hygiene Factors are those that do not provide the incentive for potential employees to join your company, but their absence will cause them to leave or not join you. Competitive salary and benefits, safety, potential for advancement, and fair employment practices are some examples of attributes that fall into this category. So, in the employment analogy, and using the Herzberg's model, the Hygiene Factors are similar to product requirements. Referring back to Figure-7, Customer Management Hierarchy, this area covers the bottom three rungs of the "loyalty ladder."

The next level of features is the Expected features. These are typically features that customers come to expect as a result of competitive and market forces. In the case of an automobile, these include gas economy (MPG), frequency-of-repair, and sample defects per 1000 cars. How these features influence customer satisfaction and buying decisions, are shown by the straight line in Figure-9. This means that there is no particular leverage in the way a parameter in this class can influence customers' buying decision. The effort required to improve the impact of this class of features in the final buying decision, is linear. Referring back to Figure-7 again, this area covers the first four rungs of the ladder.

The final category of features—Exceptional—is an entirely different class in itself. They have a tremendous "wow" power because their impact on customer value perception is highly leveraged, and is often at an emotional level. As the curve pointing upwards indicated in Figure-8, the appeal of the benefits resulting from this class of features is exponential. In keeping with the automobile metaphor, one feature that can perhaps provide this hit in today's cars could be a self-parking automobile that backs up in a slot so that the driver does not have to do the dreaded parallel parking along a curb in a limited space. Working in this area covers the entire "loyalty ladder," all the way up to the final loyalty step.

Where a feature belongs in the scheme of things for a product is a matter of time. For example, when the electric self-starter was introduced in the 1930s, this was a major breakthrough, and might have been regarded as an exceptional feature then. Before its invention, cars used a hand crank to get going. Today, its absence will prevent a car from being sold. The same holds true for cars with automatic transmission.

The Kano diagram, Figure-8, offers an elegant means of discriminating between different features of design. Everyone works hard at finding the "wow" features in their products and

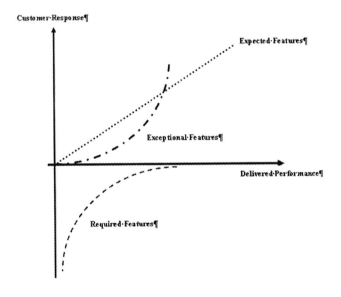

Figure-8 The Kano Diagram

services to get the customer to buy their product before they do their competitors'. This issue really gets to the crux of the problems that very quickly emerge, once the importance of the 'excitement' features is recognized. Very simply, what excites one person will often not excite someone else. Or, more seriously, can it ever be possible to define something that would excite everyone. In other words, finding the "excitement features" is generally considered to be highly desirable. Often, it is also highly unpredictable.

The Relationship Engine

To understand where a customer stands in their perception of the three categories of "satisfiers" described in the Kano diagram, a thorough knowledge of customer mindset is essential. One such tool for getting this insight is the relationship engine. The relationship engine is a model that drives exemplary and highly loyal relationships with those customers that deserve your most attention and who can significantly contribute to the success of your business and organization. As we presented before, not all customers are the same, and they must be treated accordingly with regards to what makes the best use of your resources and, in turn, provide the best return on your investment. In fact, treating customers this way can be one on the most lucrative strategies available to any business.

The relationship engine is based on a carefully orchestrated customer discovery that results in selective actions to improve customer experience, as a result of this process. It is schematically presented below (Figure-9):

The first element of this engine is Discovery. It is a carefully designed and orchestrated process of digging into customer accounts in ways that are highly insightful, leveraged, and unambiguous in its message. Surveys and focus groups are the most used approaches for assessing customer reaction. Focus groups are typically reserved for identifying new products, concepts, and offerings a company is considering. Surveys, on the other hand, are administered with almost religious fervor in most companies. Typically, surveys are administered by third parties, with their design conducted in collaboration with key employees of the company that is sponsoring it.

Both the focus groups and surveys have their limitations, which often make headlines when they misdirect a major product strategy. Consider "New Coke" (focus groups) and Instant Movies that Polaroid dabbled with (surveys) as well as other lesser-known flops. The basic premise of the survey design is flawed. The assumption companies often make is that their own customers would be unwilling to share candidly their experiences in dealing with them. The third party, which is ostensibly an expert in survey design and administration, is perceived to be better at gleaning customer perspectives from the process that they administer. Most companies automatically assume that customers would be candid in sharing with them directly their experiences.

Nothing could be further from the truth. The survey-taking organization has no knowledge of the company and even less about the product or services it sells its customers. It also has no insight into customers, other than perhaps the segment to which they, as a class belong. Done this way, the entire process becomes robotic and almost meaningless in its actionability or effectiveness. And yet, many companies routinely engage in such surveys and spend large sums of money getting information that does not help improve customer relationships long term. In many companies, bonuses are tied to how the survey results tally and, as a result, there are instances where surveys, and how they are analyzed, get manipulated to serve whomever they benefit—customer excepted—the most!

The discovery process, on the other hand, involves a company's own key employees who are chartered with designing the process and managing it inside the company. Here, key customers are identified and major issues that drive the relationships with these customers are agreed upon. Based on that perspective, a tightly designed discovery script, with actionability in mind, is prepared, and those most capable and knowledgeable about the customer meet with them in pairs to complete the discovery. In this session, a candid

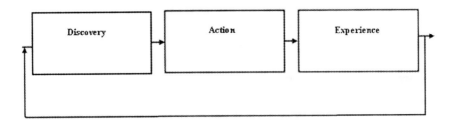

After Dee Gaeddert, QI International (Now Personnel Decisions International, Inc)

Figure-9: The Relationship Engine

exchange takes place directly between the employees and the customer, one customer at a time. Done properly, a rich and highly actionable discovery can result from such a design. The best part of this approach is that since this is done by those in the organization who have a vested interest in its outcome, there is an undeniable ownership in the outcome of this discovery. When the results of a survey conducted by an outside party, in contrast, have any adverse messages, those who should own the message, typically try to find either why the message itself is flawed, or that someone else should be responsible for why this is so.

The next step in the process is Action. This results from the discovery that prompts specific attention to those issues that are getting in the way of a good customer experience. Action is a set of outcomes, which when implemented, can result in a change that moves the customer to think differently about their new experience—in a positive way! Often, these actions are taken in conjunction with the customer, who will see the effect of these actions. Once the actions are implemented, and the affected customers notified about the impending change, the outcome should take the process to the final step.

That final step is the Experience. This relates to the customer experience that results from the changes. These changes are received in a much better light, if the affected customers are informed about what is coming, why, and how they would change customers' experience. Normally, when any change is made—positive or otherwise—the reaction is negative (see Change Curve in chapter-3). Communicating this to those who are going to be the recipients, or even the beneficiaries of this change goes a long way in anticipating what is coming. Without this groundwork the whole experience may be less than desirable. Managing the change is a major part of the Experience step, resulting from the implementation of the Relationship Engine.

An example of a change that rebounds in negative reaction, once again, is taken from the automobile industry involving anti-lock brakes. This was a major safety breakthrough in vehicle braking, where, when the wheels loose traction the braking action is modulated by the sensors that detect the traction loss. The braking system then manages the traction and safe stopping, without causing the vehicle to lose its steering ability, as often happens when the wheels lock under similar road conditions with the conventional brake systems. Initially, when the drivers were not used to this change, they continued treating the brake pedal in the same old manner, as they did before the change, often pumping it to prevent the wheels from locking on slippery roads—exactly opposite of what antilock brakes require. This driver behavior, stemming from lack of knowledge about the change, initially caused more accidents than predicted!

There is a loop that goes from the output to the input. This suggests that when a well-designed relationship engine is executed well, and the discovery and action benefit the customer—and the business, in turn—further discovery is invited. The next round, then, increases the trust, engagement, and the penetration into the customer account. This is precisely why this model is called an engine—it drives things in the right direction for both the business and its customers!

Relationship Assessment Process (RAP)

The Relationship Assessment Process is an operational implementation of the Relationship Engine just presented. Acronym apart, as a verb, *rap* also means to talk frankly and freely. What better way to create a great discovery than to have an open discussion with your key customers? Rapping with selected customers can change a relationship! The RAP is presented in the flowchart below:

A brief description of each step in the 11-element process follows (figure-10):

1. **Identify Customers:** The RAP is a potent process of discovery and action that involves resources, time, and making a commitment to improve things. In view of this, the selection of customers who will be party to this process has been done with a studied approach. Using the 80:20 rule (also known as the rule of the vital few and trivial many) is generally a good guideline. This means that 80 percent of the change can be affected by doing a discovery with 20 percent of the customers who are critical to the business at hand. If this process is handled correctly, participation is nearly `100 percent. By contrast, participation in surveys is less than 10 percent. To make matters worse, those who participate in surveys are outliers on either side of the normal distribution (deviants). What this means is that those that are extremely satisfied or those that are extremely dissatisfied tend to dominate the participant pool. The most important pool, the one that lies in the middle of the distribution, rarely participates. An additional consideration—and an important one—is the actionability of the captured data. :

2. **Define Discovery Theme:** Once the customer pool is identified, they share some common features. Using these features, and the intent of the discovery, it is a good idea to design a set of queries that will be used in the discovery. Not all discovery designs are identical, but in a pool of customers carefully identified, there is a common element. Each discovery for a segment of customers within a pool may have variations beyond the core design. This allows for a rich, and yet standardized, discovery, which helps in data analysis of themes and comparisons.

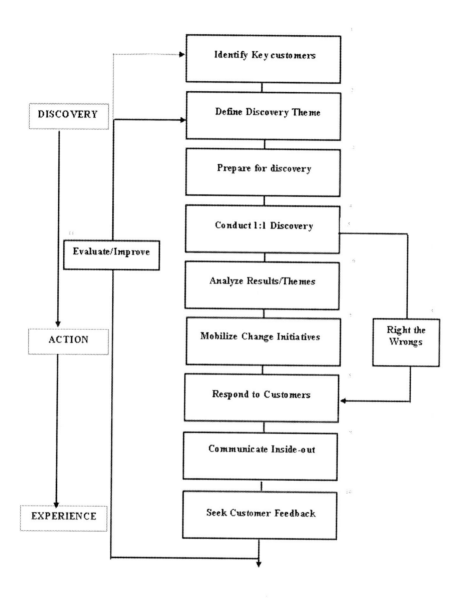

Figure-10: The Relationship Assessment Process (Adapted from *Quality on Trial*)

3   **Prepare for Discovery:** Preparation entails identifying how to match the customer/interviewer pairs and then training those who are going to go and conduct face-to-face meetings with customers. A good design is two employees per customer. Each of the employees

must have some connection with the account, as well as, the customer being interviewed. Their prior training is critical, because how to ask questions, how to dig deeper for specific information, how to be non judgmental and non defensive, are some of the key elements to learn during this training. The more non-defensive a discovery is, the more rich its outcome, and the more actionable its content.

4. **Conduct 1:1 Discovery:** This step entails a pre-selected pair of employees going to the customer site and meeting with the customer to conduct the interview. This is organized by first briefing the customer well ahead of time, explaining what the process is about, and most importantly the benefit to *them*! Typical requests may entail asking for about 45 minutes for such a meeting and then seeing how it goes from there in an actual setting. In reality, a well designed and executed interview and discovery can result in a customer spending much more time than originally scheduled. This is usually a good yardstick for its success at this stage.

5. **Righting the Wrongs:** This is a very critical step in the process. In step-4, for setting up the interview, customer benefit was the centerpiece of this request. This step is how it is immediately demonstrated. What this entails, then, is that if a customer has an urgent matter that relates to something that has gone awry in the recent past, it will come up during the interview. Probing further to explore what will allay the pain so caused, as well as, what measures can be taken to band-aid the situation, are critical to the customer experience, and to also demonstrate good faith for the discovery process. Immediate and specific interventions are two of the most important factors in this step. A follow-up after the remedy is also a good step.

6. **Analyze Results/Themes:** This is where the entire pool of data across the chosen population of clients is aggregated, analyzed, interpreted, and made actionable. Themes are identified and grouped. Specific actions by accounts are then separated out under each theme so that the changes resulting from the Action are specific to each account for which discovery was conducted.

7. **Mobilize Change Initiatives:** Once the data is converted into actionable interventions that define a change plan, it is time to present it to senior management who can agree on the priorities and scope the

change. Assignments of specific responsibilities, including communication, are then made at this stage.

8. **Respond to Customers:** This is where the change actions get specific to each account and the major change initiative agreed to in Step-7 is actualized for that account, and specifically, that customer.

9. **Communicate Inside-out:** Communication is the most critical element of the entire process. Who communicates what to whom and how this is done, and when, are all very important in maintaining the original spirit of the discovery.

10. **Seek Customer Feedback:** This is the Experience part of the Relationship Engine. At this stage, customers are asked specifics about what worked and what could be better, and why. If the Experience is positive, there will be an invitation for further discovery—a good sign of an improved relationship.

11. **Evaluate/Improve:** This is the final step that allows ongoing improvement of the RAP and making changes based on the learning from the previous discovery.

Understanding Customers

Behind any business success, its relationship with customers is at the heart of its strategy. The proverb that all customers are created equal is probably true, but to treat them as equals can be fatal to a business. Understanding the attitudes and behaviors of customers as different groups is critical to their handling. Depending on their unique behavioral attributes (prior individual biases), intensity of satisfaction or dissatisfaction (attitude), and their ability to act on their satisfaction or dissatisfaction (competitive market dynamics), customers behave in one of the five basic ways:

- Loyalists/Apostles
- Defectors
- Mercenaries
- Hostages
- Terrorists

A brief discussion of each type follows.[2]

In most cases, the **loyalist** is a completely satisfied customer, who keeps returning for more. They are the easiest customers to serve. **Apostles** are a subset of these loyalists who go out of their way to promote their experience with the company and its products, in order to recruit others to follow their path. An apostle can also be a viral marketing agent. They "infect" others with their enthusiasm about the company, its people, and its product and services. For a company to leverage its market footprint, it pays to keep these apostles happy in every encounter the company has with them.

Treating customers right is not limited to keeping them happy when everything is going well. It especially means treating them exceptionally well when something goes terribly wrong. It is at these times that a company can convert a loyalist into an apostle. It can also turn an apostle into a defector if it does not handle such episodes with special care. If a failure occurs when it relates to a loyalist or an apostle, and a company makes amends when such a failure occurs, the customers' faith in the company is not just restored, it is deepened. A loyalist with a good recovery experience can become an apostle. This is why it pays to have a good feedback system, where it is openly possible for people to communicate with the company, their experiences.

Defectors can include all customers who have suffered negative experiences from the company, its products, services, or employees. Even loyal customers who have encountered a service failure, sometimes just once, can become defectors. Letting such customers defect is perhaps the biggest mistake a company can make. When a company has strong processes in place to understand such customers' needs better, and to shower attention on them if isolated problems strike, most of them can be converted, or turned, to loyal customers, once again.

This does not mean that all defectors are worth keeping. The unreasonable demands of unhappy customers whose needs do not fit with the company's capabilities preempt excessive resources and wreak havoc on company employees and their morale. It is worth considering "firing" such customers that can be served elsewhere. It is better to send them to your competitors!

The most dangerous defectors are the **Terrorists**. These are the customers who have had a bad experience and cannot wait to tell others about it in an

---

2. In their seminal article, *Why Satisfied Customers Defect*, authors Jones and Sassar describe in details each of the categories of customers. See *Harvard Business Review*, Novemeber/Decemeber 1995 (95606).

exaggerated way to suit their own purposes. Most terrorists are emotionally charges about their experiences and they are willing go the distance to prove their plight and get sympathies from those who could be potential customers. Another flavor of a terrorist is someone who gets all charged up about trivia and go right to the top with their complaints by grossly exaggerating them just to shake things up. It is these customers that wreak havoc inside an otherwise well-run organization, and it is these that need to get "fired."

Terrorists are far more committed to their cause and are willing to go to any lengths to convey to others what they feel as an "unjust" treatment, just to shake things up in a company to get attention for their cause. When things are set right, they do nothing to acknowledge it, and continue their campaign of terror.

The **Mercenary** is a customer who, despite their high satisfaction, displays no loyalty to the company or its products/services. They are also expensive to acquire, and tend to depart easily. They chase low prices, better deals, and often, buy on impulse. They are usually not good for a long-term benefit of the company's profitability.

The **Hostage** is a stuck customer. They are at the mercy of what a company has to offer and have no choices, either because of their own situation (little money), or the competitive marketplace. Before AT&T's break-up, most customers felt hostage to its practices. Today, some feel the same about Microsoft. They may be trapped, but they still take every opportunity to complain and seek special services.

Learning from Customer Defections

Yet another opportunity to learn much about how customers see your business, is to treat each defection as a singular event of great significance, and take the courage to find out why. When a customer defects no one really wants to deal with it head on. The sales people think that it is a marketing function, the marketers feel that it is the product that the customer is disappointed about, and the product team feels that it is the service that did them in! In other words, finger pointing begins as soon as an important customer defects.

In most cases, there are warning signs everywhere when a customer is increasingly unhappy about what they are getting from a company. Usually, such a message, even coming directly from the customer, is vectored in different directions across an organization and as a result, no one takes charge of something that can be corrected relatively easily in its early stages. A company needs a disciplined process to audit a defection and then get to the bottom of it. Usually, with important accounts, the CEO should be notified, and they should take charge of finding out what went wrong, and possibly win the customer back. The process should be not to find who dropped the ball, but what in the process broke down. It is not the "who," but the "what" that caused the defection. A customer, thus recovered, is likely to be far more loyal and the process is far less expensive than finding a new customer. Studies have shown that, on average, to acquire a new customer, takes six times as much as to keep the one already on board.

The defection-learning process should be made a centerpiece of an organization's customer retention policy. Any knowledge gained from a defecting customer, even though they may not return, or be recovered, is worth the effort, and its reward is priceless in morale, leadership, and showing the true meaning of "the customer comes first."

Summary Chapter-8: Taking Care of the Customer

Every business owes its existence to its customers. So, taking care of the customer must be at the center of everyone's foremost priority. This chapter begins with the discussion of how customers can be viewed by how their needs are met. A graphic depicting customer management hierarchy shows how moving from merely meeting customer requirements, to anticipating their needs, changes how they view your role in their affairs. The graphic of Figure-8 shows how, in moving from a responsive to a preemptive strategy, shifts the customers' perception of your role in their minds.

The Kano (Kaano) diagram depicts the three classes of product features that differentiate a product in the way it appeals to the customers' buying urges: Required, Expected, and Exceptional. Once the Required and Expected features are incorporated in a product, only the Exceptional features will drive customers to stay loyal to the company's products.

To really understand a customer, a customer-discovery process is introduced. The Relationship Engine describes how this discovery can be leveraged to enhance a customer's experience. It consists of three elements: Discovery, Action, and Experience. A well executed discovery leads to specific Action that changes how a customer views your value delivery process. A focused Action results in an Experience that redefines the customer's perception of how you create value. A positive Experience invites further Discovery, which can result in the next round of Action to further enhance the experience. This is why this simple model is called the relationship engine.

A practical implementation of this relationship engine is the ten-step customer discovery process called Relationship Assessment Process (RAP). Each step of this process is defined in the discussion that presents how to implement such a process, so that successive discoveries lead to ongoing improvements in customer relationships.

Any customer pool consists of the following types of customers:

- Loyalists/Apostles

- Defectors

- Mercenaries

- Hostages

- Terrorists

Mercenaries and Terrorists impose an inordinate burden on company's resources. This includes those who work outside the customer support functions. Any company must have an active program where such customers are identified and "fired" on a regular basis.

Defections result from poor customers' experiences and when they are unable to change their relationship with the company that continues to create such experiences. There is a way to deal with defections and to turn them around from potential defectors to loyal customers.

CHAPTER 9

Working Globally

"Culture is the way in which people resolve dilemmas emerging from universal problems."

—Riding the Wave of Cultures

Yesterday's business world, that we thought was round like the earth, is now flattened by today's technology. The Internet, global travel, instant telecommunications, and the democratization of information, all have contributed to making the world a seamless trading place. But, have they really?

Despite the technology's relentless march to flatten the world, in its attempts to create a level playing field, the basic issues of human interactions stemming from cultural differences create challenges that continue to elude today's business leaders. This chapter is presented as a reminder to not just the business executives, but to all who are citizens in today's global village. It is presented as an overview of the issues that can all be lumped under the rubric of culture and geographic peculiarities.

Managers, working globally, are mystified by the cultural challenges they face in everyday business. Anyone who works with people from different cultures should be aware of the factors that drive cultural behaviors and what those behaviors can be, to better understand the people they are dealing with. Awareness of cultural differences is basic to their understanding, and the smooth interactions with people who are steeped in these cultures. Cultural differences can be systematically analyzed and understood. The best antidote for the fear stemming from cultural differences is flexibility, humanity, humility, and a sense of humor. If one can understand what the overriding drivers are in a human interaction then cultural differences can be easily codified and managed. Often, in group cultures, knowing these overriding drivers is not difficult.

No matter how objective and uniform we try to make organizations, they will not have the same meaning for individuals from a different culture. Cultural preferences create nuances of meanings, which must be understood for a harmonious workplace. Culture is a shared system of meanings within a community. It dictates what we pay attention to, how we act, and what we value. Culture organizes such values into "mental programs." How people behave in organizations is a manifestation of such programs. Each culture takes a phenomenological approach[3] This merely means that it explores how the cultural norms evolved out of human consciousness and became a preface to our working philosophy.

In any society, its product can be seen as a combination of the "content" and the "context." Here, "society" includes a business, an organization, or even a department within an organization. The "content" is what is apparent, tangible, or visible and "context" is the soul of how that comes about. This is analogous to understanding a human being by merely looking at their body; to understand a human being you must also understand their soul! Similarly, without the context, content is meaningless. In their seminal book, *Riding the Waves of Culture*, authors Fons Trompenaars and Charles Hampden-Turner identify seven factors that drive culture-oriented behaviors—behaviors that create the context:

- Universalism vs. particularism

- Individualism vs. communitarianism

- Neutral vs. emotional

- Specific vs. Diffuse

- Achievement vs. ascription

- Attitude toward time

- Attitude toward the environment

These contrasting attitudes define how different nationalities look at a given situation and then behave in a predictable way. Knowing this predilection towards certain situations and circumstances can help those who understand them, deal with people of other cultures in a constructive and accommodative ways.

---

3. See *Riding the Waves of Culture: Understanding Diversity in Global Business*, Trompenaars and Hampden-Turner

Universalism vs. Particularism refers to how certain nationalities view a way of doing things as the best. Universalits include Americans, Canadians, Australians, and the Swiss. Those from these nationalities believe that there in one best way by stating the rules and procedures that drive how things are done. Particularists include South Koreans, Malaysians, and Chinese, who advocate that circumstances dictate how ideas and practices should be applied. They focus on the peculiar nature of any given situation and the relationships.

Universalists doing business with Particularists should be patient and accepting of ritualistic ways of doing things. They should be prepared for meandering or irrelevancies that do not go anywhere. They should focus on building relationships and understanding, to conclude the business at hand.

Particularists doing business with Universalits should be mindful of their rational and professional arguments and presentations.

Communitarianism vs. Individualism contrast in how an individual is viewed in a group. The United States emphasizes the individual before the group. Countries as France and Egypt are at the other end of the spectrum. In Japan, for example, children from their kindergarten are taught to collectively conform to each other and, often, complete "individual" assignments that end up looking all alike, even drawings and doodles!

Individuals working with collectivists must tolerate time taken to consult with superiors and must understand if an accepted offer is annulled after consultation with their superiors.

Neutral vs. Emotional deals with the make-up of a group of people belonging to a nationality in how they respond to situations. For example, an Italian will respond with emotional flair, whereas an American will with phlegmatic indifference to the same situation. This means that if an Italian gets carried away with their emotions, an American should not get too excited in dealing with them. For example, if in a negotiating meeting, an Italian storms off from the negotiating table, he considers that part of posturing. An American, in the same meeting, may take offense to such behavior and conclude that the negotiations have broken down. Now, if the American walks away from this situation thinking that the deal is scuttled, it is indeed so, because there is no attempts to reconcile the irate counterpart. The Italian is expecting a rapprochement.

Specific vs. Diffuse refers to how different cultures respond to queries and challenges. The American, British, and German respond to specific issues with specificity, whereas those from India, Japan, and the Middle East will take a more diffuse approach to addressing a particular problem. So, when those who are looking for specific responses are dealing with those cultures who offer diffuse responses, they have to learn to frame their queries accordingly. Similarly, those who are diffuse in their approach are dealing with those with specific orientation, they must show tolerance when presented with information that they consider redundant.

One way to see this readily is to become aware of how those from different nationalities respond to the same email message. If an American sends a message asking for specific information about a situation, those with specific mindsets will respond to it by itemized narratives for each issue raised in the email, most likely by interspersing the response with each issue raised. Those with the diffuse culture are likely to provide a response in one place, often in general terms, without even addressing the issues raised! Such exchange can be very frustrating.

Another manifestation of this attribute is how those with diffuse perspective approach a business opportunity. Americans, typically, will go through specific research and make elaborate and slick presentation material to make their case. Those with diffuse approach may spend weeks building relationships with key people and work with them in mainly social settings. Their presentations may not even be on the mark and may not appeal to an American executive, but they may win the contract—despite their higher price and longer lead times—based on how they have built the relationships with key individuals.

Achievement vs. Ascription refers to how a society regards its population and individuals. In a meritocracy, chiefly the U.S., ascription is not an argument. So, in a business situation, someone who comes from the U.S. must learn to respect the pedigree of the person who otherwise may not be able to cut muster. Similarly, someone who comes from a class-conscious society, as in Britain, India, and some Middle Eastern countries, must learn how to deal with meritocracy. Where ascription is important, what matters is not what you studied, but what school you went to. In achievement-driven cultures where you came from is relatively unimportant.

Attitude toward time is how different nationalities deal with how fast things get done. In Japan, for example, time is considered an ally in business situations, whereas, in the U.S., people rush to get things done and concluded. In some societies, what one has achieved in the past is all important. What they are going to do in the future or even now, is less so. In the U.S., what you are doing now and in the future decide your importance.

The U.S. and the French are diametrically opposite in this regard to time. For example, what matters to an American, is what they are now and what they wish to achieve tomorrow. This is the "American Dream." The French see this as their nightmare. This is their nouveau riche. The French have an enormous sense of their past and the Americans, less so.

Attitude toward the environment is how different cultures view their environment. In some cultures the drive comes from what is within a person; the sense of personal virtues and vice. Here, motivations are derived from within. In other cultures, nature provides the inspiration for what goes on. They see nature and the world around them as more far more powerful than they are, and everything flows from that sense of awe. Which is right? Both, of course! It all depends on the context.

For an international manager to succeed in today's global culture, they must reconcile the differing views of different cultures. There are profound differences between those who show their feelings (such as Italians) and those who hide them (such as the Japanese), and those who accord status on the basis of achievement, and those who ascribe it on the basis of family and age. The international manager must show not just awareness of these differences, but also show savvy about how to address these differences to achieve a win-win situation for all and create wealth.

The approach suggested here to managing cultures and understanding international organization, is in strong contrast to the traditional approach, in which the managers decide unilaterally how the organization should be defined based on physical entities. Traditional models have been based on physical and verifiable characteristics of organizations, which are assumed to have a common understanding for all. Instead of this approach, try looking at an organization in ways in which cultures structure the perceptions of what they experience.

Cultural tensions do not limit themselves to organizational and business encounters. Perhaps their breach is brushed aside as ignorance, and out of the need to transact the business at hand. In view of this, those involved may be willing to move on with some concessions. However, with a less sophisticated populace, such concessions may not be an option. For example, when the U.S. service personnel were waving at the welcoming Iraqis after the fall of Baghdad in 2004, they were waving at them with their left hands because they were holding their weapons with their right. In that culture, the left hand is considered unholy and many took offense at this simple gesture of friendly greeting.

The Layers of Culture

In their book, *Riding the Waves of Culture*, its authors model three layers of culture: The outer layer with explicit products, the middle layer of norms and values, and the inner core layer, which comprises assumptions about existence. To understand how someone from a particular culture will behave or respond in a situation that affects an organization, all three layers are important. For detailed discussion of how to address the three layers in everyday circumstances and context of an organization, please refer to this and other cited references.

Summary Chapter-9: Working Globally

In today's environment, working with global cultures is central to how companies operate. Cultures provide the context in which business takes place and is based on the following seven factors:

- Universalism vs. particularism

- Individualism vs. communitarianism

- Neutral Vs. emotional

- Specific Vs. Diffuse

- Achievement Vs. ascription

- Attitude toward time

- Attitude toward the environment

Each factor is discussed in the light of today's global context.

- There are three layers to the context of culture:

- The outer layer which consists of physical attributes and products

- The middle layer that consists of norms and values

- The inner layer of deeply held beliefs and assumptions about our existence

CHAPTER 10

Just One More Thing: MYOB

"The less justified a man is in claiming excellence for his own self, the more ready he is to claim all excellence for his nation, his religion, his race or his holy cause. A man is likely to mind his own business when it is worth minding. When it is not, he takes his mind off his own meaningless affairs by minding other people's business."
—Eric Hoffer, philosopher and author (1902–1983)

Minding your own business (MYOB) is central to how one shows their commitment to their cause. Knowing when to keep your nose in your own affairs and when not to, in the corporate world, is important.

In business and career, minding your own business is a sign of engagement, commitment, and single-mindedness of purpose. Excellence is achieved by focus, energy, and learning from every action and task. It is when this focus is lost that one gets tempted to find faults with others and to focus on what is not happening with someone else. So, in order to achieve excellence in all that you are engaged in, it is best to keep the focus on what is on your plate and understand that obligation with singular dedication. Losing sight of this often leads to setbacks, grief, and discomposing angst.

The following list is provided as a reminder in case you wander in your ways:

1. **Getting the Job Done:** Merely doing a good—or even a great—job is a necessary condition for success, but it is not sufficient. Doing what is expected is often not enough. Delivering exceptional outcomes consistently is what creates new learning, inspiration, and a sense of purpose. Beyond this, one must learn how to play the game that everyone is expected to play in the corporate world; politics. Why? Work is *also* about politics and perception, especially in the corporate world. What this means is that someone else can, and will, take

credit for your work, and you may not even be aware of it. This is especially true if you telecommute. So much of what is done today is a team effort that, unless you remain visible to those who matter, the work that *you* did will get acknowledged, but, not you!

Sometimes, staying visible entails trumpeting your accomplishments, letting your boss know what you have done and how it creates value beyond merely what is expected, or even what everyone else is doing. Remember: If you do not blow your own horn, someone will use it for a spittoon!

2. **Using the Push-Pull System:** Much of what gets done in today's organization is through teams. The concept of teams is different in different settings: there are tandem teams, relay teams, simultaneous teams and so on. A tandem team works with members in tandem so that the output is the sum of what each contributor puts out. A relay team, on the other hand, works sequentially, so hand-off is important. Simultaneous team is akin to a surgical room team where every person has a role and it is done jointly to fulfill the obligation of the entire team.

   The concept of push-pull comes into play when you have to rely on someone to give their output to get you going; this is your input. So, if your work is delayed because the input to you is delayed then you must resort to push-pull technique. This technique entails pulling on what is due, so that when the previous team members pushes, the joint effort creates an accelerated, or at least, a timely outcome.

3. **Being respectful of others' contributions:** It is easy to criticize what you do not know or understand. So, before you complain about someone or something, make sure that you have carefully reviewed the situation and then explored the best way to create the outcome that benefits the organization. Things often look easy from a distance and when someone else is doing them.

4. **Showing Vulnerabilities:** Because, typically, organizations are so political, it is always a good idea to manage your image. This does not mean that you need a full-time PR person to escort you wherever you go inside your own company, but it does mean that you must always be on guard. Disclosing unwarranted weaknesses can land you into trouble without your even knowing it. Everyone has some weaknesses. Once you disclose them to others, you have no control over

how they are passed down to others, and how they can conduce towards actions that may hurt you now and haunt you later.

The other side of this coin is admitting your own faults or openly acknowledging when you are wrong. No one is perfect, so if you occasionally slip up, openly admit it and move on. If you inadvertently harmed someone in your anxiety to promote yourself, ask for forgiveness from those you harmed.

5. **Trashing others:** This is a typical behavior in many organizations, where people gossip behind someone's back and take pleasure in their setbacks. This behavior is so common that it even has a name: schadenfreude. Before you indulge yourself in this behavior, consider the consequences: for one, you will be branded as a gossip, you will lose your credibility and others will do the same to you.

   If you are the boss and someone comes and rats on a colleague of theirs, who also reports to you or is in your chain of command, you must take action and confront the situation. One approach is to insist that the person they are ratting on join the discussion so that they can defend themselves. Another approach is to insist that the person ratting must have a meeting with their colleague before bringing the complaint to your attention. If people are openly allowed to rat on their colleagues and the managers let this continue unchecked, the work environment becomes toxic. One of the managers' implied roles is to make others feel safe in their leadership and to develop a degree of trust, openness, and fairness among all those who report to them.

6. **Keeping Secrets:** If you know something that is private, or if you experienced something that is personal, keep it to yourself. Even if you think you trust someone, you do not know what relationship that person has with anyone else in the organization. People make strange and covert relationships in an organization all the time.

7. **Personal Ambitions:** We all have them. If they interfere with the express business of your organization, no matter how noble, keep them to yourself and work on your own time pursuing them.

8. **Being Prepared:** If you are vying for a promotion or a position, always find ways to position yourself for that opening. Don't be shy about letting the right people know about your intentions and pro-

tecting your position. Create allies and use your PR nose to promote your cause.

9. **Having a Nose:** As said already, the corporate world is a political breeding ground. If you sense something that does not seem right, trust your instincts and do not go into denial. Prepare for a course of action before the situation gets out of hand and you have to compromise yourself. Consult with a coach, mentor, or a counselor.

10. **Never Falling in Love:** Never fall in love with your company or organization. It cannot love you back! It is normal to admire your boss or a colleague. But, do not transfer that feeling to how you feel about your company. It is less painful that way when things fall apart. They sometimes do.

11. **Playing the Game:** To succeed in the corporate jungle, "fitting-in" is important. This is also called "ethos," (*eethas*) which means "I am like you" in Greek. In the corporate survival game, ethos is central to fitting in. This means that you are more likely to be accepted if you dress, talk, and walk like the rest. Many often confuse this tip with being the "yes" employee. Nothing could be further from the truth.

One central principle of success, is never losing sight of who you are and your values. So, if someone in your chain of command makes a decision that offends you, you must feel free to talk this out with your boss and to make your views known. The consequences of such action depend on what each situation is but, you must voice your objection and make known your views. In the corporate world, you must follow a decision even if you do not personally agree with it.

Ethos is why you so often see all top-level executives in a large organization coming from the same alma mater. Many often drive the same model automobiles (especially when they are not company issues). This is a terrible indictment of the social life and the culture in a corporation, but being aware of this is central to knowing how to behave. You may chose not to go along with the game, but then it is a conscious choice.

Knowing this culture is important before getting into an organization. In Chapter-9: Working Globally we introduced the three layers of culture that fall into two categories: explicit and implicit. The former category includes Artifacts and Products on the one hand and

Norms and Values on the other. These items are easy to spot during interviews and perhaps in personal encounters early on. The latter, the implicit category, include basic assumptions, which are much harder to penetrate.

To succeed in the corporate race, being aware of this expectation is critical. If you are unable to reconcile to this idea, you must honestly appraise your own chances of success in your current place of work and decide if you need to make a change.

12. **Confiding in HR:** In troubled times or when there is confusion about organizational issues, employees often resort to seeking help from their Human Resources department. Many employees also believe that, in times of trouble, the Human Resources department is their friend; someone they can go to with a problem of a personal nature and seek help. In many companies, especially those that have earned the reputation for being employee-centric, this can indeed be the case. Many HR departments also offer employee assistance programs (EAP) to help employees with their personal problems, in addition to serving as mediators in the matters that relate to controversies and conflicts. Going to HR and confiding *all* your troubles may not always be in your best interest. HR is often consulted in matters of promotions, transfers, and career advancements, as they should be. Once they know something about your past, it is their obligation to share that with the management at such times, because it *is* their job to do so. If you want confidential help, seek a personal therapist, coach, or an outsider whom you trust. Many EAP services are sourced, so you can assess for yourself the degree to which your confidence will be protected. Seek HR's help when you decide that they are best positioned to offer you their services in matters of resolving conflicts, getting clarity, or providing a perspective that comes from having encountered similar situations. In interpersonal and intra-organizational matters, often, HR expertise can be invaluable. They are professionals at handling such matters and can be a great resource if you know how best to use that resource.

Summary Chapter-10: Just One More Thing: MYOB

Surviving and even thriving in the corporate environment requires special strategies that are often counterintuitive. When uncertainties prevail and employees feel insecure, there is a growing tendency to expand your focus away from your own work and become interested in others' activities. The best strategy in such times is to keep your focus and to diligently do your own work by not just delivering expected performance, but exceptional results; going well beyond what you boss, customer, and organization expect.

The following list is provided as a reminder, in case you wander in your ways:

1. Getting the Job Done

2. Using the Push-Pull System

3. Being respectful of others' contributions

4. Showing Vulnerabilities

5. Trashing others:

6. Keeping Secrets

7. Personal Ambitions

8. Being Prepared

9. Having a Nose

10. Never Falling in Love with your company

11. Playing the Game

12. Confiding in HR

Epilogue

"Every company has two organizational structures: The formal one is depicted on the charts; the other is the everyday relationships in the organization."

—Harold S. Geneen, Chairman, ITT (1959–1979)

To the uninitiated, working in today's corporate environment and becoming successful can be a daunting challenge. One reason is, that, to many, a business or an organization can be a mystery, a hostile place where things happen over which they have no control. This sense of their mystery and lack of control are wrapped in how people interact, behave, how the business drivers shape the organization's future, how managers manage—or mismanage—how leaders lead, and how followers follow to get anything worthwhile done. So, to approach the challenge of working in today's business culture, not just in the U.S., but also anywhere in the world, is overwhelming to many corporate citizens. Since organizations are people, brought together for a common cause, those wanting to understand the rules of the corporate jungle need to understand, at least to some extent, how people behave.

Corporations run a business. A business is a system of many "components," typically comprising of the organization(s) that make its backbone, the people who make the various organizations, the economic system in which the business operates, the management systems which support its workings, the leadership processes that provide the guiding vision to the organization, and the myriad of cultural, social, and value-based rules that define its workings. Of the myriad components that constitute this system, the one perceived as most unpredictable is its people. And it is because of this, that those trying to make sense of how organizations behave focus so much on people. Ironically, people are more predictable than most believe. . It is the system in which they operate that defines their predictability. If the rules of the system are known, how people behave in is no longer a mystery. The purpose of this book is to codify the rules of organizational and business systems.

This book emerged from the overwhelming need of many who feel lost in the flux of all these factors that they find overwhelming. The approach this book has taken is to codify the systems, processes, and the social rules that make an organization and business successful. In the process, the book has attempted to codify how people behave in predictable ways, once we understand their environs.

People are poor communicators. This factor alone results in a perception that people are the most unpredictable element in an organizational setting. People often confuse the frequency of their communication with its quality. In fact, frequent communication is often known to block learning. Just look at this way, the person you are closest to—say, someone in your family—perhaps, communicates with you constantly. But, how well do you really know this person? It is the constant flow of communication that sometimes prevents you from asking the most critical questions that lead to the learning necessary to increase human understanding.

Oral, face-to-face communication is hard. What exacerbates that challenge is the myriad technological means that we routinely use in business to get things done expeditiously. For example, how a message is communicated, has much to do with its quality. An email sent to your
boss when you want to resign from your current job in normal circumstances would be inappropriate as a first piece of news to them, no matter how carefully it is phrased, as would be when someone is terminating an employee using the email as a first means of that message. Yet, it is known to take place. Most have trouble articulating their thoughts in a clear and concise language, so when the receiver lacks the ability to fully decipher a message, it creates its own dynamic. Does this mean that we should abandon everything but oral and face-to-face communication in the corporate world? Of course not!

What is suggested here, is that how we communicate, and what we say in the way we communicate, has much to do with its affect. In his now classic article, *The Human Moment at Work*, Edward Hallowell in the January-February 1999 issue of the *Harvard Business Review,* demystifies why people are so stressed out in today's world, obsessed with electronic communication in the corporate environment.

Hallowell defines the Human Moment as an authentic psychological encounter that can happen only when two people share the same physical space. He contends that the disappearing human moment is at the root of many misunderstandings and is at the start of toxic ferments that drive people crazy in today's organizations. So, one cardinal rule of survival in the corporate world today, is to manage to work in the human moment with those that affect your life. This prescription is directed to both the manager and the employee.

Communication is a two-way process. In the world now gone flat[4], where teams separated by vast distances and cultures work "seamlessly," capturing such a human moment is a challenge.

Yet another area of mystery is how the organizational and management processes work in a social setting driving a business. Chapter-2: Organizational Basics and Chapter-3: Management Basics are presented to help disabuse and demystify these areas. They provide a systemic treatment of how these processes work—or should work—and provide the foundation for their understanding. If everyone in an organization—from those in the boardroom to the ones in the mailroom—developed some awareness of these basic skills, *Dilbert* may soon become the relic of our corporate zeitgeist and will be accorded the same Jurassic curiosity as we still do with the *Flintstones*!

As technology and globalization propel ongoing changes in how organizations are evolving, human interactions are going to be disparaged. And yet, it is this very direction that is going to demand that we act more humanly in everything that we do. This is why Chapter-8: Taking Care of the Customer is presented. Today's emerging \corporate culture, with emphasis on "instant everything" is alienating customers. This is an extension of what we just discussed with the employees feeling alienated in their own daily work life. The irony here is that we communicate more with the customers than ever—more surveys, more products, more options, and more product messages—and, yet, by that very act, we are blocking building relationships with them. They are getting increasingly fed up with their impersonal treatment that they are accorded as a result. This prescription is not much different from the one presented earlier: bringing back the human moment!

In summary, the following list is provided to help those who are looking for a sound bite to help them survive the corporate jungle:

1. As you get settled in your organization, group, and job, try to really understand what the business is about, how the organization helps it deliver a better value proposition to its customers, and what your role is, in the overall scheme of things.

2. Engage fully to learn everything there is to learn in every assignment that comes your way. Take it on as a gift. You enrich your perspective

---

[4] *The World is Flat: A Brief History of the Twenty-First Century*, Thomas Freedman, Farrar, Strauss & Gerot, New York, 2005

by doing things that you love and also by doing things that you may begin to love. A thing well done, is a reward in itself.

3. Is there a good agreement between you, your team, and your immediate boss about how you create value in alignment with #1, above?

4. Do you understand the management process that drives your organization? Do you understand the leadership process that drives the people who accomplish what they set out to do? Do you understand the difference between a manager and a leader?

5. How well do you communicate? Improving communication is a lifelong endeavor. What are you doing for your part?

6. How well do you know the customer? This applies to everyone in an organization, not just those in sales, marketing, support, or a typical customer-facing function. What have you done to improve the customer bond? What have you done to stamp out the meaningless customer surveys?

7. Do you know your business ecosystem? Do you know your suppliers, partners, and alliances? What are you doing to make them a better part of your ongoing business?

8. How well do you know different cultures? What have you done today to understand someone from a different culture who works just in the next cubicle?

9. With exploding information, having to work across 24 time zones and instant access through technology, people are working longer and harder in a growingly complex environment. The actual time the knowledge worker spends at their job has gone up in the past two decades. Manage your time and work, and make work/life balance your priority.

10. What have you done today to make someone's day a little brighter, even though your own day is not all it could have been?

11. If you cannot change your fate, change your attitude!

APPENDIX I

Managing Upward: *Managing* Your Boss

"If you do not manage your boss, she cannot manage you!"

—Anonymous

Managing your boss appears like an ironic or oxymoronic phrase! Why? Most assume that it is the boss's responsibility to manage you and not the other way around. Yet, *Dilbert,* the most widely syndicated cartoon strip that pokes humor at the incompetent boss that Dilbert cannot seem to manage, is the most widely read comic strip that almost anyone who has worked in the corporate jungle can relate to. This is, perhaps, because many find the message that consistently showcases the everyday plight of a Dilbert-like worker, undeniably resonant.

Why, then, is managing your boss such an important part of a job? Although not all career ladders are full of bosses like Dilbert's, the image that cartoon strip projects of that of a mean, incompetent, inconsiderate, vindictive, and power-hungry boss is somehow identifiable to many who see vignettes of these characteristics in varying degrees in their own bosses. Often such bosses are so intent on their own welfare and advancement that they completely ignore and even trample the needs of their subordinates with impunity and total disregard.

If you feel that you are maundering through your job, getting no where, especially with your own boss, then you must become aware of how to manage your boss. Worse yet, if your boss is undermining your efforts and you are at risk of losing your job, not because of what you did or did not do, but because of what your boss did, then you must awaken to a new reality.

Before taking for granted what your boss is going to do for you, or if you feel unappreciated, frustrated, dumped on, or set up for a fall, ask yourself these questions:

➢ What is my goal with this particular job or assignment?

➢ What is my superiors' agenda and what is their style of managing?

➢ How will they know the real contribution I have made in advancing their agenda?

➢ What must I do to work within their framework so that I can be viewed as a valuable contributor without compromising my values?

➢ What can I do to rise above my colleagues to make a positive impression on my chain of command?

➢ If I stay and commit myself to the current job, what can I do to help myself and to help my boss to succeed?

➢ If I decided to move on how can I prevent getting into a similar situation—or even worse—with my next boss?

➢ Can I change my boss? (Ha! No one has changed anybody)

The following list is provided to help those who wonder about the process of managing their boss:

1. Have an initial meeting with your boss as you come on board (or if you get a new boss midstream).

2. If you have not had such a meeting to begin with, it is never too late to have one.

3. In this meeting clearly lay out roles, responsibilities, expectations, measurements, rewards, and deliverables. Boss's role and responsibilities must also be made clear in this meeting.

4. If you are in a matrix organization with two (or more) bosses, make sure that you keep them in the loop. Have individual meetings regularly. If you do not agree with the way things are going with the project boss (the one to whom you are assigned) meet with your functional boss (the one who writes your reviews and manages your salary) and get their support.

5. Agree on a scheduled reporting structure and the method of reporting. A weekly summary of progress and issues can be sent to the boss by email every Friday afternoon. If any items need attention or help, they must be at the top of this short message that is more in a bul-

letized form than as a long narrative. Also, it should be presented as an exception report than as a status report.

6. Under promise and over deliver. Move from managing expectations to managing excellence.

7. Periodically sit down with your boss and ask for their ongoing agenda and how they are driving it. Ask how you can help in their success and show how you have been helping them already. Do not *assume* that because you work for them that they already know this.

8. It is not unusual that your boss will act so busy that there is never time to sit down. Everything is a whirlwind and you are on your own most of the time. In that case send your boss a note (email) and ask for a meeting. Briefly state what the purpose is at the top and make the note short. If the boss ignores it call and leave a voice mail and, failing a response, write a follow-up note. If the boss continues to avoid meeting you, inform your boss that you are going to escalate the matter and get in touch with HR and the boss's boss. Wait a few days and then meet with them to show them your notes. Better yet, let the HR representative take care of this. By choosing to take this route you have alienated your relationship with your boss. This is a judgment call. Check with your peers to see if they are having a similar experience.

9. Without getting personally close to the boss, develop a relationship of trust and respect. The ideal relationship is when the boss comes to you asking for help in shepherding their agenda or just comes and chats with you when they are having a difficult day.

10. Every quarter schedule to have a substantial meeting (1-2 hours) with your boss. Going out to lunch is a good way to conduct such a meeting. Treat your boss to a nice lunch.

11. If you get a chance to spontaneously compliment your boss for something that they have done well, bring it in a meeting with their superiors and comment on that achievement. Nothing is more gratifying to a boss than when a subordinate conveys to their superiors their great work! Such occasions can quickly change your boss's view of your relationship with them in a very positive way. Just make sure that the compliment is genuine and deserving and not gratuitous, exaggerated, or contrived.

12. Figure out your manager's blind spots or weaknesses. Collaborate with them to neutralize those weaknesses so that your boss looks good to their chain of command.

13. If you do not agree with your boss's stand or views on an issue, do not contradict them in a public meeting, especially when superiors are present. Even if they are not, someone in the meeting will rat on you to elevate themselves.

14. Volunteer to take on jobs that your boss shuns.

15. Request a formal acknowledgement of your contribution from those who benefited from it, especially when they volunteered that information as a compliment. Ask those who can influence your chain of command with inputs about you that can set the tone of your future course of work at the employer. Asking for something in writing to be sent to your chain of command is never a bad idea. It is how you ask that sets the tone of how people respond to it. Also, acknowledging someone, whom you want, in turn, to acknowledge you, can work wonders, both ways.

16. Engage in "straight talk" with those who are undermining your efforts to make things better.

17. Keep your boss informed about what you know is happening around your own circle of awareness. Do not assume that your boss knows what you know. Although gossiping or spreading rumors should not be what you have to resort to, if there is some trouble brewing that affects your boss, keeping your eyes open and then communicating what is happening to your boss can only help your relationship.

18. Focus on the organization and place its agenda ahead of yours or your boss's. Always keep the big picture in mind in every action you take.

19. If a task or the job itself does not work out, do not personalize the failure. May be changing the place of work is your best option. Find ways to put the best face on what you have done and honestly discuss with your boss what might be done better. Move on with a positive outlook, without blaming anyone, especially your boss.

20. If your boss sees you as a threat because, perhaps, you are an overachiever or that you have more to offer than does your boss, slow

down and see if you can collaborate with others, including your boss, to improve the situation. If this does not work move on.

21. If your boss is like Dilbert's they are riddled with insecurities and self doubts. Do not openly challenge them or threaten them, this makes their insecurities worse. Because of the power they hold they can make you pay for your criticism.

22. Always show respect for your manager's position, if not for them personally. Remember, they are the manager and hold the power of employment over you!

23. In today's world, every employee is expected to do more. Always be on the look out for learning something new and increasing your value to your boss and the organization.

24. Avoid going around your boss to their superiors. If you must or that if it happens because the superiors initiate it, make sure that your boss is immediately apprised of this and the circumstances. When this happens do not get ahead of yourself by undermining your boss.

25. Find out what your boss does for fun, charity, or hobby. If you can connect that way, it is always a plus.

26. It is a good idea to explore your boss's Type (see chapter-4: Managing your own journey, Specifically Myers Briggs Type) by directly asking and then looking at how you can manage your interaction. For example if your boss is ISTP and you, an ENTJ, then make sure that when you present an idea, go with data (she is an "S"), do not force a decision (she is a "P" and you a "J"). Such strategies generally work well to increase your "compatibility."

27. Remember: An ounce of loyalty is worth more than a pound of cleverness!

28. Act positively and smile often. People often wonder about those who smile and it annoys other enough to make it worth your while.

29. If all of this sounds basic, it is. But, how many do not follow this simple prescription and suddenly get surprised by a "Notice of Concern" or a sudden and unexpected termination or a layoff?

Making *Your* Monkey Your Boss's Monkey

In a now classic *Harvard Business Review* article, Who's Got the Monkey?, the article goes into how different tasks get passed up and down an organization because of their priorities, prestige, and impact. In these days of stretched resources, overcommitted projects, and customer expectations that change day to day, it is not unusual to see your project being compromised by such forces. One way to stay on track is to try to marshal resources and get someone to help you on your derailed task, or to make up for the lost time because the project was underscoped. This is often stressful and counterproductive. A better approach is to make the problem you face, your boss's problem. Taking this stance allows you to transfer the monkey from your back to your boss's! They have the ability to control resources far better than you do. In such situations the person who makes the loudest noise gets attention.

When you get into a project deadline jam because of sudden loss of resources, the best approach is to meet with your boss (or program manager) and coolly notify them that because of what has happened your meeting with the client to report the project progress will have to be delayed. Then mention that you plan to notify the client in one or two days (depending on the meeting frequency) about the delay and a recovery plan based on your own assessment. Bosses do not like to upset clients and potentially compromise a client relationship. By this action you will be doing two things: you are making your problem your boss's problem and you are keeping the client relationship on track.

Try this approach the next time your project gets its resources suddenly yanked from under you!

APPENDIX II

Managing Meetings

"Meetings take nearly 15 percent of all white-collar time, most of which are unnecessary, unproductive, or unavoidable."
—From a report by a meeting consultant

"In a good meeting there is a momentum that comes from the spontaneous exchange of fresh ideas and produces extraordinary results."
—Harold S. Geneen, Chairman ITT (1959–1979)

A meeting is an act or process of coming together as an assembly for a common purpose. So, a meeting can involve as few as two and as many as several thousand people coming together for a common purpose. In the corporate world, meetings are the most despised and dreaded events. Yet, despite their universal abuse and waste, they continue unabated. One reason why meetings are held despite their negativity is the perception that without them things would be worse! A study conducted by Microsoft involving 1200 corporations and thousands of managers and others in 2005 revealed that nearly 5.6 hours of their time per week is spent in meetings and nearly 66 percent said that the time was wasted. This statistic is cautionary for anyone concerned with productive use of resources. In addition, there is time wasted outside the meeting room: people are often distracted by the impending event and they also linger over the meeting's fallout by talking about what the meeting really meant after it is over. All that time, before and after a meeting, is wasted in addition to the numbers just cited!

Not all meetings have an express business purpose. Some have a hidden agenda! In some instances the overriding purpose for a meeting may be its social tenor where some joyous news is announced, whereas in other instances its purpose is to communicate a serious message that affects a large population. Make no mistake; any meeting held with business associates has an implied and overriding business undertone. Even the annual company Holiday Party or similar event, too, is a business affair, although it may be obfuscated by the presence of spouses, entertainment, and lavish food in a festive ambiance. Because of this, anyone attending it must be wary of what they say and to whom and how they behave, drunk or not!

In any case, conducting an effective meeting is critical to its success. The following list describes different types of meetings:

1. Annual shareholder meeting

2. Board of Directors' meeting

3. Staff meeting

4. Working meeting

5. Status meeting

6. Training meeting/Workshop/seminar

7. Social meeting/Convivial meeting (gathering for pizza, beer, and fun)

Although this list is not inclusive, it represents the most commonly ordered *business* meetings.

The purpose of this appendix is not to provide a comprehensive meeting guide, but to present some reminders and common pitfalls so that effective meetings are not a mystery.

For Meeting Leaders

In this section what meeting leaders are responsible for is identified. In the first part the meeting process is identified. In the second, sequential steps are presented as a checklist to operationalize the process.

The Meeting Process

- Selecting Participants

- Developing Agenda

- Establishing Ground rules

- Managing flow/time

- Evaluating the Meeting

- Evaluating the overall process

- Closing the Meeting

- Canceling or postponing a meeting

The management of a meeting requires a set of skills often overlooked by those organizing it. The following information is a comprehensive set of meeting management suggestions. The reader might pick which suggestions best fit the particular culture of their organization and their own needs. Keep in mind that meetings are very expensive activities when one considers the cost of burdened labor (hourly rate X 3) for the meeting and how much can or cannot get done in the meeting. So, take meeting management very seriously.

The process used in a meeting depends on the kind of meeting you plan to have, e.g. staff meeting, planning meeting, problem solving meeting, etc. However, there are certain basics that are common to various types of meetings. These basics are described below.

Selecting Participants

The decision about who is to attend depends on what you want to accomplish in the meeting. This may seem too obvious to state, but it is surprising how many meetings occur without the right people or worse, how many attend a meeting that they should not.

Don't depend on your own judgment about who should come. Ask several other people for their opinion as well. If possible, call each person to tell them about the meeting, its overall purpose and why their attendance is important. Follow-up your call with a meeting notice, including the purpose of the meeting, where it will be held and when, the list of participants, and whom to contact if they have questions.

Send out a copy of the proposed agenda along with the meeting notice.

Have someone designated to record important actions, assignments and due dates during the meeting. This person should ensure that the information is distributed to all participants shortly after the meeting. Often, though, this task always falls on the person calling and running the meeting. The person hosting the meeting should not merely act as a facilitator but as a leader.

Developing Agenda

Develop the agenda together with key participants in the meeting. Think of what overall outcome you want from the meeting and what activities need to occur to reach that outcome. The agenda should be organized so that these activities are conducted during the meeting. In the agenda, state the overall outcome that you want from the meeting. When someone in a chain of command calls a meeting of their reports or those who are outside their chain of command, but organizationally below them, they can be more directive in such matters.

Design the agenda so that participants get involved early by having something for them to do right away and so that they come on time to the meeting as active participants and not merely as observers.

Next to each major topic, include the type of action needed, the type of output expected (decision, vote, action assigned to someone), and time estimates for addressing each topic

Ask participants if they'll commit to the agenda. Keep the agenda posted at all times.

Don't overly design meetings; be willing to adapt the meeting agenda if members are making progress in the planning process. Think about how you label an event, so people come in with that mindset; it may pay to have a short dialogue around the label to develop a common mindset among attendees, particularly if they include representatives from various cultures.

Opening Meetings

Always start on time; this respects those who showed up on time and reminds late-comers that you mean business. Welcome attendees and thank them for their time.

Review the agenda at the beginning of each meeting, giving participants a chance to understand all proposed major topics, to change them, and to accept them. Note that a meeting recorder, if used, will take minutes and provide them back to each participant shortly after the meeting.

Model the kind of energy and participation you expect from the meeting participants.

Clarify role(s) in the meeting.

Establishing Ground Rules for Meetings

Surely, you don't need to develop new ground rules each time you have a meeting. However, it pays to have a few basic ground rules that can be used for most of your meetings. These ground rules cultivate the basic ingredients needed for a successful meeting. Four powerful ground rules are: participate, get focus, maintain momentum, reach closure, and maintain confidentiality.

List your primary ground rules as an attachment to the agenda. If you have new attendees who are not used to your meetings, you might review *each* ground rule. Keep the ground rules posted at all times. Many meeting rooms have these rules framed and nailed to the walls.

Time Management

One of the most difficult facilitation tasks is time management—time seems to run out before items are completed. Therefore, the biggest challenge is keeping momentum to keep the process moving.

You might ask attendees to help you keep track of the time. A timekeeper is a good idea in a meeting.

If the planned time on the agenda is getting out of hand, present it to the group and ask for their input as to its resolution.

Evaluations of Meeting Process

It's amazing how often people will complain about a meeting being a complete waste of time—but they only say so after the meeting. Get their feedback during the meeting when you can improve the meeting process right away. Evaluating a meeting only at the end of the meeting is usually too late to do anything about participants' feedback.

In marathon meetings, every couple of hours, conduct 5-10 minutes "process" checks.

In a round-table approach, quickly have each participant indicate how they think the meeting is going. Sometimes, using a flip chart and making a "T" and writing a "+" on the left and a "?" on the right will allow you to do a "credit" and a "debit" entry respectively on each side below a horizontal line. The credit entries will list what is going well and the debit entries will list what can be improved. The same form can be used at the end of the meeting as well.

Evaluating the Overall Meeting

Leave 5-10 minutes at the end of the meeting to evaluate the meeting; don't skip this portion of the meeting.

Have each member rank the meeting from 1-5, with 5 as the highest, and have each member explain their ranking. Always use the original agenda and the purpose of the meeting to benchmark its success.

Have the chief executive/chair rank the meeting last. Use the same evaluation in the "T" format as described above.

Closing Meetings

Always end meetings on time and attempt to end on a positive note. At the end of a meeting, review actions and assignments, and set the time for the next meeting and ask each person if they can make it or not (to get their commitment)

Clarify that meeting minutes and/or actions will be reported back to members in at most a week. Make sure that you meet *that* commitment.

Canceling or Postponing a Meeting

Occasionally, a key participant is unable to attend; something gets in the way that interferes with a meeting already planned. Sometimes the reason for holding the meeting becomes irrelevant. In all such cases it is best to cancel or postpone the meeting. The best approach is to quickly notify all those already invited about the status of the meeting and why. It is best to do it before everyone gathers in the room expecting to have a meeting. Once they gather they will linger and socialize because they already have set aside that time, which is now wasted.

Checklist: Before the Meeting

Before the meeting the lion's share of the burden is on the person chairing the meeting. The person who calls a meeting must first decide if the meeting is necessary. In today's corporate world, there are many attractive surrogates for face-to-face meetings: group emails, conference calls, telecasts just to name a few. The face-to-face meetings take the most time and consume the most resources. An in-person meeting versus a virtual meeting is an option that must be weighed carefully, especially with today's myriad options available through technology for conducting a meeting. Organizing such an in-person meeting should be the last resort.

If someone calls a meeting, those attending it or those who are expected to attend must feel free to challenge having the meeting, when appropriate. The following check list is offered as a starting point for an effective meeting:

1. Clearly state the purpose of the meeting. This is different from the agenda. An agenda is a means of achieving the purpose. Be concise in stating the purpose.

2. Carefully identify those who must attend. Invite only those who can add value to the meeting. Do not invite someone just so that they feel included—idlers—or just to impress someone how well you conduct

your meetings. An idler in a meeting can bring down the momentum of an otherwise energizing meeting.

3. Make sure that you list the invitees separately from those who should merely know about the meeting by showing "ccs" next to their names.

4. Have a clear meeting agenda

5. Time, place, duration, and logistical details must be at the top of the announcement

6. If there are any action items from the last meeting that are going to be discussed, the respective actionees and the items must be listed in an appendix to the memo.

7. Ask the recipients who must attend your meeting to RSVP so that if anyone cannot make it, you can identify a substitute, who then could come fully briefed for the meeting. The RSVP loop ensures that the invitation has reached all those who must attend the meeting.

8. Be mindful of the time of the meeting and people's needs. For example, if you plan to hold a meeting that straddles a lunch break, make sure that your notice addresses how lunch will be accommodated. Such simple courtesies can make the difference between a successful meeting and its opposite.

9. Make sure that the meeting facilities are available and are in good order to conduct the meeting. Ongoing maintenance work, construction, lack of utilities in the meeting room can detract from the meeting.

10. Make sure that all physical preparations, including your own presentation material, are in good shape before the meeting. Do not go into your own meeting "winging it."

Checklist: At the Meeting

1. Arrive before the meeting time and make sure that the facility is ready for the meeting.

2. Start the meeting on time, even if some invitees are late. Waiting for others to start a meeting abets dilatory culture. One way to signal that arriving late is rude is to close the door at the appointed hour and then those who are late have to enter the room, with meeting

already in progress. Repeat offenders should be admonished lightly in the meeting and sternly in private. One idea that works is that anyone who comes late drops a dollar into a "I am late" basket. Use these funds for beverage or snack service during these meetings.

3. Once the meeting is underway, read the purpose and make sure that everyone understands it. Then read the agenda. Ask if there are any additions to the agenda items and then adjust the timing and sequence of evens.

4. At the beginning of the meeting state some rules that are obvious. Some companies post these rules in the meeting room as a reminder to all who are in the meeting:

   i.   Only one person speaks at a time

   ii.   Do not interrupt a person speaking

   iii.   Stick to the allotted time

   iv.   Do not have side meetings (see i)

   v.   Speak clearly and loudly

   vi.   Do not meander, get to the point quickly

   vii.   Do not dominate the meeting if you are not hosting it

   viii. Do not laminate a topic with your personal agenda

   ix.   Do not engage in activities that distract from the meeting

   x.   Turn off your cell phone

5. Learn how to handle those who tend to derail the meeting. This requires special skills and these skills are taught at many workshops for conducting effective meetings.

6. Carefully watch the body language of those who are *not* participating. Some participants are shy, some reticent, and some are plain intimidated by the process, although they may not be shy. Watching the body language tells much about when someone wants to say

something but is shying away for whatever reason. A good facilitator brings out the best from everyone in a productive meeting.

7. Always stay on the agenda and on time

8. At the end summarize the meeting detail the action items and the respective actionees, with timelines.

9. At the end, as the host, take a few minutes to stand up by the flipchart and solicit feedback from the participants on how the meeting went, asking them what could be improved. Going to a flipchart, as already suggested before, and drawing a "T" with "+" on the left and a "?" on the right, with a horizontal line below them, jot down participant responses to what went well on the left below the line and what can be improved on the right below the line, can provide some insights about what to repeat and what to avoid in the next meetings. Make sure that you follow this message into your next meetings. Otherwise, doing this exercise looks like it is merely done for show.

10. Make sure that you are still watching the "air time" and are still under the time limit you set for the meeting. Also, be mindful of giving equal "air time" to those who participate. Some tend to hog all the attention in a meeting, even though they have little to say of any substance.

11. Once this is done, ask again if anyone has any other comments, listen and then announce that the meeting is adjourned. If you want to linger over after the meeting with those who have time, it is up to you.

12. Leave the meeting room in the same or better shape than when you entered it before the meeting.

Checklist: After the Meeting

1) Translate your meeting notes into "Minutes of today's meeting" and summarize key points. List action items and actionees, with dates and other details.

2) If known, include the time and place for the next meeting

3) Send copies to all who attended, to the actionees, and anyone else who needs it. Do this within 24 business hours of the meeting. After that time you can no longer call it "today's meeting."

4) If anyone was disruptive in the meeting and you sense this as an ongoing behavior, meet with them one-on-one and explore what the root cause is of their negative behavior. Do not threaten.

5) If you run into anyone, who attended the meeting, pause and ask how their action item is coming, if they were assigned one. Your explaining something that needs clarification can save someone time in completing their action item.

Checklist: For Participants

Of course, the rules and protocols stated above apply to the meeting leaders as well as those who are going to attend the meeting. The participants face their own challenges in a meeting and are often unable to overcome them. As a result, many feel disenfranchised or even intimidated by the meeting process. The following suggestions are offered to those who feel lost in the process of the meeting jungle.

1) Be aware of your role in the meeting and stay within the bounds of that role so that you are not shut out.

2) If you are shy and feel under the gun to participate and articulate your view, become aware of it and seek help. There are many training courses available that can help you overcome this fear. Joining Toastmasters or a similar group and actively participating in their program can be a boon to your meeting savvy.

3) If you feel paralyzed by the fear of being made a fool if you participate, meet with the meeting leader before hand and ask for their help. Since they want the meeting to be successful, they will coach and help you to succeed in this endeavor.

4) If you are shy, seat next to someone who supports you and look for their active support during the meeting. Ignore those who signal their disapproval at your participating in the meeting.

5) If you are reticent and shy, start small and learn how to participate to gradually increase your "air time." Continue getting coached by the meeting leader.

6) Conduct your own mini-meetings to overcome the fear, shyness, and mystery of managing meeting. This is a learned and valuable skill.

7) If you have your sights on management or leadership jobs, being able to conduct effective meetings is one of the basic skills expected. In fact, if you show your skills by conducting meetings before you have to, you create visibility for yourself in ways that will help promote your agenda in ways far better than otherwise possible.

A Note: As one moves up the management ladder, communications skill is central to that move. Those who communicate effectively, both individually and in public forums, have a clear advantage over others. One of the best resources to develop communication skills is the program offered by Toastmasters International, a non-profit organization founded in 1924. Its mission: "To afford practice and training in the art of public speaking and in presiding over meetings and to promote sociability and good fellowship among its members." Today, there are over 200,000 members in 90 countries and there are dozens of Toastmasters Clubs in local communities.

APPENDIX-III

The Immigrant Professional

"Management in a global environment is increasingly affected by cultural differences."
—Geert Hofstede, cultural diversity pioneer (1928–)

The U.S. is an immigrant nation. More than any other country, people of all talents come here to pursue their dreams. In the current labor pool of 140 million workers, nearly a third is first-generation immigrants. Nearly 17 percent are their children who were born citizens in this country, also known as American Born Citizens (ABC).

First-generation immigrants face challenges that are unique. Their challenges span the gamut: social, economic, language, culture, are among the few that are prominent. As a first-generation immigrant gets integrated in to the workforce, they learn to do things differently to integrate into their place of work. Some do this well and some struggle throughout their career. This appendix is aimed at helping those who are open to learning new ways to making themselves effective quickly at their place of work.

Different immigrants face different challenges. Those who come from Western Europe are the least likely to feel these challenges, especially if they speak English well, or if it is their main language. Language is the first barrier. So, even those who are Caucasian, but come from European Common Market (ECM) countries that do not speak English, face their own set of challenges. The one who are most challenged are those who come from a diverse cultural background and those who are not able to converse well in the native language: immigrants from Eastern European block, Russia, Japan, China and parts of the Pacific Rim are just a few typical in this category.

As it relates to the workplace the following suggestions are offered to all first-generation immigrants as a group. The ones that do not apply to a particular group, for example, mastering English as a Second Language (ESL), are provided merely as a reminders to those who should consider themselves lucky that they have one less thing to conquer in fully integrating themselves in the U.S. workforce to be effective:

1. In most organizations immigrants are a minority. This means that an immigrant worker must make efforts to integrate into the work culture and become part of the group to which they are assigned.

2. One of the first impressions with which the work group deals with you, as an immigrant, is their preconceived notions—stereotypes— about a certain nationality or culture. This stereotyping is rampant in almost every country, not just in the U.S. What this means is that your colleagues are going to approach you with their preconceived notions (Mostly negative. That is what stereotyping is) about you, without even ever having met you. It is important to know what they are for a particular group of immigrants. Generalizations are different from stereotyping. These are generalized observations (both positive and negative) about a certain ethnic group. Once you know how you are being perceived then you can manage that perception by compensating for it.

   How? One approach is to go out of the way to show that you are not what your colleagues already think about you in a stereotypical way— often out of ignorance and arrogance—and compensate for that perception. For example, if they see you, as a part of the group that is perceived as rude, then you can learn to show your politeness in an overt way in every encounter that you have with your colleagues, at least initially. Knowing these perceptions is invaluable. One source of such information is the late night TV shows and comedy. Many such shows and comics poke fun at different cultures and nationalities by scripting their shows or dialogs in an exaggerated way to make a point. Watching such shows provide an avenue of becoming aware of what such perceptions are. Once you become aware, it is easy to manage how you compensate for them in your own way. If you practice the right behaviors long enough, you may internalize the "right" ones and never have to worry about them again!

3. Much of the treatment accorded to immigrant workers is a matter of their own attitude. The old saw, you attract what you project is true even here. For example, if you perceive yourself as someone who is not being included in the social events of your group, then you must

make efforts to be included in social events by making special efforts. One way is to volunteer to do something for a group. What usually compounds the problem is when the person withdraws, sulks, or just becomes passive aggressive. Such tactics will only exacerbate the situation and further alienate you from the rest.

4. Immigrants often bring their own strengths to a work group, either as technical skills, social skills, or something that makes them interesting and valuable. The best way for you to ingratiate yourself with the others is to make use of those skills to the benefit of the group. Once you are seen as a valuable member of the work group who can create value beyond just doing your job well you will be able to integrate better with the rest.

5. Pride in one's ethnic and national heritage is normal. Imposing your preferences on others unilaterally can be seen as inconsiderate and, done often, may even alienate you from the group. For example, if you are from China or of a Chinese descent, organizing a group lunch at a Chinese restaurant on your own may come across as someone who imposes their preferences on others. Chinese food is often favored by many anyway. So, the best way to organize such a lunch is to ask the group openly to choose a place. If this turns out to be a Chinese restaurant, then you are not the one who came up with that suggestion.

6. Many cultures, especially Asian, are steeped in deferential treatments of the superiors and elders. Some even believe that what the boss says is to be obeyed unconditionally. This may not always work to your advantage. Having a healthy dose of doubt about what your boss wants you to do and how can be a good thing. This attitude can be learned by watching those who know how to do this well and, at the same time, having a healthy respect for their own work.

7. Many immigrant professionals believe that they are being held back because of their origins. They also perceive that others, less capable than they, get ahead at their cost. Often, such perceptions are misguided. Many immigrants mainly focus on their work, which is good. But, in many organizations, more is expected. This can be an ability to socially do things well, speak well, and having the right image. Some do not make an attempt to change their image by consciously working on it. Image consultants, coaches, and professional organi-

zations as Toastmasters can help many who feel that they can benefit from an intervention. See a brief write-up in Appendix-II: Managing Meetings, on Toastmasters.

8. It is normal for an immigrant to socialize at work with those of their own background. This often limits their social circle and, over time, can be to their detriment. Although it is beneficial to join a group of individuals who come from the same cultural or national background as a support group, it is a good idea to keep such associations outside the place of immediate work.

9. Those who are not raised with English as their native or main language find an extra level of difficulty in being accepted as part of a group. Being able to speak and understand colloquially is one of the easiest ways to ingratiate oneself with a group. But, being able to do this requires diligent effort. Even though you may have an accent, speaking fluently and understanding everyday conversational English is one of the easiest ways to break into a group. Joining a community college to take a course on ESL, attending and participating at a Toastmasters meeting, learning new words, watching and learning from popular TV shows are some of the ways this process can be accelerated. Forcing yourself to speak English at home is yet another way to improve your language.

10. Reading about the everyday cultural events and society's problems can be a good avenue to learn about the norms. Reading syndicated advice columns in newspapers can provide such avenues.

11. One of the areas many non-English speaking immigrants find themselves challenged is in meetings. They often feel left out and complain that they are unable to get their message across in a meeting. Their common complaint is that they do not get a chance to speak because others dominate the meetings. Speaking up in meetings requires confidence, an ability to forcefully state your point, and an ability to listen well. All of these can be learned skills. Starting out small and then gradually increasing your participation can be a good way to overcome this apprehension.

12. Many immigrants often complain that they do not get included in social groups because their inability to talk about sports, politics, or local happenings. There is no substitute for having the knowledge of

the topic and then having some opinion on it to become part of the conversation in a group.

13. One avenue for rapid integration is to find a mentor. There could be a multiplicity of mentors. But, having one at work who is from the majority ethnic group can be a good way to integrate into a work group. This is also a good way to enrich the mentor by sharing your values and culture with them.

APPENDIX IV

The Human Moment at Work

"The human moment has two prerequisites: peoples' physical presence and their emotional and intellectual attention."
—Edward Hallowell, author of The Human Moment

In a business world increasingly going virtual, humans have become growingly more alienated. What has accelerated the disappearance of simple human contact in many business interactions and transactions is growing use of technology in almost every thing that a business does. At the core of it, though, it is the humans who actually make intelligent decisions, build relationships, and come up with creative ways of expanding a business. Increasing absence of simple human interactions has greatly increased the levels of stress in an everyday existence as it relates to work life. This toxic stress spills over into our personal life and there is no escaping of the vicious cycle of increased stress leading to not having time for human contact, which leads to even greater stress.

With increasing use of emails, instant messages, voice mails, and distant communication, human beings on the one hand have been brought closer. The advent of email alone has resulted in more frequent communication between people who did not even communicate before. People reach across the globe just to touch base with those that matter to them in ways that they did not before. But, the irony in this development is that it has created an illusion of a relationship that is, in fact, purely transactional. This is the case of good communication that blocks relationship building!

Most business communications tend to be transactional in nature. As a result, they tend to be functional more than having any emotional component. Personal communication that has greatly increased as a result of the email becoming ubiquitous, on the other hand, tends to be more intimate and emotional.

In the business world this increasingly impersonal, functional, and harried way of communicating has alienated those who engage in these communications. Emails are notoriously casual, cryptic, or even abrupt—hence rude in may instances. Recipients of such emails often interpret such messages as emotional assaults on their sensibilities and they become gradually isolated from those who unwittingly engage in such communications. It is because of these instances and their growing trend in business that the human moment is becoming so critical in its need. Without such a human moment those who are involved in ongoing communications that avoid the human touch, become too isolated, gradually becoming less resilient. Once they lose their resilience, they gradually become brittle and stressed, reaching a breaking point. This now starts a vicious cycle as their own outgoing messages become the very examples of what got them in this space in the first place.

An antidote for this vicious cycle and the feeling of isolation is the creating and nurturing of the human moment. As the quote at the top suggests, it requires two or more humans in the same physical space willing to share their thoughts and emotions in an open and mindful ways.

The following list suggests how to avoid a brownout and an eventual burnout resulting from the ongoing lack of the human moment and how to prolong the period between the need for the human moment in our increasingly virtual world:

1. When sending email messages, especially those that disparage the recipient in some way or demean what they have done, crafting the message with care can be a great way to prevent premature burnout for its recipients and, in turn, for you. Remember, for every action there is equal and opposite reaction!

2. Do not send angry or upset emails. Instead, pick up the phone and talk to the person one-on-one. Do not leave an angry voice mail, either.

3. Sending a message down the chain of command, the higher-ups have to be particularly careful in crafting their messages as they are typically read and re-read many times. Each subsequent reading can increase the perception of the severity of a message. For more tips see Appendix-X: Job Etiquette: eMails.

4. Make a point of regularly meeting with those with whom you frequently communicate by distant methods, as emails, voice mail, video conferencing, etc. Make a scheduled meeting that periodically allows you to have a face-to-face discussion in an intimate and personal way. If this is not doable schedule a meeting where you connect

just to chat without an express agenda and openly discuss what is working and what can change in the way you conduct business and in your relationship.

5. When in doubt about a message and its delivery mode, always decide in favor of a more personal way to communicate: from email to phone, from phone to a group meeting and from a group meeting to a personal meeting.

6. Much of the pent-up anger and resentment can be diffused with an occasional message of encouragement and good news. Catch someone doing something right and send a warm message of appreciation.

7. Send a note in a memorable way: a Thank You! note in the mail sent to their desk or office, a card in the interoffice envelope, or a greeting card to the home address.

APPENDIX V

Emotional Intelligence

"Weakness of character is the only defect which cannot be amended."
—Francois De La Rochefoucauld (1613–1680)
French Classical Writer

"Life cannot be classified in terms of a simple neurological ladder, with human beings at the top; it is more accurate to talk of different forms of intelligence, each with its strengths and weaknesses. This point was well demonstrated in the minutes before last December's (2004) tsunami, when tourists grabbed their digital cameras and ran after the ebbing surf, and all the 'dumb' animals made for the hills."
—B.R. Myers, author (1963–)

Emotional Intelligence (EQ) is increasingly being regarded as a major factor in professional and personal success, not just in the corporate world, but in general. Many regard this single factor as being more important than the Intelligence Quotient (IQ). Some of the more successful people today in various areas of human endeavor are those regarded as having a high level of emotional intelligence, whatever their IQ. The concept of EQ has to do with how you relate to other people and to yourself successfully. This is one of the factors in the portfolio of soft skills that have become increasingly important in today's world, growingly dehumanized by the ubiquity of high-technology in our everyday life. With the growing emphasis on soft skills, employees and managers alike are expected to have the EQ savvy to be able to relate well to others socially and in a business situation. A survey of 1200 successful leaders conducted in late 2005 revealed that the one characteristic that stands out common among all is "affection." This implies their ability to show affection—even "tough love"—and, in return, be loved stands out as a single attribute that defines a successful leader. This does not mean that they are also a successful manager. That entails a different filter, with characteristics such as creating shareholder value, profitability, and other "Wall Street" yardsticks. But, to be a successful manager, the ingredients of a leader are required.

John D. Mayer, a noted psychologist, defined Emotional Intelligence as the ability to perceive, integrate, understand, and reflectively manager one's own and other people's feelings.

Most people experience a range of both positive and negative emotions at work. For example:

- Satisfaction: You have done a great job at work

- Exhilaration: You just won a major contract or a recognition award

- Pride: You have helped someone out of a difficult situation

- Anger: Someone has sabotaged your work and taken credit for it. Your contribution is not acknowledged properly. Someone trashed your work.

- Frustration: Your recommendation get enthusiastic nod, but then they go nowhere

- Anxiety: You are having trouble keeping up

- Worry: You are wondering if you are next on the chopping block

- Paranoia: You wonder if everyone is talking negatively about you behind your back

- Disappointment: Your project did not get funded and a lesser one did

We, as humans, are bundles of emotional energy first, intelligent machines second. When any one or more of these emotions bubble up during the course of our everyday work experience, an emotional response is triggered first as a result of even how our brain—the source of our intelligence—is programmed. Acting on such impulses can lead to a response that can cause us regrets later. Emotional intelligence is acknowledging such feeling—positive and negative—but is not acting on them behaviorally. In this regard what Socrates said nearly 2500 years ago still holds true in the context of this topic: "*Remember that there is nothing stable in human affairs. Therefore, avoid undue elation in prosperity or undue depression in adversity.*" The implication of this suggestion is twofold: It behooves us to always *act* rationally in our own behavior, but to show emotion and concern when it relates to our dealing with others.

Emotional intelligence is not a natural gift but a nurtured one. This is why it is worth the effort to understand how to increase your awareness of this factor. The advantages of developing your emotional intelligence are several:

- ➢ Improve your self awareness

- ➢ Improve your relationships with colleagues, partners, and associates

- ➢ Help you keep yourself under control and centered

- ➢ Help you lower your stress and keep your emotions under check

- ➢ Improve your approachability: this is particularly important for managers and senior executives

- ➢ Enable your communication: Dialog openly with others and influence others with less conflict

- ➢ Enhance your standing: Influence your colleagues, managers, and customers

- ➢ Develop trust: In times of anxiety and turbulence, people will look up to you for guidance, not because you are smarter, but because they will trust you to be centered.

Theories of Emotional Intelligence

The phrase "emotional intelligence" was first coined by two U.S. psychologists John D. Mayer and Peter Salovy in the 1980s. Daniel Goleman, another U.S. psychologist built on their work and later published several books on this topic. He proposed a five-element framework to define EQ:

- ➢ Self-awareness: An understanding of yourself, your strengths and weaknesses, and how you appear to others.

- ➢ Self-regulation: the ability to manage yourself and think before you act

- ➢ Motivation: the drive to work and succeed

- ➢ Empathy: how you understand other people's view points

- ➢ Social skills: the ability to communicate and relate to others

Other contributors have expanded on this model and added more elements to the list.

To be able to relate to others, managers, especially, must possess the following competencies in today's corporate environment:

- ➤ To be able to manage themselves and not vent their frustrations on their staff

- ➤ Have self-awareness of their *real* strengths and weaknesses

- ➤ Have self confidence in their ability to lead

- ➤ Counsel or coach others within their organization and offer advice

- ➤ Encourage and mentor others

- ➤ Develop good working relationships

Despite a plethora of literature there is no standard way to test for emotional intelligence. There are many free tests available on the Internet and they reflect the flux of where this whole notion is in terms of different views and how EQ is measured. The tests are useful in making people aware of different factors and how they influence the final outcome. Developing your EQ is a lifelong process and hence needs constant attention and vigilance in your everyday social interactions. IQ, on the other hand, is a natural gift, not a nurtured one

For more information visit any of these sites: www.eip.org; www.eiconsortium.org; or www.eicenter.org

APPENDIX VI

The Annual Review and Raise

"Money could not buy you friends, but you got a better class of enemy."
—Spike Milligan, comic (1918–2002)

The annual performance review and the associated salary adjustment is one of the most poorly managed and understood of processes in today's organizations. Why? Most companies do not have a disciplined performance management process that is respected by its employees and management both. Even major players who were considered paragons of employee management and darlings of the Wall Street have been caught flatfooted when their performance management comes under the microscope of legal scrutiny. One Fortune-50 company, known for its employee orientation and focus on performance, was embarrassed to discover that when it was time to layoff nearly 10 percent of its world-wide workforce of nearly 110,000, following the meltdown of the high-tech sector in 2001, it really did not have a uniform performance management and rating system. They originally set out to lay-off the bottom 10 percent of the performers. But, the company discovered that its performance rating and ranking system was not legally defensible. The company finally ended up picking names randomly from the employee roster, losing many valuable employees and demoralizing the rest. What a waste!

Performance review is a controversial topic in organizational contexts. Management guru, W. Edward Deming railed against it in all his writings. This is primarily because the way performance management is administered in most companies. The system often tends to be subjective, arbitrary, and political. Few employees have faith in its integrity and few managers diligently carry out their responsibility well in this area. Yet, in chapter-3 Management Basics, we presented as one of the key activities of management under the functions of *Leading* and *Setting up controls*.

From both managers' and employees' view point, performance reviews must be done in earnest. The process does not start when the due date for a review approaches, but it starts a year prior to that event. The following suggestions are offered to make the overall performance review process more meaningful, productive, and timely:

1. Performance evaluation is an annual process. For the upcoming year, the performance plan must be set in motion in a meeting with your manager about a year prior to the due date.

2. In this meeting identify key performance measures and define key goals that you plan to achieve. Normally, these goals devolve down from the manager's objectives (some companies call it their Hoshin plan) and are specific to your area of responsibility. See Accountability Agreement in chapter-3: Management Basics, to understand how this can be made a part of the performance review process.

3. Agree to a realistic performance plan and define measurements. These measures must be mutually agreed upon and must be easy to accomplish. For example, merely saying "improve employee morale during next year," is not enough. But, stating that employee morale as measured through annual company surveys broken down at the department and section level is more meaningful. Then specifically stating that a 10 percent improvement in certain factor that measures morale through such a survey can lead to unambiguous measurement.

4. In case of project deliverables and milestones it is easier to state what they are and how their completion is measured. Make sure that all assumptions related to such deliverables are clearly stated.

5. In most cases SMART goals are a good way to quantify objectives to achieve. They stand for Specific, Measurable, Achievable, and Time bound.

6. Keeping the achievements to a few key goals is all that is required. In case of personal development areas clearly stating what they are and how they will be measured is critical for an unambiguous outcome. For example, if you have not taken an in-house course on team building, then successful completion of such a course with a certificate in your hand is a good way to have achieved that objective.

7. As the year progresses it is a good idea to visit the key objectives to make sure that they are on track. If an adjustment is needed it must

be made then, otherwise the original commitment stands and it creates a problem, when, at the end of the year, the goals are not met.

8. Most companies carry out their annual review with a 360 degree process. Most employees deliberately choose only those members who will guarantee them a good feedback. Although this is not skullduggery, it defeats the purpose of the annual review, because if everyone gave you a great review, then you do not get the critical input to grow in the areas where your performance is lacking. Such reviews mask blind spots. Please read Key Principles in Chapter-3 as they relate to Developing controls.

9. It is a good idea to include those who normally would not be included in a 360-degree review process. These include suppliers, customers, and anyone else who touches what you do and is affected by your style and performance.

10. If someone gives you a critical input and you guess who that person is, do not call or see that person and attack them for their input. Meet with them personally and discuss the whole report and see where they go with their thoughts during your meeting with them. If you vitiate this process by becoming defensive, belligerent, or otherwise difficult, you have just shut yourself out of a valuable ongoing feedback and growth opportunity.

11. When you meet with your manager, be open to candid feedback. Many get defensive and focus on the ratings and scores. I know many engineers, who reported to me when I was heading the department, quibbled about a few decimal points in their scores! This is irrelevant and even captious. Learning comes from listening to where the areas of growth are and not by focusing on minutia. Always keep the bigger picture in mind. Managers also need to learn how to handle this process well. Many companies do not even train their managers well on how to handle difficult people during this stage and end up compromising the entire process.

12. If any disciplinary action results from the review such as remedial measures, corrective actions, make sure that it is handled constructively. Recipients have spent their entire year looking forward to this meeting; focusing too much on the negative can bring down a person in ways that can make it difficult for them to regroup and jump start their ongoing efforts to be a good employee.

13. Always keep the tone of the entire meeting constructive even though there may be road bumps in the process due to things that did not go well or things that were misperceived. Always figure out how to constructively move forward and improve things so that the next review would be stronger. This applies to both the manager and the person being reviewed.

14. At the end agree on the next year's performance plan and how that can be achieved.

Salary Discussion

In most companies the salary discussion is handled in conjunction with the annual performance review. It is best to have the performance discussion first and, after agreeing on the areas of contribution and improvement, the salary discussion can be held. Never hold the salary discussion before the performance review is presented and concluded. This is because if the salary discussion is held first, it drowns out any constructive performance discussion.

Negotiating a Raise

If you are looking for a raise and are disappointed with the salary increase that was just presented, this is not the time to argue for a bigger increase. A company is not obligated to increase your salary every year or even periodically. Unless you want to have an adversarial discussion on this topic you must plan for this way in advance of this event. The following guidelines are provided on how to approach this sensitive area, where most feel unprepared or ill equipped:

1. The best way to ask for a higher salary is to present a compelling value message that reflects your worth to the organization. One way to do this is to make a list of special contributions you have made during the past year (or period) and monetize them. If you have helped identify pain points and taken the initiatives to eliminate them, then monetizing them as well is a good way to bolster your value to your manager.

2. Do not compare what you currently make with someone else's salary in your own organization. You are not supposed to know other salaries, even if some person told you theirs. What matters is not how you perceive that person creates value for the organization, but how your manager does. This is often non negotiable and taking this approach can create more problems for you than it is worth.

3. Never stake your claim for a higher salary based on your personal needs (sick parents, old car, need to buy first home, etc.). The only consideration for a higher salary is your higher level of value contribution to the organization.

4. If you have salary surveys, especially in your geography, make them as one point of your argument, but not your only argument. It is, after all, about how much value you create for your organization. In many cases the manager is in a better position to assess this than you.

5. Never threaten to quit or leave if you do not get what you want. Never threaten unless you plan to execute that threat. For this to happen, you must already have a job in hand to be using this tactic.

6. Whenever possible do not throw out a number. Let that come from the manager. Giving a percentage range is always appropriate. Once you throw out a number you cannot negotiate it; it is *your* number!

APPENDIX VII

When Is it Time to Move On?

"The secret to survival is knowing when to hold 'em and when to fold."
—Kenny Rogers, singer

"How you leave a job can say more about you than all the work you ever did—particularly if leave badly."

—A CTO

Few people realize that there comes a time in their job when work is no longer fun, but a drag. Sometimes, this happens suddenly, when they get a new boss who does not like them, or that working conditions suddenly change due to a variety of reasons. In most cases, though, reaching this state of no fun happens over time for most and that is why most even do not recognize it. Their pent-up stress eventually become unbearable.

The following list of warning signs is a good check to assess if you are ready to make a transition to a different job (inside or out):

1. **You do not get energized to go to work on Mondays.** Mondays are good barometers of how much you like your job. If you dread going to work on Mondays this is a good sign that you have run the course with your job and that you must move on or make a change. Yet another symptom: once the week gets going, you cannot wait for the weekend and you start planning for that from the first day of the week. Mondays, especially seem to drag on, right from the first hour on the job. For some, this feeling is not just limited to Mondays but every day that they have to go to work. Many seek respite by frequent visits to the restroom, reading material in their hands! Some even

take up smoking so that they get to go out to have a puff or two, away from their desk.

2. **You have a lot on your mind, just not work.** The work doesn't challenge you and time hangs. In meetings you day dream and do not participate. You dread going to meetings to which you are invited and wonder about those where you are not.

3. **In meetings your inputs get ignored.** This is another sign that you are no longer an important part of the team. Even if you suggest something great, it is looked upon with furrowed brow, ignored, or worse, attributed to someone else for credit a bit later.

4. **You do not get important memos/emails.** This is yet another sign that you are on your way out—or should be—and that your existence is tantamount to that of a "parasite."

5. **You get no-win assignments.** If you see yourself being set up for a series of no-win assignments, then you can assume that your boss is setting you up for a "special review" that documents how you have flubbed a series of assignments in a row.

6. **Nearly completed assignments get yanked.** You are about to complete an important project. The project is a bit late for no fault of yours and your boss knows that. Just before you are about to put the final piece of the puzzle in place to complete the project, your boss yanks you from the project and gives it to someone else, who then finishes "on schedule," taking full credit for it.

7. **Someone more junior acts as the boss's proxy.** Someone you regarded as your junior will bring a message from the boss telling you to do something on their behalf.

8. **Things change, not to your advantage.** The boss you got along with so well leaves, or worse, takes on a new favorite employee. Eventually, that person gets layered in above you on the corporate ladder, intercepting your access to the boss, taking over plum projects and moving you out of the decision-making loop. The change is subtle at first, but your loss of status compounds over time.

   Yet another unmistakable sign that you are superfluous is that when your company merges or acquires other companies, those less experienced than you, come to your organization with titles higher than yours.

9. **Your boss takes you for granted.** You do something well and you get pigeonholed as the company expert in that area. Or you're no longer seen as having potential for new projects. Or, just as bad, you're known as the good corporate citizen who'll do whatever you're asked—including relocating multiple times. Another unmistakable sign of your redundancy is that your boss does not include you on a committee that is set up to review something in your area of expertise. When you confront them, a typical rationalization is "I did not want to distract you from what you were doing."

10. **You pigeonhole yourself.** Some top performers stay at their jobs because they don't believe they could succeed elsewhere. The longer you're at a place, the more you think that success depends on your environment, or you lose confidence that you can do anything else. This is particularly true of senior professionals in their mid 40s who are otherwise ready for a promotion (Director, VP)

11. **Your mood ranges from angry to angrier.** No matter how well-regarded your work is, or once was, if you develop a reputation as a querulous crank, colleagues will distance themselves. And that isolation can make you more vulnerable in a layoff.

12. **You feel like hell.** Unhappiness can undermine your health. Early signs of excess stress: stomachaches, headaches and insomnia.

13. **Everyone looks like they're having fun.** You sulk and isolate yourself because no one comes to you for advice.

Hiring may be sparse in your field. You may be supporting a family and need the money—to say nothing of the health insurance. You only have a few years before fully vesting in your stock options. Or you're retiring in less than 15 years and want to maximize the pension you get.

If that's the case and you plan to stay, do more than just sucking it up.

Don't see yourself as a wage slave. See your job as a funding source for what you want to do next. Do what's required and do it as quickly as you can, then network with those who can give you the growth you need for the next job.

And try to develop new skills that will serve you well when you do leave.

Because the trouble with waiting—to vest, to retire, to get promoted—is that it doesn't always pay off. There's nothing stopping employers from letting you go five minutes before you reach your goal. And the terms of your exit will be theirs, not yours.

Sticky Wickets

In any working environment it is not uncommon to encounter situations where important relationships are compromised and you become vulnerable. Your dream job becomes your nightmare and you are suddenly exposed to the threat of termination or that you can no longer perform effectively or in a dignified manner. Let's look at some typical circumstances where such a possibility can arise:

1. The CEO or someone in the chain of command assigns their family member (child, wife, brother/sister) to work under you; the person does not deliver and they do their own thing.

2. An important customer inveigles the CEO to hire one of their family members reporting to you

3. Your boss hits on you

4. Your colleagues/associates hit on you

5. Your colleagues/associates make ongoing attempts to hijack your project

6. Your initiative that has helped the company in a major way is hijacked away from you; you are "reassigned."

7. Your colleagues treat you in a demeaning way

8. You have a fleeting affair with your boss or someone in the direct chain of command

9. You catch a higher-up in a compromising situation (fraud, sexual encounter)

10. You see shenanigans going on that is hurting the company

11. Your boss (or someone higher up) is engaged in a repugnant—even illegal—activity

12. Your organization suddenly gets a new boss who disliked you at a previous job.

Although this is not an inclusive list of misfortunes that can cross your career path or even derail your plans, if not your career, they are representative of today's workplace. They, actually, go back to prehistoric times as their existence stems from the basic human condition. The incidence of aberrant behaviors in the corporate world is no different than what you'd see in the world as a whole. If you are morally centered and have a good sense of balance between "right" and "wrong," you will be outraged by such encounters. Somehow, people think that inside the walls of the corporate world, you should be insulated from anything aberrant. But, when you see this within the confines of the hallowed walls of your own company, all your enthusiasm about your work and about making a difference will be sucked out from you and you may find it difficult getting up and going to work.

This, however, is an emotional reaction to what is happening and the best strategy is to drain the emotion and to deal with it rationally—a very difficult thing to do when you are in the middle of an experience. The following suggestions my help in moving ahead:

1. Do not react in ways that can put you at a disadvantage as far as how others perceive you in your reaction to what has happened to you. You have witnessed what happened to you first hand, but others are merely a party to your reaction to it. Your emotional reaction alone may vitiate the injustice and the outrage you feel. You must keep it bottled up and deal with it in a coolly calculated and rational way. An indignant or even hysterical response may seem appropriate, but it can diminish your power to pursue the correct course of action. Often, as time passes, people merely remember only the affect of your hysteria; the event that triggered it may by undermined by it.

2. Before going to someone within your own organization and giving them an earful, be mindful that everyone has their own agenda. Someone may use this opportunity to further their own agenda by making your situation worse for you. Even if they act with an altruistic motive to help, you do not know how they are going to do it and how that is going to affect your situation. In an emotionally charged situation what is said and what is communicated are often in disagreement.

3. Talk it over immediately with someone you trust—preferably from the outside—so that you can get an objective assessment of what is happening. Be truthful so that you can get an honest assessment of what is happening. Do not embellish or hide parts of what you did if they were less than honorable.

4. If you are going to react to an episode in a continuing saga, pick your battles and use your judgment to take appropriate action. Do not cry wolf!

5. If the person causing you grief is a peer or is at a level below you, dealing with them is easier. Either go to them directly, their immediate superior, or to the HR representative.

6. Some companies have ombudsman function that is assigned to a high-level executive, often off-site. If you trust this process, make an appointment. It is not uncommon, though, to not have the kind of secrecy or even privacy you expect from such meetings. After all, everyone is somehow connected in a company.

7. If you assess that you are fighting an uphill battle, chose a path that allows you to stay for a while, but make your résumé and start looking *outside*.

8. While you are there, placate those who can help you—especially if they happen to be your boss or superior—and pretend like nothing is wrong, even if you are seething with outrage from within. Interestingly, those who are morally corrupt, expect others to be like them!

9. Get out at the first chance and do not raise a stink.

10. Just in case the entire matter suddenly takes on a legal turn, keep all your 'evidence" in a safe and accessible place (not the company computer) and write your own notes to document what is happening. If you maintain a calendar make entries of appointments with peoples' names and topics of the meeting.

11. Do not threaten legal action unless you have an attorney first. Assay the merits of the case first with your attorney.

Some Exit Strategies

Nearly everyone goes through phases in their jobs and careers where they doubt their future and value to their organization. If this feeling becomes chronic there is a time to reflect and act. Of course, your response to what is happening to you depends on the level at which you participate. For example a fresh graduate receiving an occasional heave-ho from their teammates or even their boss every now and then may not be a cause of concern. But, if a senior manager receives a series of signals, despite their ongoing and great contributions, must weigh their situation against the options and act on them with some studied reflection.

The following list is provided as a preparation to getting ready when a combination of circumstances, outlined in the 13 warning signs presented previously, become everyday part of your job:

1. Always have your résumé up to date. Find what assignments you can get in your current job that will enhance your résumé if you were to

move on. On an ongoing basis look for such assignments and ask your boss before anyone else gets them.

2. Go above and beyond what is expected: provide the exceptional! This will give you a great avenue to write your leadership stories in the résumé and make you marketable on an ongoing basis.

3. Work quietly and stay in the background. Visible employees tend to get into trouble when things shift. Always focus on your work and not on your politics.

4. Do not speak ill of anyone. In an organization rumor mill is the main means of communication. Do not become a part of rumormongers.

5. Always stay positive. Even if you do not agree with a decision, carry out the assignment without complaining and to the best of your abilities.

6. Always make yourself dispensable by sharing what you do with others and leaving a trail of "what to do in case of...," so that the organization does not suffer because you become unavailable. Share this with others so they know where to find the trail. Acting this way shows confidence in your own worth. Those who keep secrets about how they do things often get booted out, contrary to what they expect.

7. Always stay positive and optimistic, smiling often. It may not make you successful and let you get what you want, but how it annoys others might alone make it worthwhile to act this way!

8. If someone is undermining your efforts, observe carefully and then confront the person. Practice straight talk and see if you can understand their motives. Do not reciprocate by doing the same to them. Always be in your element. If undermining others and engaging in subterfuge is not your game, do not learn it just to survive in the changed circumstances; you will do poorly and get exposed.

9. If you do not believe in your boss's leadership you must answer the question: can I live with this person as my manager? As we discussed in Chapter-3 leadership and being a manger are two entirely different relationships. Leaders inspire and make you forget that you are working. Instead they create an environment where their followers spontaneously do their best in ways they cannot explain. True leadership is a magical force. Is this happening in your everyday existence?

If the answer is no, then you must ask yourself the next obvious question of being able to tolerate your manager.

10. The best way to really understand the relationship you have with your boss is to have a heart-to-heart talk where you discuss the deeper issues of your relationship with them in a non-confrontational way. Having a "straight talk" and seeking responses to your issues is the best way to understand the relationship between you and your boss. After all, leadership is about relationship, inspiration, and trust. If you do not see a flow of that energy then your boss is not a leader. It is difficult to sustain and be creative in such an environment. You must decide what your real options are from then on. Going in denial over what is happening merely prolongs the agony.

11. In some cases, a boss will sense your unhappiness after such a meeting (# 10 above) and may try to placate you by giving you a "promotion" and a title to go with it. But, in terms of real authority you may have little or none. Once the allure of the fancy title is vitiated by the lack of commensurate authority and power, you may start feeling worse than you did before your change of status. Now, if you are sidelined, you gradually lose your career momentum and paint yourself in a corner, with no place to go. The best strategy in such cases is to confront such situations early and keep your career momentum by either looking for other opportunities inside or going out aggressively after what you really want.

12. If the CEO or someone at or near the top ostracizes you because of a personal grudge and that you cannot repair that damage, do not expect even your most loyal colleagues to go to bat for you. They may feign that loyalty, but their own loyalty is to their job. Do not be misled by a misplaced sense of false loyalty.

13. If the source of the wrath is from really high place (s), but your boss likes you and your work, see if they will shield you and let you continue in a diminished role.

14. If, in spite of your good work and behavior, you start seeing the 13 warning signs listed at the beginning of this Appendix, prepare to leave.

15. Leave with dignity and grace.

Leaving with Dignity

Regardless of what prompts your departure you must remain unemotional about the whole process of leaving your employer (see Emotional Intelligence in Appendix-IV). The following tips are offered to make your departure not a liability on your career balance sheet:

1. Meet with your boss and state that you need to move on. Do not complain do not explain.

2. If you have something in hand already lined up that is great. If not do not lie. It is always a good idea to look for a job when you have one. Looking for a job when out of work often puts you at a disadvantage, but sometimes this becomes an inevitable reality. In such a case see if you can work out an arrangement with your boss, so that you can "park" yourself looking for work, inside or out, and get reassigned for a reasonable period.

3. Make oral presentation of your departure plans, the status of projects, etc. and explain that you plan to provide details when you present your letter of resignation. This is generally done in a day or so after the initial meeting.

4. Give at least two weeks' notice

5. Ask whom you should brief on your pending assignments so that they can continue as you leave your job.

6. Give details of how your boss may be able to reach you in case something crops up after you depart. Set the parameters of your availability.

7. Thank your boss for the opportunities and their support. This may be difficult if the situation is causing a forced departure. Mention that for the most part you enjoyed working at the place. Do not let your immediate experience taint your entire tenure at the company.

8. Do not take parting shots at any one or any thing.

9. Do not expect a bon voyage party.

10. Do not loan your items to anyone with the excuse of coming back to visit and retrieving them once you leave. Most loaned items—especially books—are usually never returned.

11. Take all your personal files, belongings, and items with you on your way out. Do not expect them to be available later for you to retrieve.

Appendix VIII

Résumés and Cover Letters

"Do not pray for tasks equal to your powers; pray for powers equal to your tasks."

—Phillip Brock, author (1835–1893)

Résumés

During a career the need to look around is compelling and often inevitable. In view of this it is always a good idea to keep your résumé growing as you navigate through your career. Identifying plum projects, finding ways to get on them or even lead them, getting challenging assignments are all parts of advancing your momentum in your career. Many do not do this well. Many wait until some trigger prompts them to dust off their résumé and then look for a job outside. Often, by the time they get going on their campaign, they are out of their job and are at a considerable disadvantage then. The best time to look for a job is when you already have one!

This appendix is not presented here to be tutorial on writing résumés and cover letters. A more complete treatment on these topics is presented in authors *The 7 Keys to a Dream Job: A Career Nirvana Playbook!* and *Reinvention through Messaging: The Write Message for the Right Job!*. This appendix is provided merely to show how a well-written résumé and cover letter can be fashioned so that they serve as touchstones in your endeavors to pursue an opportunity. This can be even an in-company position that you have decided to pursue. An insider opportunity must be treated with as much care and respect as its outside counterpart. Do not rely on your personnel records to let the hiring manager figure out what you have done; you must showcase it the way you feel fit!

In order for a résumé to be different it must have a compelling message presented in a differentiated way. One way to achieve this is to make the résumé a *forward-looking* message of value that is centered on your unique skills and leadership stories that define your style. The following elements of a typical résumé can be incorporated in a forward-looking message as is shown in the example presented here:

- **Career Objective:** Your forward-looking value proposition

- **Experience Summary:** A few lines that capture your history in a compelling way

- **Unique Skills:** Your genius that defines what is unique about you; your gifts

- **Professional Experience:** Your chronological narration of your leadership stories

- **Education:** Your formal education

- **Professional Development:** What you have done to professionally grow since finishing formal schooling

A well-laid, two-page format, cleanly presented can make for a compelling résumé as can be seen in the attached example.

Nick Packard

(510)555-0000: email@email.com

CAREER OBJECTIVE:

Director, IT Applications Development, in a large organization responsible for: translating strategic imperatives into specific applications for use in its businesses, dramatically improving enterprise-wide processes to make them efficient, improve decision making, and enhance overall customer experience.

EXPERIENCE SUMMARY

Four years as CTO and founding partner of an IT consulting firm responsible for identifying client needs and then translating them into applications solutions; previous ten years as software architect and engineer responsible for developing innovative applications to dramatically improve business processes

UNIQUE SKILLS

- **Strategic Alignment:** Understand the corporate vision and then create initiatives to deploy this vision by identifying what needs to be developed to make it easier for businesses to succeed.

- **Technology Management:** Collaborate with executives to identify how IT can best serve their business needs. Integrate diverse views and shepherd common and unified solutions to complex problems. Establish robust metrics to assess impact of technology on business outcomes.

- **Understanding Customers:** Understand the clients and help them make technology decisions by collaboration and by helping them express their unarticulated needs. Translate solutions in to retail customer experience that is exceptional rather than expected. Create Best-in-class systems.

- **Innovative Mindset:** Spot emerging IT trends and identify how they will increase store traffic, customer experience, and manager leadership. Provide innovative solutions to individual stores.

- **Seamless Communication:** Communicate across a broad constituency: from top executives to store clerks to learn what stands in the way of exceptional customer experience. Implement.

Nick Packard   510-555-0000   email@email.com   Page 2/2

PROFESSIONAL EXPERIENCE

Pathfinder Associates, Chicago, IL
CTO, Founding Partner   2001-2004
Overall leadership in client-specific software products development. Identify clients' needs and deliver turnkey solutions. Develop robust processes for translating client needs into business solutions.

- The election results reporting system for a national Chicago newspaper was in disarray, comprising of a lash-up of various systems purchased and internally developed over the years. The news editing and reporting staff would rely on the programmers and technical experts to do their last-minute fixes to get the critical reports, always hampered by technical glitches and delays. Using new tools and integrating them with existing software, developed a user-friendly interface, allowing access to final outcomes without technical intervention. Result: Technical team remained in background and election results got reported, beating the rival newspaper, even during the highly visible and close 2004 Presidential Election. This paper now continues its edge.

- Our own client Web development process was inconsistent across different teams, causing quality problems in final delivery. Additionally, clients could not make even minor Website changes due to lack of tools. Identified a robust process for unified development and delivered final output to clients with easy-to-use tools. Results: Greatly accelerated overall development cycle, client satisfaction soared, resulting in over $3 M in additional business per year, increasing profitability.

- Developed a process to identify ongoing client needs and how their existing needs were met through a face-to-face discovery. The end process resulted in actionable outcomes.

Avenue A, Inc. Seattle, WA   2000-2001
Software R&D Engineer
As R&D specialist, helped develop leading-edge application and provided system software support

- A major client threatened defection due to company's inability to match a competitor offering critical to its business future. Quickly assessed what was required to meet or beat competitor's offering, and working with the CTO, formed a team of developers and defined the needed elements to beat out competitor's offering. Within a record

Nick Packard   510-555-0000   email@email.com   Page 3/3

one month developed a fully functional demonstration that convinced client superiority of overall approach. Client continued business, which increased revenues and profitability. Client was able to exceed its business goals using this approach. Future engagements with clients were exclusive and high margin.

- Identified opportunities to improve development processes and implemented several ongoing initiatives. Coached and mentored others to improve leadership and technical effectiveness.

Independent Consultant, Seattle, WA   1997-2000

Identified business opportunities and collaborated with clients to deliver cost-effective business software.

- A regional financial services company was threatened by looming high net worth-client defections due to lack of online account information. Its system evolved over many years comprising of many disparate elements integrated with legacy data sources. Using up-to-date tools, minimized new development, and adopting a three-tier architecture, made the new online system robust to interface and maintain. Result: Within four months new user-friendly data was on line for all 140,000 end users. No defections occurred and current clients increased activity.

- A multinational financial services company was hampered by lack of a common language and understanding in selecting the appropriate technical architecture for new systems development. Authored a document that defined current technical architecture landscape and best practices, resulting in time savings and more consistent application architecture company-wide.

Kaufer Miller Communications, Seattle, WA   1996-1997
Technology Manager

Provide technology leadership and advise top management on overall technology issues. Design systems.

- Driven by business vision and overall strategy, developed a detailed plan to implement IT infrastructure and software development process. Within six months entire infrastructure was in place, allowing growing staff to service clients with highly responsive services

Nick Packard   510-555-0000   **email@email.com**   Page 4/4

that beat out the competition repeatedly. KMC's IT capability became one of its competitive advantages.

- Developed a complete remote networked office to seamlessly connect to main operations. The remote office was online within weeks and was able to seamlessly deliver client solutions.

Software and system development specialist at various organizations
Prior-1995

EDUCATION

Bachelor of Science, Business Administration, California State University, Sacramento, CA

Major in Management Information Systems, Minor in Communications

Product Experience

Languages: Java/JSP/Servlets, C++, XML, Perl, Visual Basic (VB), IIS/ASP, SQL, HTML, JavaScript

Databases: Oracle, Sybase, Microsoft, SQL Server, MySQL, and Microsoft Access

System Software: UNIX, Solaris, Microsoft Windows, Linux, and DEC VMS

Other: NetBeans, Eclipse, Jbuilder, Microsoft Visual Basic, expert at all Microsoft Office Applications

Cover Letters

Cover letters are critical to getting the attention of a decision maker during a job search. Good cover letters are well researched and well crafted as is shown in the example. There is no short cut to writing compelling cover letters.

Letters serve a dual purpose during a transition. One is to bridge the messaging gap between the résumé and the intended job opportunity. When sent without a résumé, it serves its other purpose as your proxy, to entice its targeted reader to take the intended next step.

Many think that letters are a waste of time when pursuing job opportunities! This view is shared on both sides: those on the receiving end find most letters redundant; those on the sending end find it an unnecessary step that is more a burden than help. This is probably because it takes an effort to write a compelling letter. Most take the easy way out and cobble together something that is copied from an existing template. Worse yet, many cut and paste what is already in their résumé with what is worthy of plagiarizing from the job posting itself and create a message that clearly shows its pedigree. With each of these approaches, the job seeker is sending a message, Don't bother reading mine; I am too lazy! In taking this easy route, it provides an opportunity for those, who take the time and effort to write a good letter to differentiate themselves in a campaign!

Another rationale advanced by poor letter writers is that, in a tough market, there are many opportunities to which responses need to be sent. In order to get maximum coverage of targets, it is difficult to write all these customized letters. So, they take the shotgun approach and send many mediocre letters. As a result, none of them create any impact. If, on the other hand, job seekers selected just a few choice targets, researched the opportunities and then sent select few letters, their chances of success are greatly increased. Remember, you need only one job!

In a tough job market a *good* cover letter is a must. It further differentiates those that send it from those who do not. If the letter is well written and goes beyond what is in the job description, it commands attention and action. In the previous chapter on résumés, we emphasized that a résumé is not about you; it is about them—the employer. In the case of the letter, it is even more so. Typically, cover letters are an intimate and personal way to draw the decision-maker into *your* world by talking about *theirs*. Done this way, it resonates with their needs. A good cover letter should grab the target reader by their shoulders, look them in the eye and convey to them, I know you!

1. Find out who the hiring manager is. Use your network, commonly-available databases, or some research to find out the name and its correct spelling.

2. Research why the position is open. Also research what business cycle the company is in their industry and any particular challenges it is facing. For example, customer defections, product recalls, slow to market, quality problems, product costs, etc.

3. Talk to the company's customers, suppliers, and alliances to learn more about how it does business and what perceptions those who touch the company have about it.

4. Learn how to read company financials and read the CEO's annual/quarterly statement to glean what challenges the company is facing. Also learn how to interpret SEC filings, 10-K and 10-Q, which are available for a publicly traded company from its Website. Ask your stockbroker for investor insights.

5. Use this research to draft a letter with a Point-of-View (POV) that clearly shows how, by hiring you for the open position, you will be a change agent and make the company's pain go away.

6. Spend time polishing this draft and reduce your letter to about a ¾ page of cogent message. Show how you intend to create change that will improve things.

7. Send the letter, along with the résumé, in a differentiated way, as FedEx, *in addition* to Website submittal. Local companies will get the FedEx (Ground delivery, about $5 the next day)

8. Follow-up with the person to whom you sent the original response with diligence. This particular step is even more important (and difficult for most) than anything else in this process.

9. If all this sounds like much trouble, it is. And, *that* is the point. Very few go through this effort to send a cover letter; those who do get attention.

Yes, it is time consuming! But, then again, how many jobs do you need?

A great cover letter is also a must for an internal position. Those who are looking for an inside opportunity, either in sunny times or in times that create turmoil during mergers or economic hardships, believe that merely shopping around with their résumé is sufficient because their records are openly available to any hiring manager. It is precisely because of this view that many hold that pursuing an inside position in times, good and tough, with an impeccable résumé and a great cover letter is to your advantage.

Since your being inside the company gives you so much insight, it is relatively easy to translate that insight and craft a great cover letter. When a potential hiring manger sees an exceptional résumé and compelling cover letter, looking at the existing personnel records is only done more as validation and not as a primary way to explore your fit for an open position. Any inside opportunity must be treated in the same way as an "A" job that you might be pursuing outside. For more discussion on why this is so, please see author's *The 7 Keys to a Dream Job: A Career Nirvana Playbook!*, Key-2: Starting at the Start.

Nick Packard
(510)555-0000: email@email.com

March 22, 2005

Mr. David T. Chancellor
Senior Vice President, CIO
GroceryChain
5918 Stab Way
Oakland, CA 99999

Dear Mr. Chancellor,

I am pleased to respond to the open position of Director, Application Development, Tracking code #342210-04, at GroceryChain. I meet or exceed all your job requirements.

With the highly competitive markets in the space in which GroceryChain operates, IT can play a key role in combating inroads by aggressive super chains as Wal-Mart and Costco. Driving costs down is key in successfully establishing a brand for a grocery store chain in the emerging competitive markets and then creating an exceptional customer experience. With GroceryChain's employee growth at nearly 10 times its revenue growth, there is a great avenue to increase productivity gains and automation. I see the following factors as critical to this goal:

- Constantly evaluate how the overall vision for the organization is being implemented through technology initiatives and identify opportunities that remain untapped.

- Identify where costs can be driven down through automation and develop an agenda for prioritizing this across the entire value chain

- Automate as many of the manual functions as are customer friendly, while continually evaluate customers' preferences to provide an exceptional experience than what is expected.

- Develop a community-specific technology implementation plan that provides most productive and cost effective store operations.

- Constantly evaluate if the current technology infrastructure provides the best ROI and then recommend appropriate initiatives to make sure that this does take place.

- Develop a highly disciplined software development and implementation process that makes businesses drive technology and not the other way around.

My track record shows you how I have used my technology insights and customer/client knowledge to provide the best solutions in an effective and timely way.

I am excited about working for GroceryChain and looking forward to exploring this opportunity further.

Cordially,
Nick Packard
Enclosure: Resume

APPENDIX-IX

Leveraging Your Genius

Everyone is born a genius. The process of everyday living de-geniuses us."
—Buckminster Fuller

One of the central themes in all my previous books and my ongoing coaching practice is that we are at our best when we are able to operate with our genius or innate gifts fully engaged in what we do. Although most acknowledge the existence of powers that stem from their genius, many dismiss it because they are afraid to acknowledge that there is something special about them. Often, if they do acknowledge such a condition, they fear that it would entail their having to do something about it. This scares off people from pursuing it further in any serious vein. Yet, many go to expensive seminars that deal with finding your inner voice or buy books that write about it! The other challenge in discovering and articulating one's genius is that there are very few practical tools that can be used to make its discovery and application a reality.

Everyone knows that you perform your best when you are passionate about what you do. In passionately engaging in any endeavor you put in a much greater energy, *effortlessly!* "Work" becomes a source of joy and energy. In such endeavors you apply all your energies in a much focused way, producing results that are otherwise difficult to achieve. Those who engage in activities merely for the mercenary intentions, often disappoint themselves in what they get out of it beyond just the economic benefit. Applying your genius in what you engage changes that outlook, allowing you to be passionate about your work, nourishing your soul.

♠ Me? Genius? How?

Many often wonder how knowing their genius can help them. In other words, if they are operating with their genius already on their side, engaging them in their pursuits, how is it going to help them in their further professional growth? Here we define genius, not as some transcendent intellectual capacity, but rather, as something that creates a unique value, your gift to do something better than others can do it.

Many consciously think of their genius as their gift that allows them to do what they do better, differently than others, and aligned with their own purpose. No amount of extra effort can compensate for what your genius can help you create. When your genius is aligned with your work, things flow naturally and create amazing outcomes, effortlessly. Additionally, being aligned with the natural genius, work seems joyous. This means that there is no work-related stress that is causing so much grief to so many as they continue to drudge through their jobs. Aligned with your work with ability to manifest your genius is the state of *nirvana* that everyone yearns for. You resonate!

What does this mean in terms of a career, job search, and particularly how to go about this process of discovering your genius? It simply means that the sooner one is able to extract their genius articulate it, own it, and translate it into a compelling value proposition, the better their chances are of finding this elusive nirvanic joy that everyone is after. For more details on the Genius Extraction Tool, see the author's *Reinvention through Messaging: The Write Message for the Right Job!*.

Once this genius is discovered, owned, and applied, its manifestations are many. Genius, consciously recognized, mobilizes new opportunities. It is the catalyst that provides a new dimension to your job search. Unlike merely job-driven skills, which have limited reach across different jobs, your genius is truly a universal currency that sees no job-related boundaries. This means that you are able to mold your value proposition, to the opportunity at hand, in a versatile way to apply it to create value. Merely having job-focused skills—even transferable skills—does not allow this versatility; it does not make for a compelling résumé message. In the absence of this critical element in a résumé, it tends to lack soul. No amount of flowery language can then compensate for it as its proxy.

♠ Unique Skills (Your Genius)

Our genius is a *universal* endowment. This genius can be defined as a special gift that differentiates us from others in what we do well, by describing *how we* do it. Putting this in the résumé, gives it the extra element of differentiation early, up-front, and allows us to define our individual brand. Unique skills are a portfolio of five to seven differentiators listed in rank order of importance—to the employer—that are unique and that set you apart from others. Each is presented typically as a two-word phrase that is intriguing and is followed by a one or two line description of what that phrase means in the context of the target. Crafting the bolded two-word phrases that capture your uniqueness is one of the most creative—and differentiating—elements of writing a résumé. Each phrase, when read, immediately conveys the message of how unique value is created, *without* a need to read the descriptor. Intrigue, pith, crispness, and uniqueness are all at the heart of this phrase. The résumé example presented in the previous Appendix is illustrative of how this can be done.

In thinking and articulating Unique Skills, the focus should be on the *how* and not the *what!* This is difficult for most to appreciate. One reason perhaps is because our thinking is deeply ingrained in describing the *what* in our communication; *how* that is done is not a natural thing to think about, especially when writing a résumé. Why we focus so much on the *what* is, perhaps, because we want to present our accomplishments in a manner that is in a language regarded as currency of the value message. It is easy to see why this became the standard expression, especially in résumé writing: accomplishments presented that describe the *what* tend to be objective in their tone, hence are easier to compare to others' accomplishments.

Let's take an example. If two candidates in sales are writing their accomplishments, the one that states a 12 percent increase in sales is regarded as a "less than" the one who lists a higher number. But, let's take a closer look at their two statements:

Statement #1: *Achieved a 15 percent increase in sales by calling customer more frequently and selling them higher-margin products.*

Statement #2: *Achieved a 12 percent increase in sales by developing closer relationships with existing accounts, which resulted in having to make fewer sales calls. Leveraged each customer visit by collaborating with systems architects to develop business and technology solutions that met customers' long-term business needs*

On the surface, Statement #1 belongs to a person who achieved higher sales that year. But, if you look deeper in the *how*, it is not difficult to agree that this salesman was mortgaging the future account relationships. Why? He was selling more expensive products to make himself look good, perhaps without keeping the customers' interest foremost. Secondly, he was working hard making frequent calls, just pushing products that the customers may not have needed. This is a myopic sales strategy, bound to tank quickly. In this example, salesperson #2 is going to have a time advantage. Her sales are going to increase geometrically with time. The salesman #1 is likely to experience an opposite fate!

Thus, focusing on the *what*, does not always tell the right story. Sometimes, it tells the wrong story, as it is illustrated here!

For many, writing this part of the résumé is difficult and frustrating. They invariably end up with statements that do not create differentiation and that lack any excitement. One way to overcome this difficulty is to collaborate with someone who can help you dig out your inner passions and gifts and then help you articulate them in a compelling way. This also requires trial and error and command of being able to write concisely.

Although these statements are not what describe the Unique Skills, they are the basis for them. Unique Skills are extracted from such statements, which provide the proof, as will be presented in the Professional Experience part of the résumé.

For example, someone has a genius for understanding complexity and then breaking it down to its elements, so that it can be analyzed for easy understanding. This Unique Skill could read:

Simplifying Complexity: *Quickly analyze complex systems, situations, and environment; reduce them to their most elemental blocks by identifying patterns to show how they interact, so that they can be easily understood and tackled.*

The following tool is presented to help craft stories that are an integral part of the Professional Experience section in a résumé. The tool—**The SIMPLE Tool**—helps story telling. These stories are at the heart of what constitutes the evidence part of the Unique Skills in the résumé. They provide the evidence of how Unique Skills translate into measurable benefits. Most have difficulties writing this part of their résumé.

The second tool (not presented here) is the **Genius Extraction Tool.** Although the Unique Skills (based on your genius) appear first in the résumé presentation, from a résumé development viewpoint, they are the *result* of the stories that are worth telling. So, as a process for developing a résumé, it is best to start with the SIMPLE stories and then use the Genius Extraction Tool to develop the cluster of Unique Skills that are presented in the top part of the résumé.

Of the many labels that can be attributed to this tool, why was the Genius Extraction Tool chosen as its name? The operative word here is *extraction.*

Those who remember their visit to the dentist will know the metaphor. The process is painful but you feel better afterwards. Pulling out our own genius is somewhat akin to this process. Once the genius gets identified, the process of giving it life in words is fun and exciting.

For more details about how to apply these tools, see the author's *Reinvention through Messaging: The Write Message for the Right Job!*

♠ The SIMPLE Tool (Tool-13)

This tool is designed to help write leadership stories in a résumé's Professional Experience part. **Understanding this tool is central to delving into your genius,** as shown on the following page.

Instead of writing each bullet as a typical Task/Responsibility format, the SIMPLE format allows for a better presentation of the leadership story, showcased as evidence of Unique Skills, one at a time. Keep this write-up to refer back to when going for an interview.

SIMPLE is an acronym that stands for:

Symptom	State what was going on. (Don't confuse symptom with root cause)
Impediment	What was getting in the way?
Measurement	What specific parameters were measured from this impediment?
Plan	What was the Plan of action? (This eliminates the root cause)
Leverage	What was leveraged that showcased your leadership?
Effect	What outcome did you create and how do they measure? Connect this to any claim you want to make during a career transition for a credible leadership story.
	See Making the SIMPLE Connection.

Illustrative example:

Symptom	At El Camino Hospital, the nursing staff was taking too long to get patients to change their hygiene habits. Patients were coming back with repeat illnesses related to poor hygiene and its fallout.

Impediment   Hospital's refusal to provide authoritative training materials and Internet resources to patients and nurses on how to educate clients to research their needs

Measurement   Repeat client visits costs $1.3 M annually because they revisit the hospital every two months. With properly trained patients they should stop after the first two visits.

Plan   Proposed a comprehensive plan that involved using existing Internet resources within El Camino Hospital with others, on a time-shared basis.

Leverage   First trained nurses on how to use this resource and then equipped them so that they, in turn, could train their clients. Prepared a simple tracking log, where clients could record what they researched and how it helped their needs.

Effect   Within three months, 150 nurses were fully trained on how to look up resources and train their clients. Within six months, clients came for two visits and were then self sufficient to manage their own hygiene. An informal survey indicated that their overall wellness had increased substantially within one year. As a result of this initiative, freeing nursing time saved $1.3M annually. In addition the client quality of life increasing substantially

Reducing to a résumé bullet:

✓ Led a major initiative to change patient habits resulting from poor hygiene. Discovered that lack of coordination resulted in nurses wasting time treating repeat-visit patients. Proposed a comprehensive plan, freeing up available Internet resources to train nurses, who, in turn trained their clients. Within one year, repeat visits virtually eliminated, saving $1.3M in nursing wages. (This is the *After* version)

✓ Helped clients change their habits by implementing training using Internet resources. This cut down on repeat visits, reducing nursing workload. (This is the *Before* version)

It is easy to see the impact a well-written statement (the *After* version) makes using the SIMPLE tool.

Note: For an impactful résumé, only a few stories are needed. Because they take space, the remaining stories can be one sentence, telegraphic accomplishments, typically seen in any conventional write-up.

SIMPLE Tool for Career Transition

One of the major challenges during a career transition is the ability to connect, in a meaningful way, the past experience with the skills needed for the next career. This is reinvention. The same holds true when switching jobs that are not a mere extension of the past assignments. Such discontinuous transitions not only require imagination but also the ability to clearly demonstrate the value to the employer, where bringing you on board outweighs the risk by the benefits that come with it. What tool is effective in making such discontinuous transitions?

The SIMPLE tool has proven to be most helpful in this process. How? Using the tool as illustrated in the previous example and then specifically focusing on the final *E* for effect can do the trick. For more detailed discussion on how this is done and examples of how Unique Skills are developed and showcased in winning résumés, please see author's *Reinvention through Messaging: The Write Message for the Right Job!* and *The 7 Keys to a Dream Job: A Career Nirvana Playbook!*

The process just outlined for presenting your genius appears backwards. Why? The Unique Skills are extracted from the stories that appear in the Professional Experience section of the résumé. These are the résumé bullets points. So, to discover your genius you must first identify those stories in your past that vivified your existence and brought spark to what you did. This happens when you are operating within your genius. So, knowing what these instances are certainly help pursue the genius. This is why the process of discovering one's genius is "backwards" in the sequence in which one writes their résumé.

APPENDIX-X

Psychometric Tests: A Survivor's Guide

*"Good decisions come from wisdom. Wisdom comes from experience.
Experience comes from making bad decisions."*

—Anonymous

Psychometric tests[5] are often used to help in career assessment, guidance, and counseling. They are also used in selection, promotion, and ongoing development of an individual. There are two types of psychometric tests: aptitude tests and achievement tests. Aptitude tests measure a person's interests and their abilities to acquire a new skill or learn new skills. Achievement tests, on the other hand, score what a person already knows and can do now—much like the licensing tests given by the DMV. This appendix is provided to give an overview of the different types of tests that you may run across during your own career journey and is aimed at giving you some tips to dispel any apprehension you may have around these testes.

The following questions are typical of those who are confronted with taking such tests:

- How should I prepare for the different types of psychometric tests?

- What resources are available to prepare for such tests?

- Are there test-taking skills that I can learn?

- What can I do if I do not like the results of the tests?

---

5 Adapted from *Business: The Ultimate Source*™ (2002) Perseus Publishing

Preparation: The two most common achievement tests are those that measure verbal reasoning and mathematical ability. Because of their long-standing use in both business and academic domains, they are considered valid and reliable. Validity deals with the test measuring the right parameter for which it is designed. Reliability deals with how consistent are the results across different subjects and conditions. Since there is a myriad of such tests designed and administered by different institutions, it is perhaps best to take different tests to compare the results. This can be expensive and confusing. One outcome that may beneficial is the existence of patterns and themes.

Before going to any of these tests it is best to know what skills and knowledge are being tested. Of the many books on the market, find the best one that addresses your needs and tests that you would be taking. The books typically explain how the questions are typically structured, provide test taking strategies, and provide sample tests that you can take so that you can evaluate your own level of skills and knowledge. The books provide ways to strengthen your scores in the areas where you have weaknesses. Using this approach can significantly improve test scores and the readiness for taking tests.

Preparing for aptitude tests, on the other hand, does not entail getting ready in any other way than simply being physically and mentally alert. Since aptitude tests measure your interests and your ability to acquire and learn new skills, you cannot really prepare for these tests the same way you would for achievement tests or a math or history exam. Career-related aptitude tests are based on self-awareness, so the more you know yourself, your passions, interests, and gifts, the more likely the test results are to be useful to you. There are many books that deal with self-awareness tests.

Skills-related aptitude tests generally test your problem-solving ability in a particular field. The best preparation is to be well rested and relaxed so that you can focus on the questions and provide your best answerers.

The following list provides some guidance on how to successfully take psychometric tests and what to do with the outcomes:

1. Read the instructions carefully before commencing your test. The instructions often tell how you can achieve a higher score and what strategies can work best. For example, guessing vs. leaving the answers blank.

2. First go through the entire test and answer only those questions that you are sure of. Then go over the unanswered questions and tackle the ones that you are pretty sure of. If you still have time, you can go through the questions one more time, really taking the time to think the questions through and providing your best answers.

3. If you are taking the test for career guidance, carefully analyze the test results. No test is completely accurate. If the career advice provided by the test is too far afield, trust your own intuition. You may want to take a different test as a "second opinion."

4. If the tests are a part of a job application process, the employer should at least tell you if you passed or failed the test, even if they don't tell you the specific results. If the placement in a job is inappropriate, you have the right to question the test.

5. Never make a major career decision based on the test results alone.

6. Even if you know people inside the company that you are pursuing, take the tests seriously.

7. Some do not take tests well. So, do not feel inadequate because you did not score well. Taking a test is a skill in itself!

8. Do not stay up all night cramming for the tests. You must be rested, relaxed and ready for the tests to get the best results.

Appendix XI

Mentors: Developing Relationship with Powerful People

"A strong mentor/mentee relationship is the basis for forging tomorrow's leaders."
                                    —Jack Welch, Chairman, General Electric (1982–2002)

Navigating successfully through a career requires many ingredients. Hard work, planning, being there at the right time, knowing the right people, among factors, all play a role in a successful career. But, even then a career is filled with road bumps, unpredictable events, and situations that are sometimes hard to decipher. No matter how smart you are in what you do, having a perspective from an outsider and who can also give you the right insight at critical times are invaluable in keeping your career on track.

Being successful in a career is experiencing growth. Part of the growth comes from overcoming difficult situations that are personal in nature or from the way they affect your well being in an organization. Having someone you can implicitly trust and to whom you can reveal professional insecurities and personal inadequacies comfortably and confidentially are critical to a successful career. This is what a mentor can provide.

A mentor must be removed from your day-to-day life. This provides the objectivity to the mentoring process. This is where you talk to the mentor and communicate the challenge you face and try to get their objective advice. This is why your boss, colleague, or subordinate cannot be your mentor. They lack the proper clinical distance to give you objective advice.

A mentor is someone who takes personal interest in your professional success. A mentor is, therefore, who is committed to helping you find a path to success. A good mentor uses the Socratic Method to develop you professionally and personally and provides the following:

- An objective perspective

- An industry and business insight coming from personal experience

- Wisdom from having lived through tough times

- A network of contacts

- Guiding you to other resources when they do not have the answers

- Personal intervention when your actions are undermining your welfare

Using the Socratic Method entails asking questions in a sequence to the person who comes seeking answers. The way questions are asked back reveal insights that can benefit the one seeking answers. Often, no one person can provide all these benefits. Some provide them to a varying degree. It is not uncommon to have different mentors that provide different inputs. Developing mentor/mentee relationship is one of the most challenging prospects in a career. A good mentor can make a difference in the success of a career.

Making it Happen

Decide what you want from a mentor/mentee relationship: What is your objective in this relationship? Are you looking for organizational guidance or are you looking for professional
and personal development through this relationship? Are you looking for relationships? Answers to these and other questions can help in deciding whom to pursue for this relationship.

Assess what you bring: A good mentor/mentee relationship is a give and take. You must give something in return for what you get out of the relationship. Be very clear with the person so that there is no surprise or disappointment.

Make a list: Ask around and check out for yourself. The most important element of a good mentor/mentee relationship is personal chemistry. This is usually established in a series of meetings not just one encounter. Some companies have an official mentoring program. Enroll in the program and see what is available. Interview candidates so that you can get a good picture of the relationship you will develop over the long term.

The problem with a company-sponsored program is that once you leave the company the relationship ends.

Establish ground rules: When do you see each other? How often? How long? Where (home)? These are some of the logistical issues that must be addressed? Often, they evolve just as the mentor/mentee relationship evolves.

Young Mentors

Although mentor in the dictionary sense means someone who acts as your trusted counselor or a guide, it has a connotation of seniority. A mentor is usually an experienced professional full of wisdom stemming from their years of having lived a life of adventure, accomplishments, and learning. They are also pursued because of their power, influence, and stature in the business community in which they play. In today's context that definition of a mentor may be limiting. Why? Many young professionals these days are highly driven, accomplished, and savvy. The rapid growth of technologies has made mastering these technologies a challenge for most. Somehow, the younger generation seems to master them well and, as a result, is a great resource for learning. They are also well versed with how their generation deals with the fast-changing world, which the older generation seems to find challenging.

Having a young mentor may seem like a contradiction, but in today's world it is a necessity. There is no rule that says you must have only one mentor. One of your mentors could be someone (or several) who is savvy at something that you want to learn. Jack Welch, the legendary chairman of General Electric, often courted Gen-Y (and even Gen-X) professionals and called them his mentors. He learned much about the Internet and how they look at the exploding commerce in this new paradigm.

Common Mistakes

The following is a short list of common mistakes made in developing a mentor/mentee relationship:

- You look to your boss to be your mentor.

- You and your mentor are frustrated with the lack of progress made. A mentor/mentee relationship is more about personal growth and maturity and not project deliverables.

- Having a blind faith in the mentor. Mentors are humans, too. They, too, need mentors. Do not expect too much from a mentor. They do not have all the answers.

- Not knowing when to move on. Every relationship plays out. Once you start seeing the end of a relationship because of your own growth or the stagnation of the mentor, gradually move on and do not make a big deal about it. Graduating to a different mentor is a sign of growth

Coaching

Coaching and mentoring are considered kindred needs in the corporate world. Although they are complementary in their application, nothing could be further from the truth. While mentoring involves someone who can guide you in your career and who brings both the content and the context of what is happening in your situation to the relationship, coaching invariably involves someone who gets paid for understanding the *context* of your predicament. A mentor can be a person inside your organization, if not in your company, but a coach is usually a professional who comes from the "outside." Yes, some companies employ executive coaches who are on their staff, often they are a stable of professionals retained to serve an ongoing need when a company is doing well.

Coaching came into vogue in the mid 90s when the full impact of the newly-launched 360 degree review became growingly popular in the corporate culture. Annual reviews based on the 360 degree instruments typically highlight areas for an employee where they need to grow and increase their value in those areas. Managers typically do not have the time or the skill to help their direct reports to achieve this development. So, companies started hiring coaches to help employees in the specific areas of their needs. Many employees hire their own counselors or coaches to develop themselves, much like a physical trainer or sports coach.

The following guidelines are provided to help you select a coach that you may want to engage in your ongoing development:

1. The best sources of getting names for potential coaches is referrals from someone you know and someone who has shown progress that is visible to you.

2. Have a meeting with yourself and ask yourself introspective questions that articulate your need for development and the areas in which you see the need.

3. Meet with the coach for an initial session and explore their approach, compatibility, and style.

4. Do not sign up for a package deal no matter how much you save by paying in advance. Have a few sessions before you decide.

5. Make sure that the coach has real experience working in the corporate world and has shown career growth, reinventions, and has dealt with challenges that are typical in the corporate world. If they come from recruiting and HR staff or academic backgrounds they are less likely to be effective in what they have to offer.

6. If a coach cannot offer you specific and actionable guidance you are probably talking to a frustrated therapist who could not get their license.

7. If the guidance that you get in your sessions is not working for you, bring it up immediately in the next session and seek a course correction. If things are not working fire the coach and find another one.

8. Seek feedback from your colleagues and check for changes in your own self.

9. If you do not see things changing for yourself do not delude yourself by waiting longer.

10. If you do not respect the coach, you have lost the edge in your relationship and you must move on.

APPENDIX XII

Work-Life Balance

"The real voyage of discovery consists not in seeking new landscapes, but in having new eyes."
—Marcel Proust, French novelist, psychologist (1871–1922)

Today's knowledge worker appears to be in a rat race at work. Those who feel caught in it think that they are alone and that all others are having a "normal" existence. They look for new landscapes—even looking elsewhere—for a respite of normalcy, only to discover no greener pastures. What they fail to see is that they have the power to change their own patterns of work and create the kind of balance they are striving for. Their eyes betray them, however, because they fail to see the obvious! Those who are oblivious to the lack of balance in their work-life, as many brash, young, and ambitious professionals are in their early careers, continue on their path until some life-altering event, as a marriage, or a newborn, reminds them of their new obligations.

Many factors have contributed to this contagion, not the least of which is the technology itself that has helped boost the productivity of an average worker some 75 percent during the past 25 years. And yet workers are working longer and harder than ever. A number of factors have contributed to this escalating race between productivity and the actual hours spent at work. Some of these factors are:

- Increased collaboration across geographically dispersed teams

- Time and cultural differences across geographies that have made communications more difficult

- Flatter organizations with fewer workers

- Higher expectations from customers

- Expectations of instant responses because of improved communications

- Initiatives as JIT (just in time) manufacturing with the need for rapid responses

- The Damoclean sword of headcount cutbacks and outsourcing

- Personal communication tools as IMs (instant messaging, cell phones, and wireless devices) with insatiable demand for instant responses

- Increased debt due to constantly rising costs of the basic human needs as housing, food, healthcare, and transportation have forced people to weld their lives to their paychecks just to protect their lifestyles.

The result is that we have lost our sense of work-life-balance that was so critical to maintaining a harmonious and healthy life. Fifty years back this phrase was not even bandied about in the then prevalent lexicon.

One reason for the existence of this "work harder" expectation is driven by the need to succeed in today's economy and business climate, which require lightening fast reflexes and the ability to communicate and collaborate across the globe. Coming up with innovative ideas, products, and services require getting people across different geographies to work together. More value is created through global networks these days than ever before, so clocks have become less relevant to when things happen—they happen on demand, no matter what time it is. Instant communications have helped—and exacerbated—this condition. Because the organizations have become flatter, who all are involved in communication and decision making have become less important—everyone must know and give their input to the evolving scenario so that no one feels alienated. Democratic decision-making has its own price tag and we are paying for it in our getting involved in every bit of communication message that happens. Now we are slaved to it and simply cannot extricate ourselves from its tyranny.

The Importance of Work-life Balance

Spending too much time at work at the expense of meeting the needs of the personal life as family, health, and the need to expand horizons through new skills and explorations can result in dysfunctional existence. For a comer in their 20s, after graduation, and in their first job, such fierce commitment to their work may be understandable in consideration of their ambitions and youthful energy. But, as one gets more settled in life, a better work-life balance is critical to a long and productive work life.

We all contribute to the problem of overworking by not changing our own work habits, despite strides in technology and organizational design. The following is a summary of some of our habits that we refuse to surrender to today's reality:

1. Most managers spend nearly a full day out of their week (40 hours) on managing their communications that are not valuable. Listening to voice mails messages that go on forever, emails that choke their mailboxes, not to mention the "social" office activities and other distractions

2. Nearly a full day (15 percent) is lost per week in meetings that are not productive

3. Reworking a task because of lack of planning and understanding of the requirements of the task or project. It is estimated that a full 25 percent of what is done gets redone because of such factors.

4. Managers do not spend enough time on productive and high-performing workers to support their needs and make them even better because they are too busy paying attention to the non performers. Getting rid of non-performers early will save much time and boost morale of those who are productive. Managers must learn how to initiate an ironclad process of terminating an employee—or salvaging them—so that morale and productivity remain high.

5. Creating unambiguous accountabilities is at the heart of productive workforce. Communicating these to those involved and then tracking progress can be done far more efficiently than by adopting any other management method. See Chapter-3: Management Basics, specifically Accountability Contract.

Some Strategies for Work-Life Balance

The following is a list of some avenues that are worth following for a better balance between your work and personal life:

1. **Manage Output than Hours:** Eliminate or defer low-value activities and meetings. Manage you email and send your message to those

who must have it. Avoid hitting the "Reply All" button when responding to emails. Use the saved time on productive and creative activities or go home early.

2. **Understand the Functions of Managing:** See Chapter-3 and understand the concept of the Management Work Gap. Most managers work at level far below their charter. This wastes everyone's time, because they all follow the tone set by their boss. This management work gap now reverberates throughout the organization.

3. **Delegate:** Pushing decisions further down the chain of command builds bench strength and frees you to do more creative work.

4. **Use New Technology:** To foster collaboration use available technology to know what operations and colleagues are doing at far-flung locations. This avoids duplication.

5. **Shift Emphasis from Supervision to Collaboration:** Because of the networked workplace managers do not create value in all that they do, facilitators do. Re-examine your organizational design to make sure that you have enough catalysts and fewer managers.

6. **Seek out Right Employers:** Some employers are creating an environment that aid work-life-balance. Flex hours, having on-site nurseries, job sharing, telecommuting, providing personal services and facilities as valet, haircuts, medical checkups, gyms, and dry-cleaning at the place of work have helped relieve some of the pressures for those living under the tyranny of the clock. If your employer does not provide any relief in any of the areas mentioned, it does not hurt to bring it up.

7. **Manage Time-Off:** Long family vacations have become the thing of the past. You spend much time getting organized and clearing your work backlog before you go on such long trips, away from work, and, then, upon return, you have to work even harder to catch up, wondering, all the while, if you still have your job when you get back! Short vacations are now becoming the norm.

8. **Re-evaluate Promotion:** Before you go after the promotion, evaluate if the added responsibilities are worth the extra hassle.

9. **Move Down the Value Chain:** Companies that provide outsourcing services to their clients provide a work environment far different

from that available at their clients'. Why? Most outsourced services are provided on a contract basis and clients are charged for the time during which the services are provided. Thus, working for companies that provide such services generally have an environment where a "normal" work week—or one even tailor made to suit your needs— is easy to structure. On the contrary working for organizations that provide consulting or contract services can invariably result in grueling work schedules that often include frequent travel to client sites. In the growing outsourcing industry such opportunities are now plentiful.

10. **The Economics of Two Paychecks:** Audit the true benefits of the two paychecks, where both spouses are working. In many instances, after taxes, expenses, and the hassles the second paycheck was a mere illusion and the price paid in not having either parent home to tend to the household was dear.

11. **Reduce Personal Debt:** Rearrange your lifestyle to reduce your financial burden and obligations. Once you scale back your needs and live within your means having a smaller net income may not look that bad for the benefits that it provides. How much time you have to do comparison shopping has much to do with the kind of bargains you can get. So, if your work-life does not allow you that latitude what you are earning is perhaps getting sucked into your having to pay more because you cannot afford that time to shop properly.

APPENDIX XIII

Work Etiquette

"Proper etiquette is the lubrication that makes for smooth human relationships"

—Peter Drucker (1909–2005)

Business Etiquette

The dictionary defines etiquette as conduct or procedure required by good breeding or prescribed by authority in social or official life. This definition can be used as a guiding principle. It suggests that etiquette is even more important in a job environment than it is in others. This is perhaps because, often, most do not even realize that their churlish social behaviors make it difficult for their employers, colleagues, and subordinates to be gracious about being considerate. This consideration can range from returning a repeated phone message left on their voice mail, to explaining something that puzzles them. Why?

Etiquettes are the lubrication that makes things move smoothly. Ignoring them can create unnecessary friction and hurt, damaging relationships. Regardless of where one is in life, one needs to be aware of the appropriate etiquette. This is because, particularly for those in a transition or at a difficult juncture, their focus shifts to their own needs, and they become less aware of how they may be coming across to others. Being unaware common social courtesies can go against their moving forward and getting what they are looking for. It does not matter if you are out of work looking for a job or if you already have one and are looking for a change. The level of stress is the same; it may just have a different level of urgency! To be able to display grace under fire requires having grace at all to begin with. To display your social polish, the behaviors must be manifest in "normal" times, where they become hardwired patterns. If you cannot manifest such behaviors during "rough" times, it is because that you have not internalized them at all.

In today's workplace increased uncertainty has created an ongoing environment of paranoia and competition. Those trying to get ahead are now bolder in their overtures and more aggressive in their intent. This condition has led workers to be more self-centric in their attitude towards their colleagues. As a result, etiquettes have taken a back seat. Recent survey by AOL (October 2005) reveals that the workplace behavior has reached unprecedented levels of rudeness. In just five years, those who believe that the workplace shows lack of good manners amongst colleagues has gone up nearly 20 points (from 62 to 82).

Practicing the right etiquette will not only get what you want, it will also help you position yourself in a differentiated way in the eyes of others. You will enjoy better relationships to boot. The converse is that if you are clumsy in the etiquette department, you may not only lose an opportunity that is yours to claim, you may permanently alienate the potential benefactor beyond the immediate context! If you are a talented person, otherwise fully qualified to claim an opportunity, you will always wonder what went sour in your attaining what you so wanted and were so fit for! Ironically, etiquette demands that those who see your boorish behavior in the process, keep mum about it!

In limited space it is impossible to provide a complete guide to job etiquette. The flavor of the tips provided here can be used to understand the basic behavioral principles that you can leverage in similar situations. When in doubt, think of the other person, not yourself. Etiquette is about making others feel comfortable about being with you or interacting with you!

Oblivious Oliver!

How etiquette—or just plain civility—influences peoples' behavior towards you came into sharper focus in my own experience when I gave a talk the other day on career transition to a group of local professionals who were looking for some advice. One participant, Oliver, came to me after my talk and started pleading about his hardship and how he needed a job right away to get back on his feet again. He did not want to wait to get on my calendar and wanted me to meet with him out of turn. As I was watching his behavior after my speech, I realized that he was not letting others come and share their experiences with me by interfering with them as they tried to get my attention.

Finally, as I was getting organized to leave and was gathering my boxes of presentation materials and personal belongings, with both hands loaded, heading to my car, Oliver followed me to the parking lot and continued pleading his case. As we approached my car, I realized that I could not open my unlocked trunk as both my hands were loaded and I was carrying some stuff pressed in my armpits to boot. I was expecting Oliver to offer help opening my trunk; but he did not even register that need and kept on talking about his own plight, as he stood there talking my ear off, hands in his pockets. Finally, I put down on the ground the things that I was carrying, freed my hands, and opened the trunk as he continued to talk and plead his case, completely oblivious to what he might have done to ingratiate himself with me. As I loaded my trunk and drove off I said to myself, shaking my head in disbelief, there was no way I would want to help this person, so consumed by his own needs that he simply could not even see other's obvious needs.

Being etiquette savvy opens your eyes to what others need even when you have your own ongoing needs. By simply offering to help me open my trunk, Oliver might have got what he came looking for!

The etiquette varies from situation to situation in a job or business environment. However, within a certain situation, a particular etiquette can be considered a norm. The following discussion is presented for a typical business environment:

eMails

Over time, emails have become the lifeblood of communication in business, even in formal exchanges. Initially emails were considered an informal and a more intimate means of communication. As a result, those using them were relaxed about their use; usage: spelling and other solecisms were considered excusable. Now that emails have become ubiquitous and the basic lifeblood of all business communications, more attention must be paid to such messages.

The list of suggestions below for emailing is not just limited to internal exchanges; following this etiquette will enhance your social and business savvy as well:

1. eMails have become the single most driving factor for employee stress in today's organization. Why? One reason is that most send their emails with little or no thought to how they are creating and deliver-

ing their messages. This is not just about sloppy writing, or incorrect usage, or grammatical errors, but it is about the humanity of your message. It is common to see angry, terse, cryptic, or even offensive emails in a business setting (See Appendix-IV: The Human Moment at Work). The main reason why this happens is because, often, the writers of the emails perpetuate—even amplify—the spirit of the incoming message. For example, if they receive an agitated or upset email from a colleague, they will immediately respond to it defensively or in kind and even escalate the tone of anger in their reply. If a mildly angry email comes from up above, it creates a cauldron of emotions as the reader tries to decipher the cause of the asperity. Somehow, emails have a tendency to amplify the anger and the brittleness of the message, particularly when it is coming *down* from the chain of command.

An antidote for this common problem is not to send angry emails. If you are not sure, compose the email, sleep over it and then send it the next day. Another test for this is to check and assess if you would read the email message you intend to send, out loud on the company's public address system! If you must display your displeasure, do it in person or in a phone conversation, preferably without anger. This mode of communication prevents from escalating the tone of the emotion by the recipient playing it back over or over, as it might be done with an email or with a voice mail message.

2. A more basic issue in email communications is to first ask if it is the right way to get done what needs to be done. Ostensibly well-intentioned email messages have a tendency to often insinuate doubts in an organizational setting that is otherwise trusting. In one case a senior executive sent an innocent email to my client when she was just a newly hired analyst with some special skills. The executive suggested in his message that she could work with another team, led by his colleague, to help them improve their analytical capability. He copied (cc) the message to his colleague. When the colleague saw his copy of the message, he was at once offended by the insinuation that his team lacked such capability. The result was that this other executive never allowed my client to come near his team!

In this example, the executive might have personally explored with his colleague first by offering to him the talents of his new analyst in a face-to-face encounter. Then, depending on how his colleague responded—watching his body language and words—he could have assessed if such a gesture was earnestly received. Then he could have sent that email with a copy to my client! Of course, this route takes more time and personal involvement, but that is what relationships are and that is how things get done in a productive environment. Promiscuous and indiscriminate use of emails, even well intentioned, can vitiate an organization's fabric and permeate a toxic environment.

3. When composing *important* emails, use a good word-processing application and compose the message as if writing a letter. This discipline will force your having to write with care. Using the more sophisticated features of the word-processing applications, as grammar and spell check will formalize the message. This approach also provides a retrievable record of the file that can be stored on the hard drive under a suitably named folder, as *Important emails*. Do not compose an important message in an email browser for these reasons. Once the message in the word-processing browser is satisfactory, cut and paste the message in the outgoing email window and put the final touches on the entire message, including the Subject line.

4. Make sure that the subject line is crafted with as much care as the message it captures, as a courtesy to the readers. It also serves your purpose in getting that message opened and read.

5. Every email should be spell-checked to ensure no obvious spelling problems. Messages composed within an email application allow for a limited ability to check for errors. Reading a spell-checked message can further assure a more correct outgoing message. Spell-check programs do not differentiate between words that sound similar but have different spellings such as "to" and "too."

6. To prevent an accidental transmittal of an incomplete or unvetted message, especially for critical emails, insert the recipient address *after* you have completed writing the entire message. Your sending a blind copy (bcc) of the outgoing email to yourself will further ensure how the transmitted message actually looks.

7. Some email browsers allow retrieving messages, if the retrieval is done before the recipient opens your message. Avoid this practice for critical emails. Using the above tips will prevent many errors and inadvertent oversights that prompt these retrievals. The reason for avoiding email retrievals is that the recipient is notified that you are

retrieving your message. For important emails, this may not be to
your best advantage.

8. If you are not sure if a certain message is appropriate or that it may be
    misconstrued, wait before sending it and then read it again. If possi-
    ble, ask someone else to read it to be sure. If still in doubt see if it is
    possible to personally deliver the message in a conversation or a
    phone call.

9. Do not send toxic, offensive, angry, or derogatory messages to some-
    one before the start of a weekend, where they cannot get hold of you
    until the following business day. Such messages can often ruin some-
    one's weekend.

10. It is a good idea to avoid attachments to emails—especially out-
    bound messages—because of the computer viruses. If the message in
    the body of the email was composed using a word processor applica-
    tion, as in #3, a recommended practice is to copy and paste this mes-
    sage, in the email body, in preference to attaching that file to the
    email. If you are sending a résumé, make sure that the recipient will
    accept it as an attachment.
        A safer bet is to compose the body of the message and below the
    message pasting the electronic version of the attachment as a
    résumé, in addition to attaching the file in its original version to the
    same email message. This leader message could be your cover letter
    (if you are sending your résumé in response to an opportunity).
    Mentioning this fact in the body of the email, or even in the Subject
    line of the email, prevents any confusion as to what the attachment
    is. This approach gives the recipient an option to deal with the
    attachment, the way they prefer, and you have a better chance of
    your attachment getting read.

11. Choose the email Subject carefully. Most people get a plethora of
    emails. It is estimated that managers typically get over 250 messages
    every day (including voice mails). For your email—especially if you
    are targeting this person as your prospective hiring manager—to get
    noticed, it must have a compelling subject line to get their attention,
    as they scan their inbox for important messages. So, instead of
    choosing the subject line as *An Update*, using *A situation in need of
    help*, may create enough intrigue to the manager to take a look at
    your email. One fresh graduate from Stanford had his résumé

opened by a recruiter because she felt that the subject line *Fresh meat from Stanford* was curious and creative.

12. Do not rely on the screen name (also known as User ID or email address) to identify you to the reader, especially for outbound messages. You must have a complete identifier in the Signature block so that the reader does not have to guess who the sender is. In addition to your name and contact information it is a good idea to have other relevant details. This common courtesy should be extended to *all* emails. Having a complete signature block as a template created for all outgoing emails is a good practice. This block should have your fill name, telephone contact information, and any other detail that you consider relevant. It is also a good idea to have your email address as a part of this template. Why? Often, emails are forwarded, and in some browsers, the originating email header is dropped. In such cases, the person to whom the email was forwarded does not have the originating address, other than that of the person who forwarded the message. In such cases you miss the opportunity to hear back directly from this person.

13. It is a good idea to choose your screen name for personal emails carefully without making a statement. Avoid sending negative messages (broke@yahoo.com, divorced@hotmail.com) with your screen name; also avoid making a statement, political, social, or otherwise (Democrat@aol.com, antiwar@sbcglobal.net, atheist@Webtv.net), even if you feel strongly about how it ought to be. In the stages of making a first impression, your identification should not make an impact; your message should. How you choose to identify yourself may prevent your message from ever getting through, no matter how compelling.

14. It is good idea to maintain the original subject header in responding to someone's email. This allows for an easy message thread. It is also a good idea to include the original message, above or below your text in the body of the email. Often, many keep the same subject header for emails long after the original context becomes irrelevant. For example, someone looking for an email address from an old message may locate the old message and use a "Reply to" to create a new message, now with a completely different subject matter, without changing what pops up in the email window with the old subject heading. Avoid this practice. It shows laziness.

15. Avoid sending email messages with large files especially those that are going outside. Some graphic files, even in the body of an email, can easily hold megabits of data, which can clog mailboxes and create problems loading the messages, especially with a slow Internet connection.

16. Use "Reply All" button carefully and sparingly. Make sure that your response does need to go to all whose names appear in the original message.

17. When you can use a more personal means of communication, as a telephone call, a handwritten note, or a face-to-face meeting consider it. It makes you stand out. Remember, too, that many employees do not check their mail slots regularly, since such messages are becoming rare. So, if you do send a message by mail (US Mail, for example), mention that in an email to alert the person to look for it. Doing so, also will make you stand out.

18. When an email message requires you to do some research before responding, and the response will be delayed beyond a day or two because of this, *acknowledge* the message immediately and mention when you might be getting back with the *response* and state the reason briefly. Once you make this commitment, make sure you meet or beat the scheduled response date.

19. When you are on vacation, make sure your auto response is turned on, notifying the email senders of your unavailability. It is a good idea to give an avenue for connecting for urgent matters.

20. It is difficult to know whether an organization has a dominant email or voice mail culture. The best defense against this quandary, when sending a message, is to do both: whenever possible, leave a voice mail after sending an email to a person, using the same Subject header as the one in the email. Also be *very brief* in the voice mail message. This simple expedient and courtesy will create a memory jog for the recipient when looking at a barrage of unopened emails.

21. If you have not received a response from someone to whom you had sent an email, do not assume that they have received it or seen it. I once received an angry message from a jobseeker. I had presented a seminar to his group and had volunteered to help with their résumés. He had sent me his résumé, attached to an email, which was lost in a

sea of other emails. There was no mention of a résumé in the body of the message. The subject header was: Nice meeting you! He had a cryptic screen name to boot, which made it even more difficult to identify who he was and no signature block, just his first name—Joe. To prevent such mishaps, always make it easy for the email recipient to know what they are getting, and how to get at it quickly. Clearly stating what you expect from them at the top of the message also helps.

22. It is common to have multiple email boxes. If you send an email from one mailbox, make sure that when the response is received to that box, your system will accept it. Many email addresses that are available for free, limit the size of the incoming messages. Even mentioning the email box to which you want response sent in the body of the message, will not prevent a mishap, because most respondent just hit the "Reply" button in response to an incoming message.

Telephone Calls

Telephone calls are mainstay of business and networking communication. And yet, few follow the etiquettes to make this a pleasant and productive experience! The following etiquettes are a summary of some of the key telephone etiquettes:

Incoming calls (Home phone)

1. Have a businesslike greeting on your voice mail. Identify yourself and your telephone number in the greeting for your private line at home and follow the company guidelines for your office greetings at work.

2. With the caller ID a standard feature now, especially for residential phones, do not install security screens on incoming calls. These filters can be barriers to callers trying to reach you, including your potential employers. Use voice screening instead, available on recording machines.

3. Have a separate line for all your Internet activity. An Internet connection on a line can block it for hours and frustrate those who are trying to reach you, including your potential employers. With the growing use of wireless and DSL connections, this is now becoming less of a problem.

4. If a call comes at a time when it is inconvenient for you to take it, explain why and ask if you can call them back at a time that is best for *them*.

5. If you are angry, upset, or feel that you are not in balance, let the machine take the incoming call.

6. Do not betray your emotions or state of mind to the caller. Telephone, as a medium, is notoriously sensitive to the way your tone comes across in a conversation. In a telephone conversation your voice is "naked." Be very aware of this and manage your emotional state for all calls, incoming and outgoing!

Outgoing calls

1. Make outgoing calls at a time that does not impose on the called party. For a business call it is usually the times of business hours for the recipient. For personal calls these times are on a weekday: 9:00 AM to 10:00 PM (9:00 PM is preferred) for calls made to a home, and during regular business hours for all business calls; weekends 10 AM to 6 PM for all home calls. Avoid dinner or lunch hours even for home calling.

2. If you are calling someone on their cell phone, ask if they can talk or politely ask where they are, so that, if they are driving, you may want to ask them for a more convenient time for that call. With the one-number system now in place, it is difficult to ascertain if the person you are calling is on the cell phone or wired phone. Always ask, after identifying yourself and stating your reason for the call, if they can talk. Do not assume that they can, even if you are returning their call *within* minutes of receiving their message.

3. When the called person answers your call, immediately identify yourself fully—and not by merely saying, "Hi this is Dave"—so that you can engage in a conversation without the called person having to wonder "which Dave is this?" and losing time in engaging with you right away. Also, do not assume that even though you are calling someone in response to their message that they will immediately recognize who you are and why they should be talking to you.

4. If you called someone and the line gets disconnected, no matter what the reason, *you* re-initiate the call. The called person waits for the

phone to ring again for a few minutes; otherwise they will go about their business.

5. Do not discuss sensitive, gossipy, personally offensive, or insinuating information on the phone. If you want to give some adverse feedback, ask them to meet you and do it in person. Likewise, do not leave messages of similar nature on someone's voicemail. Sometimes, in an emotional state, people misdial and leave an offensive or abusive message on a wrong voice mail!

6. When leaving a voice mail, state your call-back telephone number twice, once at the beginning and once again at the end, even for a very short message.

   Keep your calls brief and to the point.

Office phones

There are many common elements of etiquettes between the home and the business phone calls. The following etiquettes are especially presented with today's business situation in mind:

1. Many business "offices" are closely-spaced open cubicles these days, which present special challenge for those who use telephone as a main part of their work day. To keep the voice level within the limits of infringement on your neighboring cubicle, using a headset can be a boon to this consideration. Some routinely use speakerphone to allow themselves a hands free operation without considering how it is going to affect their neighbor. Speaker phones should be reserved for conference room calls and their use should be avoided in a regular setting, where adjacent cubicles can be affected by the sound.

2. Some develop a habit of coming early in the day and checking their voice mail via their speaker phone, so that they can settle down as they sip on their morning coffee. Not only does this disturb nearby occupants, it is also impolite to have your messages heard by those around you. Using a headset is more appropriate.

3. Have a brief voice greeting that identifies you by name. For security reasons, you may not want to repeat your extension or phone number for an outside caller.

4. If you have a vacation or time-away greeting, make sure that it is changed as soon as you return. There is nothing more annoying to a

caller than to hear a greeting that announces that you should have been back already, leaving them wondering if you are *that* lazy or inconsiderate.

5. Do not leave angry, upset, or cryptic voice mail messages for others. Similar to the suggestion made earlier of not sending such messages via emails, go in person or call and talk to them live to convey such messages.

6. Do not leave messages longer than one minute. Announce your number at the beginning and then repeat your number at the end of the message, especially for outside callers.

Meetings

Meetings are the single most dreaded events and the most wasteful of activities in the corporate jungle. It is estimated that 76 percent of the meetings are not needed and could be replaced by more efficient ways of getting things done. Even in the remaining 24 percent that may have marginal need, as much as 40 percent of the time is used unproductively. Surveys show that nearly half of the time people spend in the meeting is wasted in their daydreaming, making irrelevant comments, not being prepared for the topics on the agenda, or using the forum as a socializing occasion. This is why having a good and effective meeting is so important. See Appendix-II: Managing Meetings for more details on this topic. The following guidelines go beyond mere etiquettes, but are presented to help those who are interested in making meetings more effective:

1. Do not call a meeting merely because you can. Some senior managers call meetings to show others how busy they are and how many people can come to their meetings. The higher up the attendees are in a meeting, the greater the feeling of being respected for the hosting manger. Avoid these ego trips and save others the agony of having to attend such spectacles.

2. If you can accomplish the same objective by sending emails, do not call a meeting.

3. Have the fewest number of attendees to accomplish what you set out to do

4. Publish timed agenda for the upcoming meeting and the status of the action items from the previous meeting, with names and responsibilities.

5. Always start on time. Waiting for everyone to show to start the meeting merely punishes those who are on time. At the beginning state the purpose of the meeting and then jump right into the agenda. Stick to the timed agenda

6. As the leader of the meeting you must summarize each major step so that everyone is aware of what is happening

7. Assign a scribe or do it yourself. Read the action items and responsible names before the meeting is adjourned.

8. End the meeting on time and thank everyone.

9. Leave the meeting room and facilities in the same order as you would want them for yourself, even though they were not so before you started your meeting.

Appreciating someone

One of the most powerful and potent weapons of influence in any organization is formally appreciating someone. This interesting opportunity does not require any position, reason, or time to do it. When someone goes out of their way to do something exceptional—not expected—it gives a reason for the person to whom it was done to appreciate the person who did this great act. The best approach is to do this within a reasonable time of the act—in a few days, while it is still fresh—and doing it by sending a message, typically, an email to the manager of the person. Sending copies of this email to others, such as the manager's boss is also a good idea. This simple act of writing a special note of appreciation has a power all its own. Just try it and see how magical it is, not just for the person receiving it, but for many others, who also then go out of the way to do exceptional things for you, just to get a similar acknowledgment from you for their efforts.

Disciplinary Process

In today's harried corporate environment disciplinary actions and their end point, a termination, are inevitable. Most of the people involved handle it awkwardly, making it difficult for all to be a part of this process in a constructive way. The purpose of the disciplinary process is to remedy a wrong and set the course for bringing the "wayward" employee back on track. However, because of the timing and how this is usually handled, almost everyone involved ends up looking bad.

The timing entails taking disciplinary action, soon following the employee's errant act. First, there is a verbal warning. If the employee does not show progress, they receive a written warning with a specific remedy to get back on track. The final act is termination. By their nature, these events and the entire process are filled with emotions and their volatility make rational actions difficult. It is because of this that both parties must handle the process in a constructive way. The following list may be a guide for how to handle this delicate situation constructively:

1. If an employee has done something untoward—as a malapropos comment, flubbing an assignment, or any other act that compromises an organization—the immediate supervisor has the responsibility to privately talk with the employee and clear the air. Many wait until this escalates into a bigger problem and then intervening. This is not constructive.

2. If this meeting ends up being a verbal warning, then the employee must be told this and a remark entered in the personnel file to that effect.

3. If the behavior continues, written warning comes next. Some consider this the Notice of Concern. Others have this Notice as the next step after the written warning. It is entirely appropriate for the manager to ask the employee if they need help in remedying the situation and getting back on track. The manager has the obligation to provide the necessary resources to help the employee, assuming that such an intervention can, indeed, help the situation.

4. If the Notice of Concern does not result in any progress and action on the part of the employee that convinces the manager that the situation is going to improve, the manager has the last resort of terminating the employee. The manager must involve the HR representative from step #1 listed above

5. If there is termination for any reason, including a lay-off. The manager must take the direct responsibility to handle this in a humane manner and explain to the employee the reason for the termination. Most managers do this poorly.

Job-Search Etiquette

This section is included to help those who are in transition looking for a job. The reason for including this section is to help those who are in the job market understand the finer points of job-search etiquette and give them an edge.

Responding to Posted Jobs

Posted jobs can be either published in the print media or on the job boards. Jobs posted on company bulletin boards and Websites have the same etiquette considerations:

1. Respond to a posting only if you are a strong candidate. Marginal match of your skill to the competencies posted on the open position is a disservice to the process, even if the résumé is sent electronically. In the era of the Internet, where it costs nothing to post your résumé and it takes a few seconds to respond to a position, it is all the more important that you follow this discipline. Merely flooding a Website with yet another marginal résumé is a good way to ensure that you are making the process difficult for others, who may be more qualified than you.

2. Sending an overnight courier package to get attention is a good idea. It takes some effort to find the name of the hiring manager or recipient where you want to send such a response. However, before sending your response in such an impactful way, make sure that your message has enough clout to warrant this special delivery. As more and more find out that sending a FedEx—or other courier—package in the hands of a decision maker can get an audience, the more and more vigilant the recipients are going to become. If this mode of sending a response is just to hector the recipient with the same trite message, that might as well have been sent by email, or not at all, the impact of the FedEx approach diminishes quickly for all those who rely on it. Ergo, use an appropriate method of sending your message to create an impact commensurate with your message. Do not use a sledgehammer to kill a fly!

3. Do not send a response to a posted opening to everyone in sight. Send it to the recipient named in the posting, unless you have a compelling case for sending it to someone higher up for an impact and action that the response deserves. Use your judgment.

4. Do not call immediately to verify receipt of what you sent. Remember the more common the approach to sending what is asked, the less your "right" to follow-up. You should not even bother to follow-up, where you sent a conventional email response to a job posting, in a tough market, where there are potentially a large number of respondents.

5. Even if the target employer is nearby, do not go personally to hand the résumé to someone there. You may be able to leave it, in the in-basket, at the lobby at best. Unless your response has something compelling, do not waste someone's time by having them come down to the lobby, just so that they have your résumé!

6. Comply with all the *requirements* of the posted position, when sending your response in a familiar way—email. Employers do not like it when respondents do not comply with clearly spelled out requirements. This does not mean just the job requirements, but the process that the posted opening wants you to follow. If you want to use some of the approaches suggested in this book, as guerilla tactics or unconventional methods, use appropriate means of transmittal and connecting with the decision maker.

7. Do not send your response in a format, color, or package that may appear to the recipient as off-the-wall, or presented just to get their attention. The message must have the same attention-getting power. Remember the saying: the medium is the message.

Following-up

After sending the response to an opportunity, following up depends on how you responded and what the original opportunity was. If you responded to a job with a résumé and cover letter, in a routine way to a generic address, you have no recourse to any specific follow up. This is why sending such responses put you at a disadvantage. The list below summarizes etiquettes for following-up on what you have already sent:

1. If you know the name of the person to whom the response was sent, leave a message with details, so that the person can easily track your response without having to research it further. For example, if you are David Smith—or have a similarly common name—don't just say, "Sally this Dave Smith and I am calling about the résumé I sent about a month ago. Could you please call me and tell me what the status of that job is?" A more actionable message might be, "Hi Sally this is

David Smith. About a month back, I sent my résumé, in connection with your posting for a shipping clerk, job # 22342. I would really appreciate your calling me at 123-555-2212 and leaving me a message about the status of that job. Once again, that number is 123-555-2212 and thank you!" Preferably this telephone number should be the same that you used on the résumé. Do not expect to hear if your original response was a routine one and do not keep calling, if you did not hear back the first time.

2. If you are calling to follow-up on a courier package you sent in response to a job opening, do not assume that the package is with the addressee. Look at the delivery signature commonly available for courier deliveries, and start with that person. Then sequentially trace the package and see where it might be in the chain. Then call that person. Sometimes, a package is redirected after it is opened.

3. Once you connect with the person who has your package, gently explore whether they had a chance to read it. Give them a reason to open the package, by saying something intriguing and suggest that you may call later. Be brief and diplomatic and assess where you need to begin so that the person is obliged to open it and take the next steps—your original intent behind sending such a message.

4. If the person with whom you connected asks you to call back or suggests that they would call you back at a certain time, give some additional time to reconnect if they fail to call you, so that you do not look overly anxious.

5. If you are navigating through a battery of administrators, to get to someone higher up in an organization, treat them with courtesy and respect. They may decide to "disconnect" you if, they see you as a pest. There is a thin line between being persistent and being a pest!

6. Always be thankful for any information you get and any courtesy you are accorded, no matter who that person is at the other end, where you are trying to get in.

7. After two rounds of reminders and follow-ups, find some alternate approach to getting the attention to be called back.

Networking

Networking etiquettes are flouted most frequently with unwitting consequences! How? It is perhaps because people are not even aware of the simple slipups that can cascade into a full-blown avoidance by the person at the other end of the network; amity can turn into enmity with a simple oversight, especially if you are looking to the other person to do you a favor! The following tips are a good starting point to adopt proper "netiquettes":

1. Your successful networking is based on giving more than you take. Always keep track of what is coming your way from your network and make sure that you maintain the balance with the network owing you. Not the other way around! For example if you get two leads from your network in a week, give three or more back to the same network. Always manage to give in kind.

2. If you want to contact someone, based on a tip you got from within your network, make sure that you tell the person, how you came about their name. Always reveal the source of the referral when making new contacts.

3. Make sure you keep the boundaries of your expectations with each person within your network. Do not push these boundaries. Your desperation, in getting what you want, does not constitute an emergency on the part of the person who is trying to help you! This is why it is a good idea to make networking a habit, in times, good and bad.

4. If your source gives you the name of a hiring manager, do not assume that you can directly contact that manager. Some companies have strict rules about keeping the hiring managers away from the flux of inquiries and persistent calls from interested candidates. Ask the person if it would be appropriate for you to contact the manager or if they are able to present your response to that manager. All things being equal, you should prefer the former. It lets you keep track of what is going on and you eliminate a third person from getting in the way of your future interactions with that manager. If this were to materialize your way, always keep your contact apprised of what is going on by sending a courtesy copy of your exchanges with the manager.

5. In addition to saying "thank you," every time you get help, *call* once in a while just to thank that person and for no other reason! Also send a

thank you note in the mail. Many consider receiving such a note, much more meaningful than just receiving a "thank you" email.

6. Make sure that you keep the boundaries of when and where to call your network contact, to get what you are looking for. The only contacts you should consider calling at home and off hours are your closest contacts.

7. If you are using the Internet as a channel of communication within your networking group, do not use emails to solicit petitions, send spam, and other messages of commercial import or the ones that promote your personal agenda.

8. Do not assume that those within your networking group share your religious, political, or social beliefs. If you foist them on the group, it may retaliate by alienating you from the group!

9. Do not assume that if you subscribe to an email group, such as a Yahoo! Group, that your message posted on such a board will be read and heeded by all who receive it. Many routinely ignore such group messages. If you want someone's attention, then send at least a personal message to each one!

10. Keep your email messages brief and with a subject line carefully phrased to pique the curiosity and get action!

Interviews

Interview etiquettes range from how you appear for the interview, to what to do with your briefcase when you are ready to sit down prior to the interview, to how you leave the lobby on your way out. The following is a suggested listing of etiquette that governs these behaviors:

1. Be on time for the interview. In fact, the guideline is to arrive at least 30 minutes prior to the interview and get settled.

2. Dress appropriately for the interview: dress up and not down. You can always remove one or more pieces of your clothing or accessories and carry them with you, if you suddenly feel that you're overdressed.

3. Dress conservatively. If you need help, visit a clothing store that specializes in business attire and seek advice from the floor personnel. Do not plan to make a statement with your clothes; you may not get past it. Do not let your clothes enter the door before you do.

4. Introduce yourself to the receptionist and state why you are there, whom you are going to see and when. Mention that you are early and not to announce you quite yet. Make friends with this person by holding a casual conversation. Do not demand a beverage or any other service from this person. They have a job to do—typically, answering phone calls and greeting visitors.

5. Do not make any adverse comments about the parking facilities, temperature in the room, coffee (too strong!) or any thing else to the receptionist (Lobby Ambassador). You really do not know how this person is connected. In one instance, a candidate made an off-the-cuff, disparaging comment about who might be running the company, at which he was interviewing, not realizing that the receptionist was the CEO's daughter, doing a summer internship.

6. When your time comes for you to be announced to the host or the interviewer, do not assume that the receptionist would remember this, since you mentioned it when you checked in. A variety of duties in which they are engaged can easily distract them from your needs. If that person is on the phone for a while, wait patiently even though your time to be calling your contact is nigh, and you cannot get this person's attention. If appropriate, hand the person a note politely and unobtrusively.

7. If you spill something in the lobby, as you wait for your time, clean up, even if the receptionist does not see that you caused the spill. Often, these people and others who causally come in contact with you are asked to report their impressions of you for critical hires.

8. When the interviewer or their representative comes to greet you, smile and be cordial even if they have kept you waiting. Do not suggest their lateness by looking at your watch. Smile and shake hands. Let them lead you to the place where the interview is going to take place. Practice some icebreakers with this person on the way to the interview.

9. At the place of the interview, ask to be seated and then sit down comfortably where you can put your briefcase or other interview paraphernalia. Place it down on the floor and not on the desk or table in front of you.

10. Do not interrupt the interviewer. Do not argue even if you know that the interviewer is wrong. Your anxiety and nervousness will show if you exhibit such behaviors.

11. Take notes on a notepad and not on a laptop or a handheld device close to your face!

12. Do not ask any questions about the company's woes to the interviewer, the answers to which may put that person in a compromising light. You are also likely to compromise your chances of getting in. Once a client, while being interviewed by a company's CEO asked him about the SEC investigation that was announced in the media the morning of her interview. After several rounds of successful interviews, she was a shoo-in. This question put off the CEO and the process died in its tracks.

13. When the interview is over, get up, organize your belongings, and quickly get ready to leave the area with the person escorting you out. Do not stretch their patience as you carefully organize your many belongings, if they became disheveled during the interview. Organize them later.

14. Shake hands, thank the person for their time, and ask what the next steps are and the timeline. Do not get overly obsessive about timelines or accountability in the follow-up process. Do this somewhat naturally by practicing it before the interview.

15. On the way out thank the receptionist for taking good care of you and ask the person their name.

Thank-you! Notes

Thank you notes following an interview are critical to making them remember you. They can also be used to recover from something that might have gone wrong during the interview. Mailed thank you notes are more formal and memorable than emails. In the case of important interviews sending both types of notes creates an impression. Samples of thank you email and notes are shown in Key-5 of the author's *The 7 Keys to a Dream Job: A Career Nirvana Playbook!*.

References

Etiquettes where references are concerned vary, depending on the level of the reference. Although they all deserve to be treated with consideration and courtesy, those who offer to give you a high-level reference need to be treated with special care and you should let them know that!

The following etiquette guide may help you finesse your references well:

1. Identify your references early in the process. Let them know that you are planning to include them in the reference process. Remind them about the aspect of your reference you expect them to provide.

2. Some companies have a policy of not providing a reference. Many managers, however, are willing to provide a personal reference. This is why asking early in the process can help you position your references so that there are no surprises.

3. Occasionally, some will agree to give you a written reference. If this happens while you are in the job associated with this person, it is that much more convenient. In any case, if the person agrees to a written reference, write the reference letter yourself and pass it by the person. This way you can decide what is appropriate from that reference in the context of your needs. Do not assume that this person will reference you the way you need it. Usually, it is much easier for anyone to merely edit a letter and sign it than having the need to draft it first.

4. Carry these letters of reference in your interview portfolio and when the time comes for the reference discussion, show the person asking the question. Sometimes this may obviate the need to calling your reference, hastening the process to your advantage.

5. When the potential employer asks for the references, call them, even though you had put them on notice earlier. The reason is that for final referencing, you may need to remind them again and, during this process, it also gives you a chance to prepare them to respond in line with what the needs are to bolster your case. Request the reference to highlight that aspect of the discussion that you think is relevant.

6. If appropriate, request the reference to call you upon being contacted by the potential employer. This is a courtesy to help you confirm that the process is underway. Do not expect this courtesy from all refer-

ences. Do not keep calling your references to check if they heard from your potential employer.

7. Once you know that the process is complete, either through the offer, or rejection, or any other means, promptly call each of the references or send a note (email is acceptable) of thanks. If you get the job, going the extra distance—a thank you! card, flowers, or a gift, as appropriate, can protect the references for your future needs.

8. During the process, check with the person to whom you gave the list, to see if there are any problems contacting the references on that list. It is appropriate for the references to call that person preemptively as well, if you so choose.

9. It is not appropriate to call and ask the potential employer what the references said about you, especially if you are turned down for the job.

10. If you are turned down, it a good idea to ask for a debrief. This, again, is a courtesy that the company is extending to you. If the debrief mentions any items related to a reference that surprise you, do not probe for details, unless they are volunteered as a part of the debrief.

11. After you confirm that the process is completed, call all your references and inform them that the process is complete. Tell them the outcome, if you already know it, and thank them for their support. Some of them may not have been called and they should know that they are now off the hook. You must promptly communicate with all your references and thank them, even if you did *not* get the job.

12. If you were turned down after reference checking, do not assume that it was because of what the references might have said. Do not hector references to tell you what they might have said in their conversations. You must protect your references for future needs.

Negotiating Offers

Much of the process during this step is outlined in the section on negotiations in the author's *The 7 Keys to a Dream Job: A Career Nirvana Playbook!* The following is a summary of etiquettes during this step:

1. Do not assume that you can negotiate what is being offered. Ask.

2. Always go back to the last person who made the offer and not necessarily your hiring manager.

3. Do not assume that, just because you are in negotiations, you will get what you are seeking. The offer can be withdrawn if the employer so decides.

4. Tread lightly. You should decide before entering into negotiations the down side. You should be willing to walk away if the negotiations collapse.

5. After you have been turned down, and your offer is withdrawn, do not go back begging for the same or lesser job for a lower pay!

6. Decide on which items you want to negotiate, lay them out as you enter the discussions, and then stop after the process is completed. If the outcome is not favorable, do not plan to move on to other items of the offer.

7. Above all, be pleasant, flexible, and courteous throughout the process. Always remind them that you are excited about the job.

Acknowledging Help

During your job search, many provide help, even unbeknownst to you or some even unexpectedly and pleasantly! Keep a list of all those who have helped you, going all the way back to the original lead that got you the first interview. The following etiquette lists what you can do after the process is completed:

1. Depending upon the significance of the help you received from a person, thank them appropriately. Those who provided help, above and beyond, acknowledge it commensurately: a gift, lunch, or a thank you card can be some suggestions in this department.

2. Acknowledge your gratitude in a timely way. The times following a job offer can be hectic. Within the first month of your being offered the job is a good time.

3. Be *specific* about acknowledging the help that got you the job. Merely a perfunctory "Thanks for your help" is not as impactful and proper as saying "John, your lead and the insight you gave me about what the company was looking for, and what I could present them during my interviews was instrumental in my landing this job. Thank you very much!" is far more appropriate. The person, who went out of

their way to help you, likes to know that you acknowledged correctly what that person did to help you in the process. Do not skip this detail, because you feel that the person already should know. It is not what they know; it is how you acknowledge it that makes for the proper etiquette!

4. Do not forget to thank all those with whom you came in contact during the interview process at the company, where you would be working. They are now your colleagues and associates. Even the person in the lobby who greeted you on the first interview deserves a thank you note! If you do that, it would be much easier to make them your friends, once you start working there.

Starting your New Job

Starting a new job can be exciting, especially if you are coming out of being jobless. The following etiquette is suggested at this step of the process of your transition:

1. On the first day, show up on time. Dress a bit more formally than you would normally at that company. You may be taken around and introduced to others that day; your photo might be taken. If you are senior staff (director and above), you might even be introduced to important clients and dignitaries.

2. During the initial stages of employment be patient with all the administrative work that has to be done properly. Do not show your impatience with those who are trying to get this done. Let them do their job.

3. Express to your manager that you are glad to be on board and that you are looking forward to teaming with them.

4. Many companies have initiation traditions that can be as benign as going out to lunches or to bars at the end of the day. Accommodate these rituals, even if they seem odd and infringe on your time; enjoy them.

5. If you have some habits that define how you do your job, be open to seeing how things are done at your new place.

6. Do not criticize something just because it looks odd or different to you. Wait to offer your opinion. Go with the flow, at least initially.

7. Do not to gossip and talk behind someone's back. Understand the power structure in the new place before you decide which camp you want to belong to. This can portend your future there!

8. Three months after you have started in your new job, visit all the job boards and Websites, where you had originally posted your résumé and delete it! Three months is typically the probationary period for new hires.

During the Holidays

Holidays are a great time to be showing appreciation to others and showing it in a memorable way. It is also a good time to reconnect or otherwise show that you care about the relationships. Recruiters, references, counselors, and network contacts are among those who need to be shown gratitude in a fit way. This ranges from sending holiday cards to special gift baskets and mementos with notes that express your gratitude for what they have done and what they might do for you. Use the following guidelines:

1. Make a list and segment it by how much each person in a category has done to advance your cause and present them with something appropriate. If you expect that you may need someone's help in the near future, put them on the list as well.

2. Send a personal note or greetings with a specific message of gratitude rather than a generic one. The more specific you craft a message and the more specifically you acknowledge the person, the more impact the note carries.

3. If you are on a budget, as those who are out-of-work might be, create your own gifts as baskets of goodies or a work of art that is presentable. Wrap it nicely and present it elegantly so that it looks thoughtful and expensive.

4. If you do not receive an acknowledgement, do not call to find out if they received your gift. Send a subsequent note and mention that you hope that they received the gift you had sent them. A note or email wishing them a Happy New Year is a good opportunity to do this. If they still do not acknowledge, move on.

5. If convenient and appropriate, during the holidays, take to lunch those who have done things for you. This is yet another way to make them remember you.

Where possible, hand-carry your gift, present it in person, and show your gratitude.

BIBLIOGRAPHY

"Life affords no higher pleasure than that of surmounting difficulties, passing from one stage of success to another, forming new wishes and seeing them gratified."

—Samuel Johnson, lexicographer (1709–1784)

Chapter-1: Today's Workplace

Adrienne, Carol. *The Purpose of Your Life: Finding Your Place In The World Using Synchronicity, Intuition, and Uncommon Sense.* Harper Collins, 1999.

Bronson, Po. *What Should I do with My Life? The True Story of People Who Answered the Ultimate Question.* Random House, 2003.

Buckingham, Marcus, Curt Coffman. *First, Break All the Rules: What the Worlds Greatest Managers Do Differently.* Simon & Schuster Adult Publishing Group, 1999.

Freidman, Thomas L. *It's a Flat World: A Brief History of the Twenty-first Century.* Farrar, Strauss and Geroux, 2005.

Ibarra, Herminia. *Working Identity: Unconventional strategies for reinventing your career.* Harvard Business Press. 2003

Johnson, Spencer. *Who Moved My Cheese? An Amazing Way to Deal With Change in Your Work and Your Life.* Simon & Schuster Adult Publishing Group, 1999.

Kiviat, Barbara. *The End of Management? Time,* July 12, 2004, special section, Future Shock,

Laney, Marti Olsen Laney. *The Introvert Advantage: How to Thrive in an Extraverted World.* Workman Publishing, 2002.

Schien, Edgar: *Career Dynamics Matching Individual and Organizational Needs.* Addison Wesley, Reading Mass. 1978

Schien, Edgar: Organizational Culture and Leadership, Jossey-Bass, San Francisco, CA 1997

Schien, Edgar: The corporate Culture Survival Guide, Jossey-Bass, San Francisco, CA 1997

Saraf, Dilip G. *The 7 Keys to a Dream Job: A Career Nirvana Playbook! iUniverse Publishers, Lincoln, NE,* 2004

Saraf, Dilip G. *Pathways to Career Nirvana: An Ultimate Success Sourcebook!, iUniverse Publishers, Lincoln, NE,* 2004

Saraf, Dilip G. *Reinvention through Messaging: The Write Message for the Right Job! iUniverse Publishers, Lincoln, NE,* 2004

Saraf, Dilip G. *Rehired, not Retired: Proven Strategies for the Baby-Boomers!* iUniverse Publishers, Lincoln, NE, 2005

Segal, Nina, Erich Kocher. *International Jobs and where They Are and How to Get Them.* Perseus Publishing, 2003.

Trautman, Kathryn Kraemer, Barbara Guerra (Ed.). *Ten Steps to a Federal Job! Navigating the Federal job System, writing Federal Resumes, KSAs and Cover Letters with a Mission.* The Resume Place, 2002.

Chapter-2: Organizational Basics

Adrienne, Carol. *The Purpose of Your Life: Finding Your Place In The World Using Synchronicity, Intuition, and Uncommon Sense.* Harper Collins, 1999.

Argyris, Chris, *Understanding Organizational Behavior,* Dorsey Press, Homewood, IL, 1960

Belbin, R. Meredith, *Management Teams, Why They Succeed or Fail,* Heinaman, Woburn, MA, 1981

Belbin, R. Meredith, *Changing the Way We Work,* Butterworth-Heinaman, Woburn, MA, 1997

Briggs, Isabel Myers, with Peter B. Myers. *Gifts Differing: Understanding Personality Type.* Consulting Psychologists Press, Inc., Reprint Edition, 1995.

Buckingham, Marcus, Curt Coffman: *First, Break All The Rules: What the Worlds Greatest Managers Do Differently.* Simon & Schuster Adult Publishing Group, 1999.

Carnegie, Dale, Dorothy Carnegie (Editor), Arthur R. Pell, (Editor). *How to Win Friends and Influence People,* Simon & Schuster Adult Publishing Group, Revised Edition, 1982.

Chandler, Alfred D. Jr. *Strategy and Structure*, MIT Press, Cambridge, MA, 1962

Covey, Steven R. *The 7 Habits of Highly Effective people: Powerful Lessons in Personal Change* Simon & Schuster Adult Publishing Group, 1990.

Embree, Marlowe. *Type Reporter* No. 79, 12/00. Chapel Road, Fairfax Station, VA 22039; 703-764-5370.

Osborne, Carol. *The Art of Resilience: 100 Paths to Wisdom and Strength in an Uncertain World.* Crown Publishing Group, 1997.

Ray, Michael, Rochelle Myers. *Creativity in Business.* Double Day & Company, Incorporated, a division of Bantam Doubleday, 1981.

Saraf, Dilip G. *The 7 Keys to a Dream Job: A Career Nirvana Playbook!* iUniverse Publishers, Lincoln, NE, 2004

Saraf, Dilip G. *Pathways to Career Nirvana: An Ultimate Success Sourcebook!*, iUniverse Publishers, Lincoln, NE, 2004

Saraf, Dilip G. *Reinvention through Messaging: The Write Message for the Right Job!* iUniverse Publishers, Lincoln, NE, 2004.

Saraf, Dilip G. *Rehired, not Retired: Proven Strategies for the Baby-boomers!* iUniverse Publishers, Lincoln, NE, 2005

Susan J. Jeffers. *Feel the Fear And Do It Anyway* Fawcett Book Group, 1996.

Tasca, Anthony: Organizational Consulting Workshop, SKOPOS Consulting, Foster City, CA

Tieger, Paul D., Barbara Barron-Tieger, Deborah Baker, (editor). *Do what You Are: Discover the Perfect Career for You Through the Secrets of Personality Type.* Little Brown & Company, 2001.

Chapter-3: Management Basics

Adair, John, *Action-centered Leadership*, McGraw-Hill, 1984

Adair, John, *Great Leaders*, Trans Atlantic Publications, 1997

Ansoff, Igor, *The New Corporate Strategy,* John Wiley & Sons, New York, 1988

Bennis, Warren, Leadership and Change, Perseus, Cambridge, MA; 2000

Blanchard, Kenneth and Spencer Johnson, *The One Minute Manager*, Berkeley Publishing Group, New York 1983

Chandler, Alfred D, Jr. *The Dynamic Firm*, Oxford University Press, New York, 1998

Covey, Stephen R. Principled Centered Leadership, Summit Books, New York, 1991

Deming W. Edwards, Out of the Crisis: Productivity and Competitive Position, MIT Press, Cambridge, MA 2000

Drucker, Peter F. Managing in a time of Great Change, Truman Talley Books/Dutton, New York, 1995

Hamel, Gary and C.K. Prahalad, Competing for the Future, Harvard Business School Press, Boston, MA 1994

Handy, Charles, *The Age of Paradox*, Harvard Business School Press, Boston, MA 1994

Handy, Charles, *Beyond Certainty*, Harvard Business School Press, Boston, MA, 1998

Kaplan, Robert and David P. Norton, *The Balance Scorecard, Translating Strategy into Action*, Harvard Business School Press, Boston, MA, 1996

Kouzes James and Barry Posner, *The Leadership Challenge*, 3rd Edition, Jossey-Bass, San Francisco, CA, 2003

Lewin, Kurt, *Resolving Social Conflicts*, American Psychological Association, Washington D.C. 1997

Maslow, Abraham, *Motivation and Personality*, 2nd Edition, Harper and Row, New York, 1970

Minzberg, Henry, *The Nature of Managerial Work*, Harper and Row, New York, 1973

Porter, Michael, The Competitive Advantage of Nations, Revised Ed. Free Press, New York, 1998

Senge, Peter, *The Fifth Discipline: The Art and Practice of the Learning Organization*, Doubleday, New York, 1990

Vroom, Victor, New Leadership, Managing Participation in Organizations, Prentice Hall, Upper Saddle River, NJ, 1988

Chapter-4: Managing Your Own Journey

Adrienne, Carol. *The Purpose of Your Life: Finding Your Place In The World Using Synchronicity, Intuition, and Uncommon Sense.* Harper Collins, 1999.

Bolles, Richard. *What Color is Your Parachute? A Practical Manual for Job-Hunters and Career Changers.* Ten Speed Press, 2004.

Crispin, Gary, Mark Mehler. *CareerXRoads 2003: The Directory to Job, Resume, and Career Management sites on the Web.* MMC Group, 2002.

Damp, Dennis V, Salvatore Conciald (Illustrator): *The Book of U.S. Government Jobs, 8ᵗʰ Edition, Where They Are, What's Available, and How to Get One.* Brookhaven Press, LLC, 2002.

D'Alessandro, David F., Michelle Owens: Career Warfare: *10 Rules for Building Successful Personal Brand and Fighting to Keep it.* McGraw Hill Companies, 2004.

Lucht, John: *Rites of Passage at $100,000 to $1 Million+: Your Insider's Lifetime Guide to Executive Job Changing and Faster Career Progress in the 21ˢᵗ Century.* Henry Holt & Company, Incorporated, 2000.

Krannich, Ron L., Caryl Ray Krannich, et al. *Job Hunting Guide transitioning from College to Career.* Impact Publishing, VA, 2003

Leslie, Hamilton, Robert Tragert. *100 Best non-Profits to Work For.* Thompson Learning, 2000.

Montag, William E.; *CareerJournal.com Resume Guide for $100,000 Plus Executive Jobs* John Wiley & Sons, Incorporated, 2002.

Riley, Margaret Riley Dikel, Francis E. Roehm. *Guide to Internet Job Searching.* McGraw Hill, Company, 2002.

Saraf, Dilip G. *The 7 Keys to a Dream Job: A Career Nirvana Playbook! iUniverse Publishers, Lincoln, NE,* 2004

Saraf, Dilip G, *Pathways to Career Nirvana: An Ultimate Success Sourcebook!,* iUniverse Publisher, 2004

Saraf, Dilip G., *Reinvent through Messaging: The Write Message for the Right Job!,* iUniverse, Publisher, 2004

Saraf, Dilip G. *Rehired, not Retired: Proven Strategies for the Baby-Boomers!* iUniverse Publishers, Lincoln, NE, 2005

Segal, Nina, Erich Kocher. *International Jobs and where They Are and How to Get Them.* Perseus Publishing, August 2003

Whitcomb, Susan Britton, Pat Kendall. *EResumes: Everything You Need to Know About Using Electronic Resumes to Tap into Today's Hot Job Market.* McGraw Hill Companies, 2001.

Chapter-5: Your New Job

Adrienne, Carol. *The Purpose of Your Life: Finding Your Place In The World Using Synchronicity, Intuition, and Uncommon Sense.* Harper Collins, 1999.

Black, Joe D., L. Tyler Nelson. *The Leadership of Change: A Workshop for Leaders and Managers,* 1991.

Briggs, Isabel Myers, with Peter B. Myers. *Gifts Differing: Understanding Personality Type.* Consulting Psychologists Press, Inc., Reprint Edition, 1995.

Bronson, Po. *What Should I do with My Life? The True Story of People Who Answered the Ultimate Question.* Random House, 2003.

Buckingham, Marcus, Curt Coffman. *First, Break All the Rules: What the Worlds Greatest Managers Do Differently.* Simon & Schuster Adult Publishing Group, 1999.

Carnegie, Dale, Dorothy Carnegie (Editor), Arthur R. Pell, (Editor). *How to Win Friends and Influence People.* Simon & Schuster Adult Publishing Group, Revised Edition, 1982.

Covey, Steven R. *The 7 Habits of Highly Effective people: Powerful Lessons in Personal Change.* Simon & Schuster Adult Publishing Group.1990.

Embree, Marlowe. *Type Reporter* No. 79, 12/00. Chapel Road, Fairfax Station, VA 22039; 703-764-5370.

Goldman, Daniel. *Emotional Intelligence: Why it can matter more than IQ.* Bantam Books, Inc., 1997.

Johnson, Spencer. *Who Moved My Cheese? An Amazing Way to Deal With Change in Your Work and Your Life.* Simon & Schuster Adult Publishing Group, 1999.

Laney, Marti Olsen Laney. *The Introvert Advantage: How to Thrive in an Extraverted World.* Workman Publishing, 2002.

Osborne, Carol. *The Art of Resilience: 100 Paths to Wisdom and Strength in an Uncertain World.* Crown Publishing Group, 1997.

Ray, Michael, Rochelle Myers. *Creativity in Business.* Double Day & Company, Incorporated, a division of Bantam Doubleday, 1981.

Tieger, Paul D., Barbara Barron-Tieger, Deborah Baker, (editor). *Do what You Are: Discover the Perfect Career for You Through the Secrets of Personality Type.* Little Brown & Company, 2001.

Chapter-6: Getting Settled in Your Job

Embree, Marlowe. *Type Reporter* No. 79, 12/00. Chapel Road, Fairfax Station, VA 22039; 703-764-5370.

Goldman, Daniel. *Emotional Intelligence: Why it can matter more than IQ.* Bantam Books, Inc., 1997.

Saraf, Dilip G. *The 7 Keys to a Dream Job: A Career Nirvana Playbook!* iUniverse Publishers, Lincoln, NE, 2004

Saraf, Dilip G. *Pathways to Career Nirvana: An Ultimate Success Sourcebook!,* iUniverse Publishers, Lincoln, NE, 2004

Saraf, Dilip G. *Reinvention through Messaging: The Write Message for the Right Job!!* iUniverse Publishers, Lincoln, NE, 2004.

Saraf, Dilip G. *Rehired, not Retired: Proven Strategies for the Baby-Boomers!* iUniverse Publishers, Lincoln, NE, 2005

Chapter-7: When Things Go Wrong

Saraf, Dilip G. *The 7 Keys to a Dream Job: A Career Nirvana Playbook!* iUniverse Publishers, Lincoln, NE, 2004

Saraf, Dilip G. *Pathways to Career Nirvana: An Ultimate Success Sourcebook!,* iUniverse Publishers, Lincoln, NE, 2004

Saraf, Dilip G. *Reinvention through Messaging: The Write Message for the Right Job!!* iUniverse Publishers, Lincoln, NE, 2004.

Chapter-8: Taking Care of the Customer

Burchill, Gary, Christina Hepner Brodie, *Voices into Choices,* Joiner Associates, 1997

Howe, Roger J., Gaeddert, Dee, Howe, Maynard: *Quality on Trial: Bringing Bottom-line Accountability to the Quality Effort* McGraw Hill, Inc. New York, 1995

Jones, Thomas, O and W. Earl Sasser, *Why Satisfied Customers Defect* in *Harvard Business Review* HBR Press. November December 1995.

Reichheld, Frederick F., *Learning from Customer Defections,* in *Harvard Business Review* HBR Press. January February 1996

Reichheld, Frederick F., *Loyalty Rules! How Today's Leaders Build Lasting Relationships,* Harvard Business School Press, Boston, MA

Chapter-9: Working Globally

Gundling, Ernest, *Working Global Smart: 12 People Skills for Doing Business Across Borders*. Davies-Black Publishing, Palo Alto, CA 2003

Peterson, Brooks, *Cultural Intelligence, A Guide to Working with People from Other Countries*, Intractultural Press, Yarmouth, Maine, 2004

Saraf, Dilip G. *The 7 Keys to a Dream Job: A Career Nirvana Playbook! iUniverse Publishers, Lincoln, NE, 2004*

Saraf, Dilip G. *Pathways to Career Nirvana: An Ultimate Success Sourcebook!*, iUniverse Publishers, Lincoln, NE, 2004

Saraf, Dilip G. *Reinvention through Messaging: The Write Message for the Right Job!*, iUniverse Publishers, Lincoln, NE, 2004.

Saraf, Dilip G. *Rehired, Not Retired: Proven Strategies for the Baby Boomers!*, iUniverse Publishers, Lincoln, NE, 2005

Trompenaars, Fons, and Charles Hampden-Turner, *Riding the Waves of Culture: Understanding Diversity in Global Business*, 2nd Edition, McGraw-Hill, New York, 1997

Chapter-10: Just One More Thing: MYOB

D'Alessandro, David F., Michelle Ownes. *Career Warfare: 10 Rules for Building Successful Personal Brand and Fighting to Keep it*. McGraw Hill Companies, 2004.

Jeffers, Susan J. *Feel the Fear And Do IT Anyway*. Fawcett Book Group, 1996.

Laney, Marti Olsen Laney: *The Introvert Advantage: How to Thrive in an Extraverted World*. Workman Publishing; 2002.

Ray, Michael and Rochelle Myers: *Creativity in Business*: Doubleday, A Division of Bantam Doubleday Dell Publishing Group, New York, 1989.

Saraf, Dilip G. *The 7 Keys to a Dream Job: A Career Nirvana Playbook! iUniverse Publishers, Lincoln, NE, 2004*

Saraf, Dilip G. *Pathways to Career Nirvana: An Ultimate Success Sourcebook!*, iUniverse Publishers, Lincoln, NE, 2004

Saraf, Dilip G. *Reinvention through Messaging: The Write Message for the Right Job!! iUniverse Publishers, Lincoln, NE, 2004.*

Saraf, Dilip G. *Rehired, Not Retired: Proven Strategies for the Baby Boomers!*, iUniverse Publishers, Lincoln, NE, 2005

Index

"Unless your ideas are ridiculed by experts, they are worth nothing."
—Reg Revans, author, *Action Learning*

AUTHOR BIOGRAPHY

Dilip G. Saraf

Author–Speaker–Career Coach–Life Coach

After getting his B.Tech (Honors) from IIT-Bombay and Master's in electrical engineering from Stanford, Dilip worked at various organizations, starting as an individual contributor and then progressing to head an engineering organization of a division of a high-tech company, with $2B in sales, in California's Silicon Valley. The material in this book resulted from his career experiences spanning nearly four decades, at four very diverse organizations, including a major conglomerate in India.

During the 40-plus years since his graduation, Dilip changed four careers by reinventing himself at each transition. When he left the corporate world, as head of engineering of a technology company, he started his own consulting business, helping high-tech and biotech companies streamline their product development processes. Dilip's third career was working as a marketing consultant helping Forture-500 companies dramatically improve their sales based on a novel concept. It is during this work that Dilip realized that the greatest challenge most corporations face is leadership. Dilip decided to work with corporations helping them understand the leadership process and how to increase leadership effectiveness at every level. With the job market shift that hit the Silicon Valley in 2001 like a tsunami, Dilip changed his career track again and decided to work with many high-tech refuges who wanted expert guidance in their reinvention and reemployment. Dilip, now in his fifth career, works with professionals in the Silicon Valley and around the world helping with reinvention to get their dream jobs or vocations.

As a career counselor and life coach, Dilip's focus has been career transitions for professionals at all levels. Working with them, he has developed many groundbreaking approaches to career transition that are now published in his four previous books. He has worked with those looking for a change in their careers and jobs at levels ranging from CEOs to hospital orderlies. He has developed numerous seminars and workshops to complement his individual coaching for making career and life transitions. During the Valley's worst job drought, Dilip has shown nearly 2,000 high-tech and other professionals how to reinvent themselves. Dilip's central theme in his practice is to help clients discover their genius and then build a value proposition around it.

Dilip owns two patents, has two publications in the *Harvard Business Review* and has led a CEO roundtable for *Chief Executive* on Customer Loyalty. Based on his work helping clients reinvent themselves with his groundbreaking approach, he published *Seven Keys to a Dream Job: A Career Nirvana Playbook!* released in June 2004. His second book, *Reinvention Through Messaging: The Write Message for the Right Job!* was published in November 2004, and his third, *Pathways to Career Nirvana: An Ultimate Success Sourcebook!* in January 2005. His fourth book *Rehired, Not Retired: Proven Strategies for the Baby Boomers!* was published in October 2005. *Conquering Your Workplace: From Mail Room to Board Room—A Sourcebook for Today's Workforce!* resulted from Dilip's work with clients' experiences as a result of the shifted workplace and his own experience as someone, who worked in the corporate world for 25 years and consulted for nearly 15. Dilip is also listed in *Who's Who*, has appeared several times on *CNN Headline News/Comcast Local Edition*, as well as in the *San Francisco Chronicle* in its career columns. Dilip is a contributing writer to *CareerSource*. Visit www.7keys.org for more about Dilip's background and current work.

Dilip is a sought-after speaker at public and private forums on jobs, careers, leadership challenges, and on how to be an effective leader.

"*Men are afraid to rock the boat in which they hope to drift aimlessly through life's currents, when actually they are stuck on a sandbar. They would be better off to rock the boat and try to shake it loose, or better still, and jump in the water and swim to the shore.*"

—Thomas Szasz, U.S. psychiatrist (1920–)

978-0-595-37486-1
0-595-37486-7

Printed in the United States
124664LV00003B/2/A